THE THEORY OF PAPAL MONARCHY IN THE THIRTEENTH CENTURY

THE THEORY OF
PAPAL MONARCHY IN
THE THIRTEENTH CENTURY

The Contribution of the Canonists

JOHN A. WATT

FORDHAM UNIVERSITY PRESS
NEW YORK

CONTENTS

Preface   VII

Introduction   1

Part One   THE FIRST THREE PHASES OF CANONIST THOUGHT   9
             1. Gelasius I and the Decretists   12
             2. Innocent III and the Early Decretalists   34
             3. Innocent IV, the Decretalist   58

Part Two   THE LANGUAGE OF SOVEREIGNTY   75
             1. *Plenitudo potestatis*   75
             2. *Papa est iudex ordinarius omnium*   92
             3. *Plenitudo potestatis, iudex ordinarius omnium* and
                the Secular Order   97

Part Three   HOSTIENSIS AND THE PAPAL POWER IN TEMPORAL AFFAIRS 107
             1. The Commentary on the *Per venerabilem*   110
             2. The Distinction of the Powers   118
             3. The Cooperation of the Powers   125
             4. The Superiority of the Spiritual   129

Part Four   CONTINUITY AND CHANGE   135

List of Works Cited   145

Index   155

PREFACE

From the earliest days of its emergence as a governmental institution, the papacy maintained and ever more specifically particularized, a set of principles concerning its primacy of jurisdiction. A part of this logic of church government related to the relevance of papal authority to the actions of rulers, to the exercise of political power. Certain periods of papal history have been especially fertile in developing ideas about the nature and extent of papal authority *in temporalibus*. In this connexion few centuries can claim the significance that attaches to the one which opened with the pontificate of Innocent III and closed with that of Boniface VIII. This was a time when the papacy came to occupy a position in relation to European political life which was unparalleled in papal history. With this new position and in the conflict it engendered, traditional generalities concerning the relationship of the ecclesiastical to the secular power were recast and reinterpreted according as changed political circumstances and the exigencies of new situations demanded. In the course of the thirteenth century the whole theory of papal authority in temporal affairs received a thorough overhaul.

Canonists have their significance for the historian of the papacy and the historian of political ideas for the part they played in this rethinking process. It was in canonical science that traditional papal theory was confronted with contemporary papal practice. The resulting dialectic was to produce in its synthesis a new theory designed to fit the facts of recent papal political experience. The record of the Church's governmental past—whether distant or recent—was preserved in the law books. In the light shed by it, canonists considered the principles of papal monarchy for the better understanding of present practical applications of its authority. The *Decretum* of Gratian reproduced a *compendium* of texts which represented the organizational and institutional aspects of Christian tradition. The *Decretales* represented the most recent implementation of that tradition by the papacy. Canonist commentary on this *Corpus Iuris Canonici* was a major intellectual effort to sustain a critical examination and achieve a reasoned solution of the manifold problems of ecclesiastical government. This book attempts an examination of that part of the effort which constituted the canonist contribution to the discussion of the problem of papal authority in the temporal order.

My obligation to Dr. Walter Ullmann is immense for it was he who turned the direction of my working life towards medieval studies, who supervised my initiation into technical research and on whose generous support I continue to rely. I am happy to have this opportunity of expressing my most grateful thanks to him. I am grateful too, to Rev. Professor David Knowles and Rev. Professor Aubrey Gwynn, S.J. who gave me counsel and encouragement at different stages in the progress of my work. Without the help of the published work of Professor Stephan Kuttner, manuscript study in the field of medieval canonistics would be onerous indeed. But my debt to him is also personal. It was through his unfailing generosity that I came to membership of the international community of those interested in medieval canon law and to enjoy the intellectual stimulus that attends this membership. I must record that very generous financial assistance granted by the President, Dr. Michael Tierney, and Governing Body of University College, Dublin and the Senate of the National University of Ireland helped me to participate in the International Congresses of the Institute of Canon Law. That I leave my thanks to Marianne, my wife, to the last is not to say that my debt to her is least.

I wish this were a better book to honour these persons to whom I owe so much. Its imperfections are on its author's head.

INTRODUCTION

The work of the medieval canonists has always formed a significant chapter in the histories of medieval political thought. The law of the Church and its attendant juristic science forms the proper source material for the examination of the system of ideas which lay behind the functioning of papal government. Ecclesiastical jurisprudence was the practical branch of *sapientia Christiana*. It was concerned with a constitution and the exercise of power within its terms; with an organization and the methods by which it was to be run. It had of necessity to be articulate about the nature of the papacy, the constitutional and organizational linchpin. In consequence the canonists were the acknowledged theorists of papal primacy. To them rather than to the theologians belonged that segment of ecclesiology which treated of the nature of the Church as a visible corporate society under a single ruler. In that period of nearly a century which lay between the accession of Alexander III and the death of Innocent IV, canonists were required to register the increasingly numerous and more diverse applications of papal rulership to the problems of Christian society. The concept of papal monarchy came to be reexamined in academic literature because of the accelerating tempo of papal action. Under the stimulus of an active papacy, the canonists were led to examine many of the assumptions on which the popes based their actions and claims. The world of affairs conditioned the evolution of a political theory, which in turn helped to shape the course of events.

This theory was essentially an analysis of monarchy. The canonists understood the word in its straightforward sense:

> *monarchiam:* id est, singularem et unicum principatum:
> monos enim grece, latine unus; archos, id est princeps.[1]

In this use of the term, the Roman Church could be aptly described as the '*monarcha* omnium ecclesiarum,' since the prince of the Apostles and his heirs exercised supreme and undivided jurisdiction over the universal Church.[2]

---

[1] Rufinus, *Summa* C.12 q.1 c.15 (ed. Singer p. 322).

[2] Rufinus: ' . . . sacrosancta videlicet Romana Ecclesia, quae, cum sit apex omnium cathedrarum, cum sit mater ecclesiarum omnium, magistra quoque omnium, dignissime ipsa sola omnium ecclesiarum obtinere meruit monarchiam': *Sermo habitus in Lateranensi concilio sub Alexandro Papa III* ed.G.Morin, 'Le discours d'ouverture du concile général de Latran (1179) et l'œuvre littéraire de Maître Rufin,' *Atti della Pontifica Accademia Romana di Archaeologia* ser. 3, mem. 11 (Rome 1928) 117.

This monograph, however, is not concerned primarily with the concept of papal monarchy as rulership of the ecclesiastical world. The papal *principatus* extended not only over the faithful ordered in their provinces, dioceses and parishes, but over them in their secular orderings of kingdoms, fiefs and cities as well. 'To Peter,' said Innocent III, echoing St. Bernard, 'has been entrusted the direction not only of the universal Church but of the whole world (*totum saeculum*).'[3] The papal charge was thus twofold. It was of the common welfare of the Christian world as an ecclesiastical hierarchy. It embraced also that community of kingdoms and peoples which formed the *saeculum* or *populus Christianus* — the entity which was later to be called the 'common corps of Christendom.' The present study is especially concerned with the concept of papal monarchy in so far as it had reference to this community; in a word, in so far as it was political.

Political ideas, methods of argument and terminology cannot of course be properly appreciated out of the context of the society to which they were intended to have relevance. Much of thirteenth-century thought about papal power in temporal affairs was only meaningful on the assumption that there existed a common international society of which the pope was to be head. The papal political logic developed from this premise and it was only within the framework of the idea of Christendom that it acquired much of its rationality. The idea itself was old before Gratian compiled his *Decretum*.[4] But in common with other major presuppositions of papal thought, it was subject to a new scrutiny by the canonists of the thirteenth century. This notion, perhaps the most distinctively medieval of political ideas, can be examined in the canonist tradition in a fashion that no other type of thirteenth-century writing allows. For canonist thought blended abstract principle with practical application, and traditional with contemporary ideas in a special way. That an Innocent IV as a private canonist doctor, should write commentaries on his own political acts as pope epitomizes that interplay of canonical theory and papal practice which gives the canonist tradition its unique quality.

In this work, canonists are studied primarily for the insight they afford into the thirteenth-century papal political mind. Of recent years there has been a quickening of interest in this topic due to the opening for systematic

---

[3] St. Bernard: 'Nempe signum singularis pontificii Petri, per quod non navem unam, ut caeteri quique suam, sed saeculum ipsum susceperit gubernandum. Mare enim saeculum est, naves ecclesiae': *De consideratione* 2.2.8 (PL 182.752). Innocent III: 'Petro non solum universam ecclesiam sed totum reliquit saeculum gubernandum ... Cum enim mare mundum, iuxta verbum Psalmistae dicentis: "Hoc mare magnum et spatiosum ... " (Ps. 103.105); per hoc quod Petrus se misit in mare, privilegium expressit pontificii singularis, quod universum orbem susceperat gubernandum' (PL 214.759).

[4] Cf. especially, J. Rupp, *L'idée de Chrétienté dans la pensée pontificale des origines jusqu'à Innocent III* (Paris 1939).

investigation of the literature which comprised the formative period of ecclesiastical jurisprudence in the later twelfth and early thirteenth centuries. The student now finds this region of medieval intellectual activity carefully mapped and signposted, with guide-books readily available. What was until quite recently a sector of papal history impenetrable to all but the sternest spirits has been brought to order and system.[5] Already canonist material has figured as the significant element in the reappraisal of the political thought of such major international figures as Alexander III and, especially, Innocent III.[6] New canonist sources have thrown much new light on the origin and evolution of papal ideas and terminology.[7] Its study has perhaps begun a new chapter in the interpretation of the papal aspects of the medieval problem of Church and State.[8]

As yet however, the reexamination of the political logic of the papacy in the thirteenth century has not advanced much beyond the pontificate of Innocent III. There have been occasional and relatively brief forays into later pontificates,[9] On the whole, however, concentration has been, naturally enough, on the period when the previously unworked canonist sources were thickest — the later twelfth and early thirteenth centuries. What has not so far been

---

[5] Particular mention must be made of three indispensable works: S. Kuttner, *Repertorium der Kanonistik* (1140-1234), *Prodromus corporis glossarum* I (Studi e Testi 71; Città del Vaticano 1937); A. van Hove, *Prologomena ad Codicem Iuris Canonici* (2nd ed. Rome-Malines 1945); G. Le Bras, *Institutions ecclésiastiques de la Chrétienté médiévale: Préliminaires et Ière partie, Livre I* (Histoire de l'Église, ed. Fliche et Martin; Paris 1959). Very valuable also are DDC, *Studia Gratiana* (Bologna 1953 et seq.) and the *Bulletin of the Institute of Research and Study in Medieval Canon Law* (*Traditio* 1955 et seq.)

[6] See especially M. Maccarrone, *Chiesa e Stato nella Dottrina di Papa Innocenzo III* (Rome 1940); W. Ullmann, *Medieval Papalism* (London 1949); H. Tillmann, *Papst Innocenz* III (Bonn 1954); F. Kempf, *Papsttum und Kaisertum bei Innocenz III* (Misc.hist. pontif. 19; Rome 1954); M. Pacaut, *Alexandre III. Étude sur la conception du pouvoir pontifical dans sa pensée et dans son oeuvre* (Paris 1956).

[7] The numerous articles of A.M. Stickler have made available considerable selections of decretist material which has been of great assistance in the writing of this study.

[8] On this point reference should be made to several important bibliographical articles: B. Tierney, 'Some Recent Works on the Political Theories of the Medieval Canonists,' *Traditio* 10 (1954) 594-652; R. Folz, 'La papauté médiévale vue par quelques-uns de ses historiens récents,' *Revue historique* 218 (1957) 32-63; G. Michiels, 'Pouvoir spirituel et pouvoir temporel,' *Bulletin de théologie ancienne et médiévale* 8 (1958); R.E. McNally, 'The History of the Medieval Papacy: A Survey of Research, 1954-1959,' *Theological Studies* 21 (1960) 92-132.

[9] E. g. G. Le Bras, 'Boniface VIII, symphoniste et modérateur,' *Mélanges Louis Halphen* (Paris 1951) 383-394; M. Pacaut, 'L'autorité pontificale selon Innocent IV,' *Le Moyen Age* 66 (1960) 85-119; id. *La théocratie: L'Église et le pouvoir au moyen âge* (Paris 1957), esp. chapter v. M. Maccarrone, *Vicarius Christi: Storia del titolo papale* (Rome 1952); J. A. Cantini, 'De autonomia judicis saecularis et de Romani pontificis plenitudine potestatis in temporalibus secundum Innocentium IV,' *Salesianum* 23 (1961) 407-80.

attempted is a linking of this material with the work of the post-Gregory IX
commentators. This work has always been better known to historians of
medieval thought, since most of the later thirteenth century commentaries
have been in print for some centuries. The new work on the earlier canonist
writers has made necessary a reassessment of the later writers. The present
study is primarily an attempt to evaluate the later commentators, in particular
Innocent IV and Hostiensis, in the light of the *materia politica* which the
earlier canonist tradition had put at their disposal for 'further perfection,
adaptation to changing circumstances and refinement.'[10] Put in another
way, the object of this study is to clarify the interpretation of thirteenth
century canonist thought by examining its internal evolution. It studies the
elements of continuity and change in the typical methods, ideas and terminology concerning papal power in temporal affairs that occurred in the period
broadly between Huguccio and Hostiensis. I have concentrated on throwing
into relief the essential terms of reference of canonist thought on the problem
and I have as far as possible eschewed detail in order the better to describe
its framework.

Part I of this study aims to present a chronological narrative of canonist
thought about papal power in temporal affairs up to and including Innocent
IV. Its object is to show the elements of method and doctrine that composed
the canonist discussion of the problem, with an indication of the changes that
occurred in this period. Two factors give design and form to this survey:
one an assumption about the framework of canonist thinking about the relations of the powers, the other the chronological divisions of canonist literature.

It is assumed that the medieval discussion of the problem of Church and
State, whatever the period or type of writer or his personal loyalties, had
always to reckon with three facets of the matter: that the powers were divided,
that they must cooperate with each other and that in some sense or other the
spiritual power was the higher one. These were the basic abstractions, even
with those who were challenging the political consequences of the superiority
of the spiritual power. How these three elements were reconciled could, of
course, differ very considerably. But that each aspect must find a place
somewhere in the logic, unless a man was to repudiate the law of God, was
common ground.

The narrative of canonist doctrine is accordingly shaped by the way in
which canonists considered each of these three interacting principles. They
were not, however, of equal standing, since it was the weight accorded to
sacerdotal superiority which determined the real content of the principle of

---

[10] S. Kuttner, 'The Scientific Investigation of Medieval Canon Law: the Need and the
Opportunity,' *Speculum* 24 (1949) 491-501 at 497.

divided powers and dictated the conditions of their cooperation. Particular attention must therefore be directed to this determinant.

The second factor giving shape to the narrative account is the three distinguishable phases of canonist literature in the twelfth and thirteenth centuries. The first, that of the early decretists, began with the appearance of Gratian's *Decretum* about 1140 and was terminated by Huguccio's *Summa* about 1190. The second was that of the early decretalists, the period of the reception of the new law of the *Quinque Compilationes Antiquae* and also of a series of *Apparatus* on the *Decretum* from which emerged its *glossa ordinaria* (c. 1215-17). The third phase was initiated by the supersession of the *Compilationes Antiquae* with the promulgation in 1234 of the *Decretales* by Gregory IX, which in due course were the basis of the commentaries of such men as Goffredus, Innocent IV and Hostiensis.

From the point of view of the development of ideas about the papacy particularly in its political aspects, each of the second two of these periods can be readily identified with a pope of outstanding canonistic interest — Innocent III, the most important papal legislator of the thirteenth century and an outstanding analyst of papal primacy, and Innocent IV, responsible for the most dramatic papal political act of the century, the deposition of Frederick II, and at once a significant legislator and a leading academic jurist. The activities of both these popes were of the utmost importance for the development of canonist ideas about the papacy and present themselves as obvious *foci* for the organization of a narrative account of that development (Part I, sections 2 and 3).

For the early decretist period however, no one papal name suggests itself with such readiness as a *focus* round which can be conveniently discussed the leading ideas and methods of the first chapter of the canonist story. No single pope impressed his doctrines on the *Decretum* to the extent to which Innocent III did his on the literature of the *Compilationes Antiquae*, or Innocent IV on post-Gregorian commentary. Nevertheless the suggestion that there is some special connection between the decretists and Pope Gelasius I has been made sufficiently often by historians to warrant using his name as a point of reference. It will be shown that the relationship between Gelasian and decretist thought is not altogether free from textual complications. It is doubtful how far the expression 'Gelasian doctrine' is meaningful for interpreters of canonist thought. Nonetheless to accompany the decretists in following the fortunes of texts that can be related in some way to Pope Gelasius is to obtain a view of the main features of decretist thinking about the papacy in temporal affairs (Part I, section 1).

The writing of a chronological account of the development of canonist doctrine revealed very clearly the quite fundamental place in thirteenth-century papal thought of the term *plenitudo potestatis*. In the meaning of this term lies the heart of canonist and papal thinking about the nature and exercise of papal authority. Part II is an attempt to analyze this term. It is traced from its first appearances in canonist literature to its adoption at the highest official level in the Creed professed by the Roman and Greek churches at the Second Council of Lyons in 1274. It is especially in this context that there is brought home the impossibility of divorcing the study of canonist political ideas from their ecclesiology. *Plenitudo potestatis* and the closely related term, *papa est iudex ordinarius omnium*, began their careers in a purely ecclesiastical context and they did not lose this primary meaning. In how they became by extension political terms lies one of the keys to the understanding of the essential nature of canonist thought about papal monarchy.

Part III is intended as an analysis of the thirteenth-century canonist system as it was at its fullest before the topic of papal monarchy became envenomed by later thirteenth-century controversy and the work of academics was pillaged or political ammunition. Hostiensis was probably the most outstanding academic jurist of the century. It is perhaps not fanciful to see him standing in a relationship to the thirteenth-century canonist tradition analagous to that of Aquinas to the thirteenth-century theological tradition: the culminating point of synthesis whereby the western Christian tradition absorbed one hitherto extraneous to it — Greek philosophy in the one case, Roman law in the other. However this may be, the claim of Hostiensis to be among the very front rank of ecclesiastical writers in this century will not be seriously disputed. He is an obvious subject for detailed investigation necessary in order to make a final assessment of the canonist discussion of the theory of papal monarchy.

Hostiensis did not write systematic political treatises, any more than did the other academic canonists. One cannot go to any one point in his writings and find all the material relevant to political discussion gathered together. It is scattered throughout the length of his *Summa* and of his *Apparatus*, closely linked it is true by a thorough cross-reference system, but nevertheless not given that form and order which the systematic treatise provides. The expositor of his political ideas is faced with the problem of reconstructing the logic of the argument. He must put it together in the single unified whole which Hostiensis did not himself provide.

There is an obvious danger attendant on this reconstruction process. The giving of a framework and pattern by the expositor to a mass of material undifferentiated by the author himself involves judgments as to what constitute the premises of the argument and about the emphases to be accorded to its stages. There is a danger that such judgments will be colored by the assumptions and prejudices of the expositor so that his reconstruction will be but a partial and subjective view of the logic as a whole. Hostiensis has been down the centuries a conspicuous victim of biased reading, and those who have searched his works for a point of view they wished to find there have rarely been unsuccessful. The really interesting problem here is not so much that interpreters have managed to support antithetical viewpoints with the opinions of Hostiensis — for this is a fate common enough for those who write technically and lengthily — but whether or not Hostiensis did maintain at different points in his books positions which were inconsistent. Is there in fact a political logic, a systematic, reasoned consistent theory to be reconstructed from Hostiensis' work or is there merely a mass of arguments loosely pulled together, but not refined into a coherent whole with its apparent inconsistencies resolved? Does it arise inevitably from the nature of Hostiensis' work — and by extension, of the work of canonists in general — that some should see him as a 'dualist' and others as a 'monist,' that some should judge him 'moderate' and others 'extreme'? Or has this arisen from the selection of his texts according to the subjective inclinations of the selector?

The reading of Hostiensis in the light of the antecedent canonist tradition — as it always should be to be properly appraised — has brought the conviction that the bases of his thought were rooted deeply in a century or more of the discipline of canonical science, that he was its full embodiment and logical product. He was neither more nor less inconsistent than any other ecclesiastical writer on the problem of the relations of the powers. His 'inconsistency' was itself typical of the canonist tradition for it sprang from a twofold tendency that ran through all ecclesiastical speculation about the relations of the powers in the thirteenth century. Canonist thought knew two themes: one which developed the principle and application of the distinction of the powers, and another which reflected on the unitary nature of Christian society. On the one hand it was of divine law that there was a dualism of spiritual and temporal powers and on the other, it seemed equally of divine command that there should be a single kingdom of Christendom. There was unity in the formation and direction of Christendom and duality of powers inscribed within it. Both were equally aspects of Christian politics — the former justified by arguments drawn from the doctrine of the Mystical Body, the kingship of Christ and its vicariate, the latter because of Christ's explicit injunctions that the powers should be divided. The canonist tradition had to find room for both aspects. The respective emphases placed on them in canonist literature varied according to context and to the predilections of individual canonists.

In the writings of Hostiensis, so much the product of the canonist tradition, both positions are to be found equally clearly indicated. Sometimes he wished to emphasize that the powers were one in a unity of order, imposed by the unity of the purpose of the one Christian body. In these contexts, there was a tendency for his language to become extravagant — he could speak of the pope as 'dominus spiritualium et temporalium' and to paraphrase St. Paul to claim that all kings were 'sub pedibus eius.'[11] Sometimes he wished to grapple with a practical problem of conflicting ecclesiastical and secular jurisdictions and his approach was realistically dualist, his tone moderate. Both strands of thought were equally canonistic and both must be taken into account in any interpretation of canonist thought about the papal power in temporal affairs which purports to be complete. That conviction is the basic assumption of this study.

---

[11] Cf. Eph. 1.22 and Ps. 8.8: Hostiensis, *Apparatus* 1.33.6 (*Solite*) s.v. *nihil excipiens qui dixit quodcunque*, whence to such polemical writers as Ptolomy of Lucca, *Determinatio compendiosa de iurisdictione imperii* (ed. H. Krammer, MGH, *Fontes iur. germ. antiqui separatim editi* 1; Hanover 1909) c.25, p. 50 and Henry of Cremona, *De potestate papae* ed. R. Scholz, *Die Publizistik zur Zeit Philipps des Schönen und Bonifaz VIII* (Stuttgart 1903) 465.

PART I

THE FIRST THREE PHASES OF
CANONIST THOUGHT

In the evolution of canonist views about the papal monarchy and its relationship to secular power, the work of three popes was of very great consequence: Gelasius I, Innocent III and Innocent IV. Other popes, of course,
left their mark on the *Corpus iuris canonici*, but these three made significant
contributions specifically to the principles and practice of the papal power in
temporal affairs. These three papal names also mark in a general way the
three broad chronological divisions into which our period of canonist literature
can be divided: Gelasius I, representing the *ius antiquum*, around fundamental
texts of which the decretists pursued their line of enquiry concerning the
relationship of the powers; Innocent III, by way of whose *ius novum* canonists
rethought in more contemporary terms so much of what half a century of
decretist activity had established; Innocent IV, whose own *Apparatus* and
legislation and not least whose controversy with Frederick II, brought the
canonist system very near to completion. A general survey of the contributions of each of these popes to the making of the canonist view of the papal
power in temporal affairs will serve as a narrative introduction to the nature
of canonist working methods, terminology, principles and problems in their
analysis of papal monarchy.

Gratian and his forbears culled about a hundred canons from the official
letters and theological writings of Gelasius I. His contribution to the *Decretum*
was, among papal contributors, second only in size to that of Gregory I. It
thus complemented the work of Gregory as a source wherein the eleventh
century reformers had found 'in its practical form the lofty spirit of order
and papal initiative in the affairs of all the Churches of the West which they
sought to renew.'[1]

With this emphasis on practical matters, on the *instantia quotidiana, sol-
licitudo omnium ecclesiarum*,[2] the Gelasian canons were of very varied nature

---

[1] R. W. Southern, *The Making of the Middle Ages* (London 1953) 142.

[2] 2 Cor.11.28. Cited in the very first decretal ever issued (by Pope Siricius in 385: W.

and found places throughout the whole length of Gratian's *Decretum*. It was
not a decretist practice to identify particular doctrines with particular individuals; the name of Gelasius did not personify any specific view on any judicial
matter. He was one *auctoritas* among many, more influential than most
perhaps, but nevertheless merely a part of a tradition. Examination of decretist glosses, however, suggests that the Gelasian canons of most significance were concerned with the principles of two aspects of papal primacy:
appellate jurisdiction and relationships with the temporal power. We shall
see in due time how in the evolution of the term *iudex ordinarius omnium*,
decretists built on the canons concerned with the former aspect and their work
was officially adopted by Innocent III.[3] The measurement of the influence
of Gelasius on canonist thought about the relationship of spiritual and temporal
powers is our immediate concern.

This question will be examined strictly within these stated terms. The
problem here is not what Gelasius himself meant in asserting a very general
principle about the distinction of the two powers in the context of the Roman
Empire at the end of the fifth century, nor how Gelasius has been interpreted
in post-medieval times. Whatever view may be taken either about Gelasius'
own rendering of the superiority of the spiritual power and its novelty otherwise in its own day, or about the nature of its role in the future, the question
here concerns what the canonists and popes of the twelfth and thirteenth
centuries knew of Pope Gelasius and how they used his texts. In the history
of ideas there is generally a distinction to be made between the views of the
individual thinker himself and what later ages made of them. We do not
necessarily understand the nature of Gelasius' contribution to the stock of
medieval political thinking by having an interpretation of what Gelasius has
given to the modern world. Confusion is confounded if it is not taken into
account that the scholars of periods equipped with full and critical editions
of the authentic texts of a Father of the Church are often very differently
placed from their medieval counterparts. Gratian did not know his Gelasian
texts in any critical way. By the time they were incorporated in the *Decretum* they had been through several editions in the various canonical collections
on which Gratian drew. Inevitably in this process textual errors occurred
and were perpetuated. In the case of the Gelasian texts treating of the relationship of the powers, these errors were not merely a variant of readings of
individual words and phrases. There was significant distortion of the originals
— through selection of extracts taken out of context, through quotation by a
much later writer, himself bent on a particular interpretation, through amal-

---

Ullmann, *The Growth of Papal Government in the Middle Ages* [London 1955] 5), this became
a cherished formula of papal chanceries throughout the middle ages.

[3] Below, pp. 94-95.

gamation of a part of the original with later accretions, through truncation of texts incorporated in different parts widely separated in the *Decretum*. Further, such were the errors of attribution of authorship and ignorance of the original author when a later writer was really quoting, that a decretist, if asked to study the personal views of Gelasius on the relations of the powers, could not have done so. For two of the relevant major texts attributed to him were in fact Gregory VII's and contained only three sentences of genuinely Gelasian work, while of the other two, genuinely Gelasian in full, one was attributed to Cyprian and the other to Nicholas I. It was not merely the canonists who used Gelasius in this form: the *Decretum* was common to all types of writer on this problem. 'Gelasian doctrine' is thus a dangerous category to apply to the Middle Ages. Medieval men did not think of Gelasius as typifying a particular view of Church-State relations, nor had they the equipment to do so had they wished.

This qualification having been made, however, it still remains true that the writings of Gelasius on the problem, whether the real authorship was known or not, and writings which stood in his name even if that was not exactly accurate, played a significant part in the evolution of canonist theories. Again, there will be cause to notice at a later stage the Gelasian-decretist background to some Innocentian doctrines. The important point is that all the four texts of the *Decretum* which together comprise the main body of the *auctoritates* for decretist speculation on the relations of the two powers, relate in some way or other to Pope Gelasius. A survey of the glosses based on these texts will introduce the leading themes and principal literary methods of decretist thought on this subject and thus form the necessary background to the emergence of the thirteenth-century work stemming from the decretals of Innocent III.

'Pater iuris canonici, divini et humani' was the title accorded to Innocent III by the leading canonist of the thirteenth century.[4] Hostiensis may be forgiven his exaggeration when the extent of Innocent's personal contribution to the *Gregoriana* is calculated.[5] As a formulator of profound and subtle pronouncements on papal jurisdiction over secular rulers, Innocent III needs no introduction.[6] What has to be determined is the nature and extent of the impact made on canonist thought by his 'political' decretals. Some estimation has to be made of the novelty or otherwise of early decretalist thought, stimulated by Innocent III, as compared with decretist thought. That his pontificate marked a critical stage in the development of canonist ideas is

---

[4] Hostiensis, *Summa* 5.7 § 1 'Innocentius pater iuris'; *ibid*. 5.39 § 12; 5.3 § 10.

[5] Cf. Friedberg, *Corpus iuris canonici* II, cols. xiv-xvi (516 decretals)

[6] Reference may be made to p. 3, n. 6 above, for some of the recent literature on this subject.

beyond question. What can be profitably examined perhaps is the precise degree of continuity and change represented by Innocent's work.

It is in the context of this problem of the evolution of canonist political thought that Innocent IV has especial importance. For many historians prompted by the testimonies of Frederick II and Matthew Paris and of Robert Grosseteste, Innocent IV appears as the very personification of 'aggressive Popedom.' Arrogance, cupidity, and usurpation of the rights of others were charges levelled at Innocent in his own day and, on the whole, later critics, often with a zest sharpened by religious prejudice, have endorsed them. Cast for the role of usurper of ecclesiastical and political power and held to be primarily responsible in the policies he pursued, for the debasement of the papacy's position of spiritual leadership, Innocent IV is often seen as the creator of an extreme *theory* of papal power in temporal affairs, as the 'father' of hierocracy. Even those who have sought to defend Innocent III against charges of extremism, of being a *Papstkaiser*, have shown no similar sympathy for the positions of Innocent IV. Indeed Innocent III has been defended in part by a transference of responsibility for the development of extremist views to Innocent IV.

There is a real and important problem for the history of canonist doctrines in this identification of Innocent IV with the growth of an extreme theory of papal power in temporal affairs. How far was hierocratic theory a creation of the thirteenth century and what was the precise part played in it by Innocent IV? In what sense was his thought a turning point in the development of canonist principles of the temporal effects of spiritual authority?

Such questions are among those central to this study and they underlie it as a whole. They link Innocent IV and Boniface VIII with Gelasius I or at any rate, they confront the papal theory as evolved in the thirteenth century with the thought of preceding periods. The immediate discussion, a chronological narrative of canonist thought, drawn from the three main source groups, is an essential preliminary to seeking their answers.

1. *Gelasius I and the Decretists*

In a rather artificial way four texts of the *Decretum* may be labelled Gelasian. D. 96 c.10 (*Duo sunt*) was attributed by Gratian to Gelasius. In fact it was taken from Gregory VII's famous first letter to Hermann, bishop of Metz. The first two paragraphs of the canon were a citation of the genuine Gelasian letter, the last and longest was Gregory's own. C.15 q.6 c.3 (*Alius item*) was a continuation of the same letter, carrying on where *Duo sunt* stopped. It was attributed by Gratian to Gelasius, though it related an event of the eighth century, and was in fact Gregory VII's work. D.96 c.6 (*Cum ad verum*) was taken from a genuine letter of Nicholas I and is entirely a quotation from Gelasius's *De anathematis vinculo*. D.10 c.8 (*Quoniam*), attributed to Cyprian, is the same passage minus the opening sentence of *Cum ad verum*.[7]

These four passages were not, of course, the only texts in the *Decretum* which were found relevant for the discussion of the relationship of the powers. But they were undoubtedly considered the major ones in connection with the broad principles of the relationship. It was invariably one or another of them which initiated fundamental discussion, in the course of which all other contributory canons would be introduced. Together, therefore, they formed the basis of all decretist work on the subject. Together, they established a general proposition which though never stated specifically by any decretist, underlay all canonist thinking on the relations of the two powers. It may be stated in this way: that any abstraction expressing the principle of the relationship had to take account of three aspects of it which are all divinely commanded — the powers were distinct, they had to cooperate, the spiritual power was superior. The first was commanded by the Lord Himself, albeit, as one decretist put it, 'indistincte';[8] the second followed from the divine origin of both powers, and the third from the power of binding and loosing accorded to priests for the proper exercising of which they were accountable before God. For all canonists, these three commands formed a single divine precept for the regulation of the relations of the two powers. Their literary and methodological problem was to interpret and combine each aspect in harmony with the *auctoritates*, whether those embodying earlier tradition and set out in the *Decretum*, or those reflecting current papal practices and set out in the *Decretales*, whilst preserving the unity of the divine principle that underlay them.

The interpretation of the superiority of the spiritual is obviously the critical factor in establishing an equilibrium of the three aspects. What canonists thought of that principle conditioned what they thought both about the nature of 'dualism' and about the conditions of the exercise of cooperation. It is logically necessary, therefore, to begin with some account of how decretists estimated the consequences in the temporal sphere of sacerdotal superiority.

From this point of view, the canons *Duo sunt* and *Alius item* were crucial. In the name of Gelasius stood all decretist principles concerned with the *primum caput* of sacerdotal preeminence: the papal right to depose rulers.

The *casus* or summary which Benincasa of Arezzo provided for the *glossa*

---

[7] This information concerning the origins of these texts is taken from Friedberg's notes to each of the canons in his edition of the *Decretum*.

[8] Alanus Anglicus, *Apparatus 'Ius naturale'*: 'Et indistincte docuit dominus dicens "reddite que sunt cesaris cesari" etc.': ad D. 96 c.6 s.v. *discrevit* (B.N.MS 15393, fol. 70rb). Characteristically, he added: 'Verumtamen alteri subesse non negauit.'

ordinaria on *Duo sunt* is an admirable introduction to what this text meant for decretists.[9] Gelasius and the Emperor Anastasius, he said, were in controversy about their respective preeminence. The Pope proved that his authority was the greater on two grounds: firstly, because a divine charge had been laid on him for the welfare of the soul of the emperor and all men, and for which God would hold him accountable; secondly, because emperors were juridically subject to priests, as was shown when Pope Innocent excommunicated Arcadius, and St. Ambrose, Theodosius. 'Colla regum et principum submittuntur genibus sacerdotum'; the words were drawn from the Gregorian part of the text and represented his spirit, not that of Gelasius. Far from being a 'dualist' text, *Duo sunt* as known by the canonists was designed to emphasize the subordination of the secular power. Emperors, kings, princes, every man *sine distinctione* was subject in moral matters. Sacerdotal superiority in this respect was not expressed in a purely admonitory fashion nor was its operation confined to the sphere of the consciences of individuals. It was a judicial power with public effects enforceable under a sanction which had deprivation of public office as its ultimate stage.[10]

The lesson of *Duo sunt* was reinforced by that of *Alius item*. Benincasa put this succinctly enough: 'Pope Gelasius writing against Emperor Anastasius says that he can depose him on account of his wickedness.'[11] Gelasius had said no such thing. It was again Gregory VII alleging precedent for a papal deposing power — the substitution by Pope Zachary of Pepin for

---

[9] 'Anastasius imperator et Gelasius contendebant de preheminencia unius· ad alterum. Set Gelasius ostendit quod auctoritas pontificalis longe maior est quam culmen imperiale et hoc probat duabus rationibus: scilicet quia papa de anima imperatoris et aliorum redditurus rationem et quia colla regum et principum submittuntur genibus sacerdotum; et duobus exemplis: scilicet Ambrosii et Innocentii, qui Archadium et Theodosium imperatores excommunicaverunt': ed. A. Stickler, 'Sacerdotium et Regnum nei Decretisti e primi Decretalisti,' *Salesianum* 15 (1953) 575-612, at p. 33 of the offprint.

[10] Cf. Johannes Teutonicus, *Glossa ordinaria* ad D.96 c.10 s.v. *iudicio*: 'Zacharias quoque papa regem Francorum deposuit et in locum eius Pippinum substituit, xv.q.vi. Alius.' For an earlier interpretation, cf. Huguccio, n. 14 below. For a slightly later one, cf. Raymond of Peñafort: 'Nam imperatores, reges et omnes principes, hac sine distinctione, omnis homo pertinet ad iudicium ecclesiasticum ratione peccati, Extra iii, de iud., Novit, LXIII di. Valentinianus, XCVI di. Quis dubitet, Duo sunt, XI.q.III. Si autem. Et est ratio quia ipse papa et alii prelati ecclesiastici tenentur de omnibus reddere rationem in districto examine .... ': *Summa iuris* 1.11 ed. J. Ríus Serra (Barcelona 1945) 39.

[11] 'Gelasius papa scribens contra Anastasium imperatorem dicit quod potest eum deponere propter malitiam suam. Et hoc probat exemplo Zachariae papae qui regem Francorum deposuit non tantum propter sua delicta, quantum pro eo quod inutilis erat: et loco eius Pipinum patrem Caroli posuit, et omnes Francigenas a fidelitate eius absolvit: et milites a vinculo iuramenti [sicut ecclesia frequenter absolvit milites a vinculo iuramenti] in depositionibus episcoporum.' I have here used the text of the 1561 edition of the *Casus* supplemented by the words in brackets from Stickler's text, *Salesianum* 34.

Childeric as king of the Franks. Thus history was made to support the argument of *Duo sunt* which adduced responsibility for the souls of men before the divine tribunal as the justification for bringing their bodies before the sacerdotal tribunal. Priests had the power of binding and loosing souls; they had, therefore, the power of judging men's public conduct and holding them publicly accountable and punishable. Punishment in a public way might mean exclusion from the *societas fidelium*; loss of any position of authority seemed the inescapable consequence of such exclusion. The judicial power of priests in Christian society was thus genuinely an *imperium spirituale* (as one early decretist put it):[12] an *imperium* because it was *potestas iudiciaria; spirituale*, because its basis and object were in the spiritual order. But it was not necessarily only spiritual in its practical effects.

Whether or not Gelasius intended his teaching to be understood in a way that permitted the deposition of rulers may perhaps be doubted. But it is certain that canonists read these views into texts which stood in his name and it can hardly be disputed that they reflected accurately enough the views of Gregory VII. There is no need to go here into the *minutiae* of all decretist glosses about the deposing power;[13] we may safely assume that the authoritative opinion of the twelfth century is represented by the *magna lucerna* of early decretists, Huguccio. At any rate, future work proceeded from a basis he had done most to establish, and it is for this reason, not merely because he was Innocent III's teacher of canon law, that his views on deposition deserve attention.

---

[12] *Summa Lipsiensis*: 'Quod ergo hic dicitur, quod habet utrum(que) gladium, id est tam super clericos, quam super laicos imperium habet spirituale, ut quem ligat in terra, ligatus sit in celis': ed. J. Juncker, 'Die Summa des Simon von Bisignano und seine Glossen,' *Zeitschrift der Savigny-Stiftung für Rechtsgeschichte, Kan. Abt.* 15 (1926) 492-3 n.2. It was S. Mochi Onory who first gave prominence to this expression, *Fonti canonistiche dell' idea moderna dello Stato* (Milan 1951) e.g. 6, 111, 115, 121, 122. But language of this sort was common enough when decretists were commenting on Matt. 16.19 and on Peter Damian's paraphase of it in D. 22 c.1 '(Petro) clavigero terreni simul et coelestis imperii iura commisit'; cf. e.g. *gl. anon.* (Sidney Sussex College, Cambridge MS 101): 'tam super clericos quam laicos ius spirituale commisit id est, potestatem ligandi atque soluendi' (fol. 19va: Stickler, *Salesianum* 22): *gl. anon.* (B.M. Stowe 378): 'tam super laicos quam clericos imperium habet quo ad spiritualia velud quem ligat in terra sit ligatus in celo' (fol. 12b); *gl. anon.* (Durham Cath. MS C.I.7: 'quo ad animas, scilicet ubi ait "Quodcunque ligaveris" etc. usque soluta est in celo, potestatem petro concessam dicit terrenum et celeste imperium' (fol. 11rb). This *locus* was used to debate whether the *ius* of the *terrenum* (*Romanum*) *imperium* had also been committed to the pope, see below p. 26.

[13] Cf. O. Hageneder, 'Exkommunikation und Thronfolgeverlust bei Innocenz III,' *Römische historische Mitteilungen* (Österreichisches Kulturinstitut, Rome) 2 (1959) 9-50; id. 'Das päpstliche Recht der Fürstenabsetzung: seine kanonistische Grundlegung (1150-1250),' *Archivum historiae pontificiae* I (1963) 55-95.

Huguccio was not an extremist in his notion of the papal power in temporal affairs. He held a belief about the origins of imperial power that was to be rejected in Innocent III's *Venerabilem* and of the 'two swords' to be criticized by later decretalists. Even his deposition theory envisaged a certain qualification of the exclusive right of the pope to act against rulers worthy of deposition. This very moderation makes it the more revealing of the place *Duo sunt* and *Alius item* held in early decretist thought when, on their basis, Huguccio asserted the principle, 'papa potest iudicare imperatorem in temporalibus.' They were texts which established sacerdotal supremacy and expressed it as a power to judge and punish the political conduct of secular rulers.

It was another Gelasian canon, *Cum ad verum* which prompted Huguccio to discuss the nature of the distinction of the powers. Having established to his own satisfaction the principle that 'quoad institutionem, neutra (potestas) pendet ex altera,' he introduced the question of whether one power was greater than the other. His solution was essentially an analysis of *Duo sunt.* Some had argued, he said, that this canon asserted the principle that the pope was greater than the emperor in spiritual matters and the emperor greater than the pope in temporal matters. But for Huguccio (and here his opinion was fully representative of the majority decretist view) *Duo sunt* taught that the pope had jurisdiction over the emperor *in spiritualibus,* but the emperor had no jurisdiction over the pope *in temporalibus.* If a pope was guilty of theft of property, the emperor had no power to judge him. But if an emperor were guilty of injustice to anyone or of theft, he might be compelled by ecclesiastical censure to give satisfaction or make restitution.[14] He was thus 'quodam modo'

---

[14] Huguccio: 'Set queret aliquis uter utro sit maior? Et quidem in spiritualibus papa maior est imperatore; imperator maior papa in temporalibus, sicut aperte colligitur ex eo quod sequitur et infra eo. Duo et xi.q.i. Magnum, Sacerdotibus et di.xxii.c.i. Set aliter et aliter: papa sic est maior in spiritualibus quod habet iurisdictionem in spiritualibus super imperatorem, ut in eis possit eum ligare et condempnare, ar. di. lxiii, Valentinianus et infra c. Duo; set imperator non sic est maior papa in temporalibus ut e. Duo; nullam enim iurisdictionem uel prelationem habet imperator super papam; set dicitur esse maior in temporalibus quam ille quia maiorem potestatem et iurisdictionem habet in eis quam ille, non tamen super eum, sicut episcopus alterius loci maior est quam iste privatus, qui tamen non subest ei. Sic et illud intelligitur, infra ii.q.vii. § Item cum Balaam usque Item David. Si ergo papa offenderet aliquem in temporalibus, puta auferendo ei capam vel possessionem aliquam uel huiusmodi, non posset conueniri ab illo coram imperatore; posset ibi excipere et dicere: "qui me iudicat dominus est" (1 Cor. 4.4), ar. ix.q.iii. Nemo, Aliorum, Cuncta; tamen de huiusmodi re apud concilium potest deponere querimoniam; si tamen satisfacere noluerit a nemine cogetur, contra autem Leo dicit, infra ii.q.vi, Nos; set non dicit hoc ex communi iure set ex humilitate et dispensatione. Set numquid papa potest iudicare imperatorem in temporalibus? Credo quod sic: per excommunicationem enim coget eum uel respondere coram se uel coram alio per se uel per procuratorem': ad D. 96 c.6.s.v. *officia* (Lincoln Cath. MS 2, fol. 172^{vab}).

subject to the pope *in temporalibus*.[15] It was divinely ordained that sinners should be denounced to the Church and the pope had jurisdiction to compel the attendance of the accused *coram se*. The formulation of the logic of papal jurisdiction *ratione peccati* in denunciation procedure is here very plain from Huguccio's reading of *Duo sunt*.[16] Innocent III's citation of Philip Augustus, denounced to him by King John, justified in the well-known decretal *Novit*, was but the official adoption of the view, to form the classic canonist interpretation of Gelasian-Gregorian ideas.

[Huguccio's contention was that if an errant ruler would not submit himself to the judgment of others, the pope as *iudex superior* would assert his right to judge him.] He showed a certain disposition to give the electoral princes in the empire, and the barons of kingdoms, a place in these judicial proceedings.[17] For the rest, procedure was envisaged as following a typical canonical pattern. Admonition was the first stage after conviction and if this did not produce a change of heart, major excommunication (*a communione fidelium*) followed, and release of subjects from their fealty. If the ruler remained recalcitrant, sentence of deposition might be passed, his removal by armed force be countenanced and the substitution of another be permitted. Whether this sentence of deposition was passed by the pope (with the assent of the princes) or by the princes (with the assent of the pope) did not affect materially the principle of papal authority. Whichever procedure was adopted, the pope was 'iudex superior.' For if a king was tried by his barons and condemned to deposition, this sentence needed papal assent. The status of 'iudex superior' meant that such major political changes in Christian society could not be made without recourse to the head of that society.[18]

---

[15] '*Subiectas*: in spiritualibus et quodam modo in temporalibus': ad D. 96 c.11 (MS *cit. loc.cit.*)

[16] '*Nosti itaque* .... *te pendere iudicio*: quo ad spiritualia et in secularibus etiam, papa imperatorem iudicare si alterius iudicium subire nolit; nonne dictum est de quolibet nolente satisfacere, "dic ecclesie" (Matt. 18.17)? Nonne tunc ecclesia cogit imperatorem ut satisfaciat ei quam lesit uel restituat quod male abstulit uel penitentia non debet dari quia inutilis est, ut xviii.q.vi. c.i?' ad D. 96 c.10 (*Duo*) (MS *cit.* fol. 172rb).

[17] '*Quod dictum est papa posse eum deponere, credo verum esse de voluntate et assensu principum si coram eo accusetur et convincatur; quod tunc demum intelligo si conuictus et admonitus non vult cessare et satisfacere, tunc debet excommunicari et omnes ab eius fidelitate debent remoueri, ar.xv.q.vi. Nos sanctorum, Iuratos. Si nec tunc corrigitur, tune demum sententia iuste percellitur et armata manu recte expellitur et alius legitime eligitur. Set a quo dabitur sententia? A domino papa coram quo fuit conuictus uel a principibus suis, si hoc romanus pontifex approbauerit': ad D. 96 c.6 s.v. *officia* (MS *cit.* fol. 172vb).

[18] '*Deposuit*: Set numquid papa potest deponere imperatorem uel regem qui non subest imperatori? Sic, si de uoluntate principum coram eo accusetur et conuincatur, et conuictus et admonitus nolit satisfacere, tunc debet excommunicari, et si sic non resipiscit, recte sententia depositionis percellitur a papa uel a principibus de uoluntate pape: est enim papa

Thus the 'gravius pondus sacerdotum': a principle of public law, a jurisdiction to which all political authority was subject.

But this principle was not the only one the decretists learned, or thought they learned, from Gelasius. Whether they were aware of the true source or not, they learned from him of the divine origin of temporal power and the divine command that the powers were to be distinct. It was in this context that the canons *Quoniam* and *Cum ad verum* had their special role in the evolution of canonist thought. The former was placed in D.10 of the *Decretum*, which dealt with the subject, *Constitutiones seculares ecclesiasticis subsunt.* The latter, in D.96 which sought to establish the proposition, *Nulli laici quidpiam de rebus ecclesiasticis statuant.* Both these Distinctions, the two principal *loci* in the *Decretum* for political discussion, were concerned with ecclesiastical independence, the autonomy of the clerical order in its own judicial, legislative and administrative concerns. As has been seen in considering Huguccio's deposition theory, such questions were not separable from a consideration of the nature and extent of sacerdotal superiority. In the context of decretist discussion of the exclusion of the lay power from participation in ecclesiastical business, the canons *Quoniam* and *Cum ad verum* served both to raise the level of the generality of the argument by initiating consideration of the main principles of the relationship of the two powers, and to relate those principles to very practical matters.

Their particular emphasis was on the distinction of the *officia utriusque potestatis,* and it was on the support of these texts that canonists leaned most heavily when taking account of the separation of the powers.

The general understanding of the texts (which are in fact virtually the same) may be illustrated from summaries supplied by Huguccio and Benincasa of Arezzo.[19] The Emperor Michael, it was related, had ordered on his own

---

maior eo et preest ei ut di. xcvi, Duo, Si imperator. Set nonne principes et barones si coram eis conuincatur possunt eum deponere? Credo quod sic, si habent assensum pape, aliter non, cum iudex superior, scilicet papa inuenitur; si vero iudex superior non inuenitur, tunc propter defectum iudicis possunt subditi deponere superiorem, ar. di. xl. Si papa et iii.q.i. § ult.': ad C. 15 q.6 c.3 (B.N. MS lat. 15396 [collated with lat. 3892] fol. 224vb).

[19] Huguccio on *Cum ad verum*: 'Usque ad aduentum Christi, iura imperialia et pontificalia erant indistincta quia idem erat imperator et pontifex ut di. xxi, Clericos; set a Christo distincta sunt iura et officia imperatoris et pontificis et alia sunt attributa imperatori, scilicet temporalia, et alia, scilicet spiritualia, concessa sunt pontifici, et hoc est factum causa humanitatis seruande et superbie uitande. Si enim imperator uel pontifex omnia haberet officia de facili superbiret, nunc uero cum indiget altero et videt se non plene sibi sufficere humiliatur. Et introducitur hoc capitulum ad ostendendum quod imperator non debet disponere uel iudicare de rebus ecclesiasticis, quondam enim confusa et indistincta erant officia imperatoris et pontificis' (Lincoln Cath.MS 2, fol. 172va). Benincasa on *Quoniam* (*glossa ordinaria*): 'Iulianus imperator vendicabat sibi imperium et pontificatum: quod locum habuit in veteri testamento. Sed dicit Cyprianus, quod postquam Christus venit, sic officia utriusque po-

authority that Ignatius, patriarch of Constantinople should be deposed by his bishops and was duly obeyed. Pope Nicholas pronounced that a lay ruler had no power to give such an order. Before the time of Christ, there was confusion and indistinctness about the separation of the powers and the one person was to be found exercising the functions of both king and priest. But the powers were separated by Christ Himself *causa humanitatis servande et superbie vitande.* For if one person held both powers, he risked being consumed with pride. True Christian humility demanded a separation of the powers, with the recognition that neither power was sufficient to itself, that each needed the support of the other. The lesson, then, for decretists was that the distinction of the powers and the necessity of their cooperation was a principle of divine law, as was the divine origin of temporal power.

These principles needed to be reconciled with that of the superiority of the spiritual power. D. 10, where questions were posed about the validity of secular law in ecclesiastical matters and *e converso*, provided concrete problems on which decretists could make such a reconciliation. The discussion of such practical problems as whether secular law could overrule ecclesiastical law and the circumstances in which secular law might be used in ecclesiastical courts constituted an analysis in microcosm of the relations of the powers. For they concerned the application of the principles of each of the three elements involved in the relationship — the separation of the powers, their mutual cooperation and the degree of superiority .and inferiority involved for each power.

There was some fumbling among the earlier decretists in the handling of these questions. But even before Huguccio, some decretists had begun to make the distinctions appropriate to their view of both ecclesiastical autonomy and superiority. Peter of Blois, for example, argued that the canons had unquestioned authority in ecclesiastical courts when ecclesiastical cases were being tried and ecclesiastical persons were concerned. The secular courts had a similar autonomy, with, however, an important qualification: 'canonum enim vigor se extendit ad causas seculares ex quibus et in quibus anime periculum versatur.' He instanced the use of the ordeal by boiling water and hot iron as a matter where secular law and custom should be abrogated by canonical practices.[20] Huguccio's view was a more elaborate version of the same inter-

---

testatis diserevit, ut imperator terrenis, pontifex coelestibus praesideret, ne propter duplicem potestatem homo superbiens rursum ad inferna demergatur: sed cum opus est, altera potestas vicissim alteram subleuaret. Idem casus est, xcvi. dist. Cum ad verum.' (ed. 1561: minor textual variants with the text printed by Stickler, *Salesianum* 32).

[20] 'In talibus itaque causis (scil. que coram iudice ecclesiastico tractandum est) canones legibus imponunt silentium si circa huiusmodi articulum sibi invicem leges et canones adversentur. In secularibus autem negotiis inter seculares personas agitandis, leges non cedunt canonibus. Quod tamen sine distinctione non admitto. Refert enim lex vel consuetudo

pretation. It is, however, not written as a single whole, which makes for
difficulties in summary presentation. The *résumé* of the question by Alanus
did justice to the final decretist position.[21]

He answered in a series of distinctions the implied question: when do the
leges yield place to the *canones*? A law promulgated by a lay ruler was concerned with either ecclesiastical or secular matters. If it concerned ecclesiastical affairs, it was invalid *eo ipso* because it was promulgated by one who
had no charge over such matters (invalid, *ratione constituentis*, in Huguccio's
phraseology[22]) unless it was a privilege granted to the Church. If the law pro-

---

inducat aliquid in iudicio seculari, quod importet utrique vel alteri parti dampnum tantum
pecuniarum, an etiam periculum animarum, ut sunt illa iudicia in quibus Deus temptari
videtur, scilicet aque ferventis vel candentis ferri, vel duelli. Canonum enim vigor se extendit ad causas seculares ex quibus et in quibus, anime periculum versatur. Quantum enim
ad hoc, ut anime provideatur omnes persone spectant ad forum ecclesiasticum, et in talibus
iudiciis, secundum meum iudicium, videtur per canones legibus et consuetudinibus deroga-
tum': *Speculum iuris canonici* (ed. T. A. Reimarus, Berlin, 1837), D. 10, pp. 40-41.

[21] *Apparatus 'Ius naturale'*: 'Ostenso ius positivum cedere iuri naturali ostendit legem
cedere canoni. § Constitutio a principe promulgatur aut super negotio ecclesiastico auts
super seculari. Si super ecclesiastico eo ipso quod lata a principe non valet, ut xcvi.di
Bene quidem, xvi.q.ult. Laicis, Non placuit; nisi fuerit privilegium quod ecclesie tribuit
imperator, hoc enim ipso iure valet. Talis est constitutio illa, xvi.q.i,. Generaliter, C. de
episcopis et cler.l.i. (Code 1.3.1). Si super negotio seculari lata fuerit, aut contradicit canoni
aut non. Si non, valet et ipsam ecclesia tamquam suam approbat et per eam negotia decidat,
ubi canon nichil statuit, ut di.x.c.i, et per totam distinccionem, xi.q.iii, Summopere; que
si a principe immutatur, eam immutatam ecclesia habere debet nisi per canonem specialiter
fuerit confirmata, tunc enim quantum ad ecclesiam pro canone habenda est, ar. C. de vet.
iure enuc. l.i. (Code 1.17.1). Si quedam canoni contradicat, nichilominus in secularibus et
in foro seculari valet, nisi legi et euangelio fuerit contraria; tunc enim non valet, ut sunt leges
de usuris loquentes et de divorciis. In foro autem ecclesiastico canon illi legi contradicens
debet obseruari et secundum ipsum iudicari, ut xvi.q.i, Continua, xxxiii.q.ii, Inter hec.
Exempli gratia habeatur illud quod est C. de pre.xxx.vel xl. annorum, Si quis emptionis
(Code 7.39.8), extra, de prescript. Vigilanti (X.2.6.5), que sibi contradicunt in prescriptione
mala fide possessoris. Set hec vera sunt secundum opinionis tenorem, que dicit imperatorem
quoad secularia pape non subesse. Secundum vero aliam est dicendum canonem semper
in negotiis secularibus legi sibi contrarie preiudicare, nisi expresse concedat legem illam in
secularibus obseruari, ut concedit leges precipientes cruentas ultiones quas, licet canon
non inferat, permittit tamen a secularibus potestatibus inferri, ut xxiii. q.v,. Iudex, Regum'
ad D. 10 pr. (B.N. MS lat. 15393, fol. 6va) and A. Stickler, 'Alanus Anglicus als Verteidiger
des monarchischen Papsttums,' *Salesianum* 21 [1959] 351-2).

[22] Huguccio: 'Duobus modis dicitur fieri (scil. lex) contra canones, scilicet ratione constituti et ratione constituentis: ratione constituti, quia ea constituitur quod constitui non
debet, ut ille que permittunt usuras, et separationi coniugum sine mutuorum consensu
causa religionis . . . . ratione constituentis, cum constituitur ab eo qui non habet potestatem constituendi, ut legitur de basilio, ut di.xcvi, Bene quidem': ad D. 10 c.4, s.v. *contra
canones* (Lincoln Cath. MS 2, fol. 122va). These neat formulae were adopted by other decretists throughout the thirteenth century, e.g. *gl. anon.* Caius Coll. Cambridge, MS 676,
ad *loc. cit.* (fol. 4rb); *Apparatus 'Ecce vicit leo'*, ad *loc.cit.* (B.N.MS Nouv. acq. lat. 1576,

mulgated concerned secular business, either it conformed to the canons, or it did not. If it did, it might be adopted for ecclesiastical use if needed,[23] and on ecclesiastical reception of it, not by virtue of secular imposition; if the law was changed by its promulgator, any change for ecclesiastical purposes required ecclesiastical action. But if the law did not conform to the canons, it was valid nonetheless for the secular *forum* — provided it did not run contrary to divine law. If it was in opposition to divine law (decretists commonly cited the Roman law of usury and divorce as examples) it was invalid (*ratione constituti*, as Huguccio had put it).

This view, though stated differently by different writers, was adopted by the decretalists. As St. Raymond of Peñafort phrased it, no secular laws concerning ecclesiastical persons or things were applicable in ecclesiastical courts unless approved by ecclesiastical authority. Those laws which did not contradict the canons might be used if need be *in adjutorium ecclesiae*, even in ecclesiastical cases. In secular cases heard before a secular judge, secular law had full force and might not be changed by the pope except *ratione peccati*.[24]

There can be no doubt that these views were fully representative of the usual decretist interpretation, of D. 10 in general, and of *Quoniam* in particular. The respective spheres of operation of lawmakers were clearly separated, the circumstances of how and when one law might supplement the other envisaged, and the superiority of the spiritual power moderately expressed as a veto in moral matters. Thus the decretists had produced, as their contribution to the authentic canonist tradition, a statement of the relations of the powers of a clearly 'dualist' nature.

---

fol. 26vb); Alanus, '*Ius naturale*', ad *loc. cit.* (B.N.MS 15393, fol. 7ra and ad D. 10 c.1 fol. 6vb); Guido de Baysio, *Rosarium*, ad *loc.cit.* (Venice 1578, fo. 11vb).

[23] It was apparently the canonists of this period who first spoke of 'canonized' laws — *gl. anon.* Caius Coll.MS. 676: 'per papam leges laicorum canonizate sunt': ad C.16q.7 c.24 (fol. 139va); Damasus in his *Quaestiones* spoke of 'lex canonizata' (B.N.MS lat. 14320, fol. 188rb).

[24] 'Constitutio ecclesiastica abrogat omnes leges sibi contradicentes in causis spiritualibus, et breviter in omnibus que spectant ad salutem anime, id est, sine quibus anima salvari non potest vel impeditur ad salutem. In talibus enim sacre leges non dedignantur sacros canones imitari . . . . Unde leges que permittunt usuras, vel matrimonium seu repudium, vel similia contra canones, non tenent, etiam leges que permittunt prescriptionem cum mala fide . . . . Nam imperatores, reges et omnes principes, ac sine distinctione omnis homo pertinet ad iudicium ecclesiasticum ratione peccati . . . . . Item leges omnes tractantes de personis ec-clesiasticis vel rebus non tenent nisi quatenus sunt per canones approbate. Imperator enim vel aliquis laicus nichil potest disponere de rebus vel personis ecclesiasticis . . . . Ille autem leges que non contradicunt canonibus possunt assumi in adiutorium ab ecclesia etiam in spiritualibus causis . . . . In aliis vero causis secularibus et coram iudice seculari optinent leges vigorem suum . . . . nec posset papa eas tollere nisi in casibus suprapositis vel quoad suum forum': *Summa Iuris* 1.11 (*ed. cit.* 39-40).

It would, however, distort the whole perspective of decretist thought to hold this 'dualism' to be their last word on the subject.

On the contrary, the 'dualist' interpretation, elicited very properly and usefully for practical contingencies from D. 10, far from closing discussion, really began it. For the principle of *iurisdictio divisa* had to be reconciled with many another *auctoritas* which suggested the opposite. Two of the most powerful were *Duo sunt* and *Alius* if they established the principle of the pope as *iudex superior*, was there not a self-evident inference from it, that there was one unified society over which one judicial authority was exercised? Further, there were canons in the *Decretum* which seemed to indicate a view of papal primacy which 'dualism' implicitly restricted. There were other canons which in expressing a view of the ancillary nature of secular power seemed to modify substantially that degree of independence which 'dualism' appeared to allow to it.

These were no doubt considerations which led to the heart of political thinking for they could not be solved without discussing the nature of Christian society, the role of the papacy as an international power, the function of kingship — the whole constitution of the *regimen Christianum*. But it was not until the turn of the thirteenth century that anyone was to write a formal systematic treatise specifically on this topic, and he did not do it as a canonist but as a theologian.[24a] The canonists worked on a less abstract level and contented themselves with raising these fundamental matters incidentally to the solution of a concrete problem — the burning practical one in papal politics from Besançon in 1157 to Lyons in 1245, that of the relationship of pope and emperor.

The most ambitious political *excursus* attempted by the decretists was designed to find the answer to the question, *utrum papa habeat utrumque gladium*? The *quaestio* was, of course, to become classical. By the time, perhaps, of the *glossa ordinaria* on the *Decretales*, or at any rate by the end of the thirteenth century, it had become to a high degree formalized and thus had ceased to be a vehicle for creative thought. Its constant repetition throughout the later middle ages is thus inevitably wearisome for a modern student. But in this period of the early decretists and decretalists it was a new feature in political writing, evolved for the discussion of a real problem by men who clearly felt strongly about it. It was, too, a changing form — in one way, through the increasingly comprehensive examination of all the texts of the *Decretum* and in another, through the reception of new law. Thus it did not merely become more efficient academically; it was kept in vital contact with actual contemporary papal practice as the new legislation was integrated with older traditions represented through the canons of the *Decretum*.

[24a] James of Viterbo, *De regimine Christiano* (1301-2).

There were really two problems in the *quaestio*, which were not always very clearly separated: the specific one of the nature of the relationship of pope and emperor, and the more general one of the distinction of the powers *in genere*.

The debate among canonists about the empire in the period before *Venerabilem* must be examined, at least in outline. Almost every decretist work considered the problem in some form or other, ranging from an unelaborated list of the authorities in the *Decretum* arranged *pro* and *contra*, to a fully comprehensive dialectic. Naturally there was much variation as to length and profundity of treatment and as to emphasis placed by individual writers on particular arguments; some decretists would advance the argument of one canon *pro*, where another would use it *contra*; some omit reference to authorities that others obviously regard as very important; some are strongly personal in their expression of views while others were content to reproduce earlier arguments without further comment. But by the end of the twelfth century, when Ricardus Anglicus reviewed the matter in his *Summa Quaestionum*,[24b] the major arguments and counter-arguments had been marshalled and can be summed up relatively briefly.

The issue had resolved itself into the juridical significance of the papal coronation of an emperor. Did it confer the emperor's executive powers and dignity or merely the title of *imperator* and the sanctification of the office? Did the imperial function, then, derive directly from God or mediately from the pope? Huguccio spoke for an important section of the decretists in maintaining the position which he expressed:

> Ego autem credo quod imperator potestatem gladii et dignitatem imperialem habet non ab apostolico, set a principibus et populo per eleccionem . . . ante (*scil.* unctionem et confirmationem) quidem imperator est quoad dignitatem set non quoad unctionem, licet ante non dicatur imperator et ante habet potestatem gladii et eam exercet.[25]

[24b] The importance of this review was first brought out by W. Ullmann, *Medieval Papalism* (London 1949) 211-15. The relevant *quaestio* has now been printed by A.M. Stickler, 'Sacerdotium und Regnum,' 41-42, from Monte Cassino MS 396. I have collated this text with Zwettl MS 162 to remove some ambiguities in the Monte Cassino version.

[25] Huguccio's position had been most clearly foreshadowed by another Bolognese decretist, Simon of Bisignano. Simon's main argument, which Huguccio incorporated almost literally into his more elaborate commentary, was stated: 'Propriis actibus, id est, actus utriusque potestatis, uel quod in sua persona facit: pauit enim turbas, uendentes de templo eiecit, quod ad regis officium spectat; et se seipsum in ara crucis immolat, et pro inimicis orauit dicens, "pater ignosce illis quia nesciunt quid faciant," quod sacerdotis est officium; usque *hoc habet*: quod imperator vero habet potestatem gladii; distincte enim sunt he potestates nec una pendet ex altera, unde in huius rei figuram dictum fuit, "ecce gladii duo hic"': ad D. 96 c.6 (Lambeth Palace MS 411 fol. 15[vb]). The main decretist protagonists of the position after Huguccio were the anonymous authors of the *Glossa Palatina* and the *Apparatus 'Ecce vicit leo'*.

The opposing view was put in this typical way:

> Dicimus quod apostolicus habet gladium materialem et spiritualem set aliter et aliter: spiritualem auctoritate et usu, materialem tantum auctoritate, quia quando inungitur imperator datur ei ab apostolico potestas et executio gladii materialis.[26]

The protagonists of each interpretation sought to base their case on a principle of divine law. For the first,[26a] the Huguccian position, the texts of Gelasius were of considerable importance. *Cum ad verum* and *Quoniam* laid down the principle, 'aperte' according to Huguccio,[26b] that Christ had divided the dignities

---

[26] *Summa Monacensis* ad D. 22 c.1 s.v. *terreni simul et celestis imperii iura*, ed. Stickler, 'Imperator vicarius Papae: Die Lehren der französisch-deutschen Dekretistenschule des 12. und beginnenden 13. Jahrhunderts über die Beziehungen zwischen Papst und Kaiser,' *Mitteilungen des Instituts für Österreichische Geschichtsforschung* 62 (1954) 202. The interpretative tradition which this text represents was perhaps the majority one among decretists and began with Rufinus. Some decretists repeated Rufinus almost verbatim, e.g. *Summa 'Tractaturus Magister'* (B.N.MS lat. 15594, fol. 7ra); Johannes Faventinus, *Summa* (B.M. MS Royal 9.E. VII fol. 46vb; *gl. anon.* Caius Coll. MS 676 (fo. 12b); *Summa 'Antiquitate et tempore'* (ed. Stickler, 'Imperator vicarius Papae' 201). Others express the same concept more elaborately in different language from Rufinus (e.g. *Summa Bambergensis* ed. Stickler, 'Imperator vicarius Papae' 204). In the systematic discussions of the *quaestio* 'utrum papa habet utrumque gladium' it was generally phrased according to the vocabulary of Rufinus e.g.: *Summa Lipsiensis*: 'Nota qui primam tenent sententiam dicunt quod summus pontifex utrumque habet gladium: alterum non administratione set tantum auctoritate, ut materialem; celestem vero et ecclesiasticum plena auctoritate' (ed. Juncker, 'Simon von Bisignano,' 493); Ricardus Anglicus, *Summa Quaestionum*: 'Sunt alii qui dicunt quod utrumque gladium habet summus pontifex; alterum auctoritate et amministracione, reliquum auctoritate absque amministracione': MS Zwettl 162, fol 147va-148vb and Stickler, 'Sacerdotium et Regnum' 41. It was this case which was ultimately to be successful, see below pp. 45-47.

[26a] Ricardus Anglicus summed up the position: 'Videtur quod non habet utrumque (gladium): distincte enim sunt potestates, quia nec imperator iura pontificis nec pontifex iura imperatoris usurpare potest ut di.xcvi. Cum ad verum. Item, a deo consecutus est potestatem imperator, ut di. xcvi. Si imperator. Idem dicitur xxiii.q.v. Quesitum, ubi dicitur quod meminerint homines has potestates a deo fuisse concessas. Si ergo a iudice civili ad summum pontificem appelletur non tenet appellacio ut in ex. Alexandri iii. Denique. Ex hoc ergo manifeste potest colligi quod imperator a summo pontifice non habet imperium, quia si haberet ab eo, ad illum posset appellari. Idem potest confirmari auctoritate illius capituli, ii.q.vi. Omnis oppressus, ubi dicitur de illo qui appellat quod coram patricio debent ventilari secularia negocia, coram ecclesiastico, ecclesiastica. Item, secularium negociorum prohibetur esse cognitor apostolicus, ut xi.q.i. Te quidem, quod videtur ergo quod nullum ius habeat cognoscendi super causis secularibus vel committendi cognitionem secularium aliquibus. Item antequam essent summi pontifices erant imperatores et idem ius et eamdem potestatem habebant quam nunc habent. Unde non videtur quod ab illo nacti fuerint hanc potestatem, set a deo' (MS *cit.* fol. 148ra).

[26b] '*Officia:* hinc aperte colligitur quod utraque potestas, scilicet apostolica et imperialis instituta sunt a deo et quod neutra pendet ex altera et quod imperator gladium non habet ab apostolico, ar. hic et infra ead. In scripturis, Duo, Si imperator et di. xciii. Legimus et ixxiii.q.iiii. Quesitum': ad D. 96 c.6 (Lincoln Cath.MS 2, fol. 172vb).

and functions of each power, that both were instituted by God, that neither, therefore, depended for its institution on the other and that the emperor did not hold his sword from the pope. A third Gelasian canon, *Si imperator*, asserted the principle, 'apertissime' according to Laurentius Hispanus, that the emperor, enjoying his power 'divinitus' neither had nor accepted his power from the pope.[27] These three texts were the most important of those 'canones multiplices'[28] which, it was believed, established that the empire was from God directly. To supplement this argument, Roman law made its influence felt with the view that the divine gift of imperial authority was invested in princes and people and from them transferred to the emperor.[29] Thus the argument against papal possession of both swords was based essentially on considerations of divine, natural and human law.

The 'monists,' as the upholders of the view that the pope had the *ius* of each power might be called,[30] relied on a particular reading of an exegesis of

---

[27] '*Divinitus:* id est, a deo, non a papa. Apertissime (per) hoc capitulum ostenditur imperatorem non habere nec accipere gladium et potestatem, nisi forte quo ad confirmacionem, et esse maior eo in temporalibus': ad D. 96 c.11, B.N.MS 15393, fol. 70vb.

[28] *Quaestiones Orielenses:* 'Set econtra videtur posse probari (quod imperator non habeat potestatem gladii ab apostolico): ante fuerunt principes quam apostolici et tunc gladii potestatem habebant a Deo, a quo est omnis potestas. Nam et de Pilato est dictum: "non haberes in me potestatem, nisi datum esset tibi desuper." Non ergo potestas gladii est ab apostolico. Item canones multiplices dicunt quod imperator potestatem gladii habet a Deo, ut di. XCVI, Si imperator et C.XXIII. q.iiii, Quesitum. Item Deus dixit: "Ecce duo gladii hic", id est due discrete et distincte potestates: ecclesiastica scilicet et secularis; neutra ergo istarum pendet ex altera': ed. Stickler, 'Sacerdotium et Regnum' 35.

[29] Cf. Laurentius: '*Officia potestatis discrevit*: immo pocius confundit cum utrumque adimpleuerit: set hoc fecit ut ostenderet quod utraque potestas ab eo haberet inicium, ar. xxi. Cleros, et duo nobis a deo data sunt, scilicet imperium et sacerdocium, in aut. quom. opor. epis. in prin. coll. iii. (*Nov.* 6 pr.) la(urentius)': ad D. 96 c.6 (B.N.MS lat. 15393, fol. 70rb). Cf. also *Glossa Palatina*: *officia potestatis discrevit*: immo uerum contrarium quia non discreuit set confudit, cum ipse unus et idem utrumque officium gesserit: set dic quod ipse utriusque officii per se gessit, ut notaret quod ex eadem fonte processerunt, xxi.di. Cleros. Nam dicit lex quod summa nobis dona a deo concessa sunt, scilicet sacerdocium et imperium, in aut. quoniam opor. epis. in prin. coll. iii.' (Durham Cath. MS C.III.8, fol. 36va).

[30] Ricardus Anglicus summed up their position: 'Queri solet utrum summus pontifex utrumque gladium habeat, materialem scilicet et spiritualem. Quod uidetur posse probari: utriusque enim imperii scilicet celestis et terreni ei iura concessa sunt, ut di. xxii. c.i. Si ergo habet utrumque imperium, ab eo habet imperator potestatem quam habet et eodem modo alii principes. Item fidelitatem facit ei imperator tamquam domino, ut di. lxiii. Tibi domino. Item legitur quod papa reges deposuit, puta Zacharias regem Francorum, non tam pro suis iniquitatibus quam pro eo quod tante potestati inutilis, ut xv.q.vi, Alius. Si ergo regi potuit auferre potestatem, uidetur quod ab eo habuerit. Unde a simili uidetur hodie quod si imperator abutitur potestate sua, illi possit auferri imperium et alium principatum. Hoc idem potest probari alio exemplo: Constantinus enim postquam urbem romanam et partes occidentales beato Siluestro concesserat, ad partes orientales imperium et regiam potestatem transtulit et constantinopoli constituit sedem imperii, ut di. lxxxvi. (*recte* xcvi)

the *Tu es Petrus* text as their 'argumentum optimum.'[31] Peter Damian,
seeking a strong phrase to urge the universal *praelatio* of the Roman Church
had included in a rendering of Matthew 16.18 the phrase, 'qui beato Petro
aeternae vitae clavigero terreni simul et coelestis imperii iura commisit' and
this text had passed into the *Decretum*. All decretists agreed that the first
meaning of the phrase was that the pope had been given supreme power over
the souls of all members of the Church, lay and clerical, an *utrumque imperium*
of a strictly spiritual and ecclesiastical kind. But there were many decretists,
as has been seen, who read the text in terms of *utrumque gladium*, equating
the 'terrenum imperium' of the text with the contemporary *Romanum imperium*. Once this exegetical method was indulged in, it was possible to give
a similarly contemporary political meaning to many another primatial text:
those (Gelasian) canons, for example, upholding the universal jurisdiction
of the Roman see as a general court of first instance and as a supreme court
of appeal for every Christian.[32] Similarly with other scriptural authorities:
for example, a Pauline text which had already done service for Gregory VII
in underlining the political consequences of papal power as *iudex superior*:
'Know you not that we shall judge angels? How much more things of this
world (*secularia*)?'[33]

History reinforced this interpretation of the imperial *subiectio*. There was
the matter of the oath which emperors-elect had been taking to the pope for
some centuries. Gratian had included in the *Decretum* the text of the oath
sworn by Otto I through his legates in 962. Decretists saw in this canon the
explicit recognition by the emperor that he held his sword from the pope.
It might even be read occasionally, and crudely, as a feudal oath, thus making
the emperor, 'homo pape.'[34] Then the Zachary-Childeric-Pepin episode could
be made to show that the pope had the making and unmaking of kings: if
this was the case, could it be denied that imperial power was received from
the pope?[35] A second piece of historical interpretation strengthened the in-

---

Constantinus. Sic itaque aliquando fuerat imperium apud Grecos; postea vero ab Adriano
papa Carolo est concessum et eis ablatum est, ut di. lxiii, Adrianus. Ex his ergo uidetur quod
utrumque habeat gladium, et imperator ab eo. Item, romana ecclesia potestatem habet
de omnibus iudicare, ut ix.q.iii. Cuncta. Item alibi dicitur quod omnis oppressus libere
sacerdotis vocem appellet, ut ii.q.vi. Omnis. Ex hoc uidetur quod a iudice ciuili possit
appellari ad ecclesiasticum, maxime cum causas privatorum apostolus iussit deferri ad ecclesiam, ut xi.q.i. Placuit' (MS *cit.* fol. 147va-148ra)

[31] Damasus, *Brocarda* (B.N.MS. 14320 fol. 220vo)

[32] The canons were C.9 q.3 cc. 17, 18 in reference to which decretists coined the phrase
'papa est iudex ordinarius omnium' which is discussed below, Part II section 2.

[33] 1 Cor. 6.3.

[34] Caius Coll.MS 676, ad D. 63 c.33 (*Tibi domino*) fol. 42va.

[35] This argument recurs frequently, e.g. Simon of Bisignano: '*Deponitur*: id est, deponen-
tibus ipsius regis consensit vel subditos ab eius fidelitate absoluit, quod per consequenciam

ference. The theory that the empire had been withdrawn from the Greeks by the pope and given to Charlemagne was freely canvassed by decretists.[36] In the translation of the empire from East to West lay confirmation of deposition theory and papal possession of both swords.

Innocent III's famous decretal *Venerabilem* virtually settled for canonists this argument about the status of the emperor and it will be discussed in due course.[37] What might be noticed here is a second and perhaps more important aspect of the decretist background to Innocent III's political decretals, that

---

fuit depositus. Unde hic volunt quidam colligere quod imperator potestatem gladii ab apostolico recipiat: non enim videtur posse auferre, si non dedisset': ad C.15 q.6 c.11 (Lambeth Pal.MS 411 fol. 51vb). *Summa 'Reverentia sacrorum canonum'*: 'Nam si papa regem deponere potuit, ergo potestatem gladii auferre potuit; ergo et conferre': ed. Stickler, 'Imperator vicarius Papae' 204.

[36] Notably by the *Summa 'Et est sciendum'*; Mochi Onory, *Fonti Canonistiche* 119. The glosses in Durham Cath. C.II.1 would appear to derive from this work. Compare the text given by Mochi Onory with the commentary on the same canon (D.22 c.3): '*Constantinopolitanae*: 'Quia translatum est imperium ad Greciam. Unde dicunt quidam constantinopolitanum debere esse romanum imperatorem, quod falsum est. Quodam (tempore) ecclesia ab hereticis vexabatur et tunc vocatus est constantinopolitanus qui venire contempsit, datum est imperium (genti) facienti iusticiam et datum est karolo, ut xxiii.q.ult., Hortatu et infra, di. lxiii, Adrianus. Set numquid ita potuit papa transferre imperium? Resp.: sic.' The same manuscript contains an interesting composite gloss on the two-swords question, not hitherto published: 'Terrenum imperium dicitur potestas spiritualis gladii quam habet papa super laicos terrenis inhabitantes, celestem eam quam habet super clericos: nam hos et illos potest ligare et soluere. G(andulphus?): uel proprie quia ut duo erant gladii in passione domini sic et duplex est seueritatis officium et mansuetudinis: gladium materialem commisit imperatori, et eum in hac parte uicarium constituit; gladium mansuetudinis qui non mortificat set viuificat; sibi reservavit: ideo secundum hoc videtur quod imperator habet a papa potestatem nam et si imperator ea abutatur, papa potest eum deponere, ut xv.q.vi, Alius item. Quod tamen non videtur cum prius fuerunt imperatores quam pape, et tunc potestatem habuerunt. Nam omnis potestas a deo est, quia antequam consecretur imperator potest uti gladio post eleccionem populi, qui ei et in eum omne ius transfert, ut infra, de institu. De iure scripto. Item cum papa non habet execucionem gladii qualiter illum potest transferre in alium, ut xxiii. q.ult. Sepe, Hii? Habet ergo eam a deo, ut di. xciii, Nec tempore et xxiii. q.iii. Quesitum. Regem autem hic deposuisse dicitur, quia propter contumaciam eum excommunicato domino teneatur obedire, ut xv.q.vi. Iuratos. Quid ergo de hiis iudicibus qui temporalem accipiunt iurisdiccionem a papa uel ab episcopis qui et comites sunt: a quo accipiunt tales gladii potestatem? Resp: forte ab episcopis potestatem, et a potestate execucionem, vel ab episcopis totum: quidam enim aliis concedere possumus quod nosmetipsos exercere non possumus, ut di. lxxxvii. Episcopus. Set quid si a talibus iudicibus ad tales episcopos fuerit appellatum et in causa sanguinis, de ea possint agnoscere? Resp: Quere et inquire': ad D.22 c.1 (fo. 20vab). The second gloss is clearly the *Summa 'Et est sciendum'*; compare the text printed by Stickler 'Imperator vicarius Papae' 203. Two recent studies have clarified the whole course of development of the theory of the *translatio imperii*, P.A. van den Baar, *Die kirchliche Lehre der Translatio Imperii Romani bis zur Mitte des 13. Jahrhunderts* (Rome 1956); W. Goez, *Translatio Imperii* (Tübingen 1958).   [37] Below, pp. 34-37., 46-48.

concerned with the general principles of the relations of the powers. By the end of the first phase of decretist work, the eve of the pontificate of Innocent III, canonist thought on these principles showed two especially characteristic traits. On the one hand, it had a lively sense of the dualism of the powers based as well on *Cum ad verum* as on a practical appreciation of the reality of the working of separate lay and ecclesiastical jurisdictions. Certain recent papal statements confirmed this line of thought.[38] On the other hand, however, emphasis on the superiority of the spiritual power was very strong, even with the apparently 'dualist' writers such as Huguccio. Texts like *Duo sunt* made clear that the sacerdotal power of binding and loosing, the *imperium spirituale*, was juridically enforceable under sanction. If the precise meaning of *Alius item* was sometimes disputed, it was nonetheless agreed that punishment of negligent and delinquent rulers could be taken as far as their deposition. Lay princes were subject, therefore, *in spiritualibus et quodam modo in temporalibus*, with loss of office and their expulsion by armed force the ultimate sanction enforcing their inferiority. Dualism might demand the principle that appeal did not lie from a secular court to an ecclesiastical one, but the *imperium spirituale* demanded also that the ecclesiastical judge might compel a secular judge to render justice (that is, to fulfil his function) and that in circumstances where justice was being withheld maliciously by a ruler, the oppressed might denounce his oppressor to the Church for judgment.

It cannot be said that these two trends of decretist thought, dualism and the superiority of the spiritual power, were very adequately reconciled. For the latter, with its emphasis on the pope's position as judge of all Christians — *papa, antonomastice iudex*[39] — was essentially a unitary concept. It implied a single society of all Christians, over the constitution of which one ruler enjoyed *plenitudo potestatis*. This power was held, it was beginning to be argued, by him who was *vicarius Christi*.[40] The full implications of these concepts were yet to be drawn, but by this stage of canonist thought, it was already clear that there was an innate tension in decretist thought: between the trend which considered the distinction of the powers *quoad actus utriusque* and another which, in emphasizing the universal jurisdiction of the pope, urged the unity of one society under a single head.

The position may be expressed by an interpretation of the well-known text in which Stephen of Tournai formulated the dualist position: 'secundum duos

---

[38] In particular, four decretals of Alexander III in *Comp.* I *Denique* (2.20.7 = X.2.28.7 § 2); *Si duobus* (2.20.7 = X.2.28.7 § 1); *Lator* (4.18.5 = X.4.17.5); *Causam* (4.18.7 = X.4.17.7)

[39] The expression was Huguccio's ad C.9 q.3 c.13 s.v. *iudex*.

[40] These terms are discussed in Part II below.

principatus duplex iurisdictionis ordo.'[41] But he postulated also that the society (*civitas*) wherein this division of jurisdictions was ordained was the *ecclesia* and that each order was subject *sub eodem rege*. His *rex* was Christ. But if it were claimed that there was a *vicarius Christi* specifically and uniquely charged with everyone and everything within the *ecclesia*, the whole concept would take on a different perspective. Before the end of the pontificate of Innocent III there were canonists who were prepared to carry the logic of the unitary argument to its conclusion.

Superiority of the spiritual power and distinction of the powers were then two basic principles which decretists learned especially through the words of Gelasius. They learned a third — that cooperation of the two powers was likewise a principle of divine law. *Duo sunt* (as edited by Gregory VII), *Cum ad verum*, and *Quoniam* made the point. Another Gelasian canon to figure in D. 96 of the *Decretum* reinforced it. *Si imperator* urged that cooperation with the Church was the function of the good prince and led decretists to consider more specifically the question of the aptness of the secular power for ecclesiastical service.

They were in fact quite specific: the secular power could be coerced into giving help. This was the corollary of the view that the power of spiritual authority should be used to compel inefficient or negligent rulers to exercise their royal function properly. The lending of help at need to the priesthood was a part of the royal function. Indeed some twelfth-century writers appear to argue that there was no other monarchical function than to be available as the agent of the spiritual power, so narrowly do they restrict the function of monarchy. What, however, was meant by such *dicta* as 'rex est minister sacerdotii' and 'ecclesia sibi reges constituit' and the like,[42] was the principle that the coercive power which had been given to the priesthood could in certain circumstances be exercised in no other way than through using the secular power. Clerics were forbidden to shed blood and bear arms. They could not act as their own police force nor inflict capital punishment. Nor could they easily defend themselves physically. When therefore they were

---

[41] The *Prooemium 'Sapientia edificauit'*, deriving from Stephen of Tournai, is less well known and is reproduced here as a statement essentially the same as Stephen's but somewhat more interestingly expressed: '. . . Nam ab re, quam prius Salomon domum dixerat, dehinc civitatem vocat. Pro mansionum enim multitudine civiumque multiplicitate civitas dicitur; set quia omnium inhabitantium paterfamilias unus est, quia etiam multitudinis credentium cor unum et anima una (Act. 4.32) merito domus una vocatur. In hac ergo civitate uel domo sub eodem rege et patre, i.e. Christo, duo populi sunt secundum quos duo uite, secundum quos duo principatus, secundum hoc duo iura. Populi, clerici sunt et laici; uite, spiritualis et carnalis; principatus, sacerdotium et regnum; iura, ecclesiasticum et forense': ed. Stickler, 'Sacerdotium et Regnum' 26.

[42] Cf. John of Salisbury, *Policraticus* (ed. Webb) 4.3.516a; Honorius of Autun, *Summa Gloria* (MGH *Lib. de Lite III*) 18.72; 24.75.

not able to arrest criminals nor punish those who merited the death penalty nor protect themselves adequately, they had recourse to the secular power. The king to this extent acted in a ministerial capacity. Whilst this view was commonplace among twelfth-century ecclesiastical writers as a whole, what distinguished the decretists from the others was that they considered the ministerial function in detail both in principle and in relation to particular circumstances.

The authorities for the principle itself formed a *quaestio incidens* in C.23 q.5 of the *Decretum*. The *quaestio* as a whole was a treatise on force, dealing with the legitimacy and otherwise of physical coercion in many of its public aspects — war, legal penalties, forcible conversion and so on. It was entirely logical that a subsection of this treatise should deal with the prohibition of the clergy from bearing arms and shedding blood and with the function of kings. Having considered the circumstances in which the use of force was legitimate, Gratian turned naturally to discuss its implications for the achievement of spiritual ends. More concretely, he sought to show that the two powers must cooperate to preserve Christian life and that if kings despised their duty in this regard, they were to be excommunicated.

Something of a summary of this *quaestiuncula* is provided by the rubric of the relevant texts and the *dictum* in which Gratian gave his personal comment on them:

> c. 18 (*Non frustra*). Why regal power was instituted, and legal penalties ordained (Augustine).
> c. 20 (*Principes*). What priests are powerless to accomplish by exhortation, the power of discipline may exact by fear (Isidore).
> c. 21 (*Res autem*). Both the kingly power, and the sacerdotal authority defend what pertains to the worship of God (Leo I).
> c. 22 (*Incestuosi*). Whom sacerdotal admonition is not able to correct, is corrected by the secular power (III Council of Tours).
> c. 23 (*Regnum officium*). The office of kings is to suppress evil-doers and to encourage the good (Jerome).
> [Part VI] Gratian: Wherefore, just as we are ordered to show faith and reverence to princes and powers, so the necessity of defending churches falls on the administrators of secular offices. If they despise this duty, they are to be rejected from communion.
> c. 26 (*Administratores*). Those who hold office ought to hear the complaints of churches diligently (John VIII).

The two texts here which canonists found most significant were *Administratores* and *Principes*. The former ordained that secular princes should be attentive to what ecclesiastics asked them to do and that if they were found wanting, after due warning, they would be excommunicated. The latter, a classical Isidorian text, asserted that the first duty of secular princes was to collaborate in the work of salvation in association with the priesthood: 'their power within the Church would not be necessary unless what the priest cannot make prevail through the teaching of doctrine, force implants through the dread of discipline.' Thus decretists drew a principle from tradition: secular princes were to be coerced into exercising their jurisdiction in ecclesiastical service. As Huguccio put it: secular princes were established to this end — that what the Church was unable to do alone, should be done by them *quasi ministri*. Nor were they free to refuse this duty.[43]

Principes and *Administratores*, then, declared the assumptions that underlay the term *brachium seculare* which Huguccio was among the first to use. There were especially two particular contexts where canonists of the late twelfth century insisted on the cooperation of the secular arm: the chastisement of incorrigibly criminous clergy and the arrest and punishment of heretics.

The role of the lay power in the penal code for delinquent clerics was established, to the decretists' satisfaction at any rate, at least by the time of Huguccio.[44] The solution neatly summarized the three postulates of Church-State relations: the superiority of the spiritual power, manifested in the *privilegium fori*, was emphatically maintained with the principle that the lay power should have no part in the punishment of clerical criminals who could be subjected to ecclesiastical correction: the separation of the powers, insisted on to preserve clerical autonomy, demanded that no ecclesiastically inflicted penalty had the consequence of the guilty being abandoned to the secular power: the cooperation of the powers came into the reckoning when a cleric was incorrigible, that is, could not be corrected by ecclesiastically administered discipline, in which case by license of the Church, he should be punished by the secular arm. The prince could be ordered to perform this duty.[45]

---

[43] ' .... et nota quod principes tenentur ecclesiam defendere, ut xxiii.q.v. Principes, et si admoniti nolunt hoc facere, possunt excommunicari, ut xxiii.q.v. Administratores': ad D.63 c.22 s.v. *ad defendendas* (text printed by A. Stickler, 'Der Schwerterbegriff bei Huguccio', *Ephemerides Iuris Canonici* 3 [1947] 217, a fuller version than that given in Lincoln Cath.MS 2, fol. 121ʳᵃ). 'Nam ad hoc sunt constitute seculares, quod per se nequit ecclesia, per eos quasi ministros exercetur, et per eos tuitionem et potestatem et quietem habeat ut xxiii.q.v. Principes, Administratores': ad D.96 c.16 s.v. *usque tueri* (Lincoln Cath.MS 2, fol. 172ᵛᵃ). '*Lex imperatorum*: utitur quando vult (ecclesia) ut xvii. Nec licuit et xxiii.q.v. Principes et di.lxxviiii, Si duo: non tamen uti cogitur, ut xxiii.q.ii. Inter hec. Set si uti voluit seculari brachio, ille a quo petitur auxilium tenetur ei obedire et eam defendere, ut xxiii.q.v. Principes, Administratores': ad D.10 c.1. (Pembroke Coll.MS 72, fol. 122ᵛᵇ).

[44] The penal code for heretics was discussed primarily by the decretalists, in relation especially to the canons of the third Lateran Council (in *Compilatio I*) and the fourth (in *Compilatio IV*). It is discussed below pp. 42-43 and 49. See now O. Hageneder, 'Studien zur Dekretale "Vergentis" (X, V, 7, 10): Ein Beitrag zur Häretikergesetzgebung Innocenz.' III.' *Zeitschr. der Savigny-Stiftung für Rechtsgesch. Kan. Abt.* 49 (1963) 138-73.

[45] Huguccio: ' ... cum omnino sint (clerici) incorrigibiles et per ecclesiam corrigi non possunt, tunc de licencia ecclesie iudex secularis potest eum capere et cohercere, ar. di. xvii, Nec licuit, et xxviii.q.v. De liguribus .... *et tunc curie tradatur* ..... clericus enim

Directly or indirectly, accidentally or consciously, the decretists considered the major components of the problem of the relation of the powers through the agency of Gelasius I. They divided the powers according to Gelasian terminology, though they were not aware of its Gelasian authorship; they considered sacerdotal superiority in terms of its ultimate public effect, the deposition of rulers, with reference to Gelasius though in fact the text in question had been substantially altered by Gregory VII; they recalled the duty of rulers to cooperate *ad nutum sacerdotis* by way of a genuine Gelasian canon, properly attributed to its rightful author. It is only in this general and somewhat tortuous way that it can be argued that twelfth-century canonist thought was 'Gelasian.'

Historians who have thus labelled canonist thought in this period have done so to emphasize the dualistic aspect of canonist theory and to express the view that the decretists worked on the assumption that both powers were independent and supreme in their respective spheres or *ordines*. It has been argued here that to use the name of Gelasius in this context falsifies the real nature of the Gelasian contribution to canonist political thought. But even if the label itself be rejected, does the notion that is being labelled form an acceptable generalization about the characteristic features of decretist thought?

It is fully acceptable — as far as it goes. But to say that decretists were dualists does not advance analysis very far. Innocent IV was also in a certain sense a dualist and Hostiensis enunciated the principle of the distinction of the powers with a clarity not equalled by any twelfth-century decretist. All canonists were committed to dualism, for the distinction of the powers, it was agreed, was a principle of divine law. But to let the matter rest at that begs all the real questions that must be asked about canonist thought.

The essential question concerns the understanding given by the canonists of various periods to the nature of sacerdotal superiority. For it was this principle which determined the practical content of dualism and the cooperation of the powers. It is only when the full implications of this superiority have been considered that the appropriate qualifications can be made to the principle of dualism and a final assessment made of the true position being maintained.

---

depositus non debet tradi curie statim ut in ex. Licet preter, set debet poni in monasterio vel alio loco ad agendam penitenciam, ut di. lxxxi. Dictum, et si sic contempserit resipiscere, nec ibi esse in pace voluerit factus contumax excommunicabitur; si nec sic corrigatur nec in aliquo modo corrigi possit per ecclesiam, tunc ultimo tradendus est curie, id est permittendum est,vel etiam precipiendum est iudici seculari ut eum capiat et coherceat': ad C. 11 q.1 c.18 (B.N.MS lat 3892 fol. 189ra). Canonist doctrines on the 'traditio curiae' have been well presented by C. Duggan, 'The Becket Dispute and the Criminous Clerks,' *Bulletin of the Institute of Historical Research* 35 (1962) 1-28.

When the first period of canon law commentary was completed with the *Summa* of Huguccio and 'for the moment, apparently, not much was left to be said about Gratian's work in the way of commenting and glossing,'[46] there were already significant breaches of the line which demarked the independence of the lay power.

It was postulated that the pope, 'antonomastice iudex,' had power to correct secular rulers for sin and negligence, even to the point of having a direct deposing power over emperors and kings. The line of demarcation between the powers was to be defined by the spiritual power. Secular princes were 'quasi-ministers' of the *sacerdotium*, obliged under sanction to give help when required. There was, further, a strong current of opinion in favor of papal possession of 'both swords' where the metaphor expressed the derivation of imperial power from the pope. Even those decretists such as Huguccio himself who did not agree with this view had to admit a considerable qualification of imperial autonomy: 'in multis imperialis potestas pendet ex pontificali.'[47] Perhaps most significantly of all, there was apparent a disposition both in the curia and in decretist writing to emphasize the headship of the Christian *orbis* of the vicar of Christ.[48]

It is the tension between these various principles and applications of sacerdotal superiority which so substantially modify the principle of dualism, and that principle itself which gave to the whole canonist system its unique characteristic. No other branch of ecclesiastical thought experienced so intensely the pull between *iurisdictio divisa* and sacerdotal *maioritas*. The biggest single contribution of Gelasius I to the canonist tradition was to have provided, albeit fortuitously, the primary materials whereby that tension was revealed. And it was from that tension that canonist thought drew vitality enough to rethink the whole problem of the papal monarchy of Christendom.

---

[46] S. Kuttner, 'Bernardus Compostellanus Antiquus: A Study in the Glossators of the Canon Law,' *Traditio* 1 (1943) 277-340 at 284.

[47] Huguccio: 'Neutra (potestas) pendet ex altera, uerum est quo ad institutionem, set in multis imperialis potestas pendet ex altera': ad D. 96 c.6 s.v. *principaliter* (Lincoln Cath.MS 2, fol. 172rb).

[48] *Summa Reginensis* (Petrus Beneventanus?): 'Dicebat cardinalis Johannis et Pauli (Johannes Sutrinus?) quod inde dominus papa dicitur Christi vicarius quia Jesus Christus preest toto orbi ita et papa': text published by A. Stickler, who suggests the identities of the author and of the cardinal quoted. Petrus Beneventanus became a papal *capellanus* in 1205 and was a trusted confidant of Innocent III's: 'Decretisti bolognesi dimenticati,' *Studia Gratiana* 3 (Bologna 1955) 377-410, text at 393, biographical details concerning Petrus, 408. The implications of this vicariate of the whole Christian world were brought out more fully by Alanus Anglicus, cf. below, p. 50.

2. *Innocent III and the Early Decretalists*

With the six or seven political decretals of Innocent III incorporated in the *Corpus Iuris Canonici*,* canonist thought on the relations of the powers opened a new chapter as their teachings were absorbed and integrated with those of the decretist tradition. Their assimilation into the existing canonist stream was one of the critical periods of thirteenth-century political thought when seeds were planted which were to germinate in the controversies with secular rulers in mid-century and at its close. The theories of Innocent IV and Hostiensis were, to a very considerable extent, but the comprehensive understanding of these Innocentian decretals, which, in turn, were closely linked with Huguccio and the early decretists generally. It would be misleading to portray the Innocentian decretals, in their broad lines, as anything but continuous with decretist thought, but there can be no denying their very great importance in making foundations of materials assembled by the decretists. Under the Innocentian stimulus, canonists reconsidered many aspects of Church-State relations and in so doing gave to their theory particular emphases which were to be influential throughout the century. There was a straight line of development between the ideas of Innocent III and Boniface VIII and it was the canonists who marked it out.

In a real sense, Innocent III transformed the canonist understanding of the relations of the powers. This is not to say that he changed it out of recognition. On the contrary, his political legislation emerged logically from a decretist background. There was no sharp break between decretist and decretalist thought. But the integration of the older theory based on texts, with theories drawn from cases, with solutions justified by an authoritative, up-to-date technical language, led to a thorough reexamination and restatement of canonist positions. The precise degree of continuity and change in the canonist tradition to which Innocent's pontificate gave rise, is a nice question and is one of the major interpretative questions which any examination of canonist ideas in this period should try to answer. For it is on the understanding of continuity and change at this time that the accurate charting of developments within the canonist tradition throughout the thirteenth century as a whole essentially depends.

There were at least eight ways in which Innocent III's influence on canonist political thinking was of abiding significance.

---

* The decretals of Innocent III will be cited by *initia* without further reference: *Venerabilem* (*Comp.* III 1.6.19 = X. 1.6.34); *Solite* (*Comp.* III 1.21.2 = X. 1.33.6); *Novit* (*Comp.* III 2.1.3 = X. 2. 1. 13); *Licet* (*Comp.* III 2.2.1 = X. 2.2.10); *Per venerabilem* (*Comp.* III 4.12.2 = X. 4.17.13); *Vergentis* (*Comp.* III 5.4.1 = X. 5.7.10); *Excommunicamus* (*Comp.* IV 5.5.2 = X. 5.7.13).

In the first place, with *Venerabilem*, he solved one question that the decretists had considered a major problem: the constitutive principles of the relationship between the empire and papacy. Canonists were now satisfied that in the sense of this decretal the pope had two swords. The Translation of the Empire theory, hitherto a minority opinion among decretists, became official doctrine and clinched the argument that it was the pope who conferred the power of the imperial sword, the right to administer the empire, on the emperor-elect.

The circumstances leading to the issuing of *Venerabilem* are too well known to need detailed recapitulation here. Innocent III attempted to break the deadlock between the rival candidates of the disputed election of 1198 by reducing the somewhat imprecise existing German electoral procedure to the norms of canonical electoral procedure, according to the practice of capitular election. The analogy between the papal role in the making of a bishop and the making of an emperor could be taken a long way.[1] Thus Innocent III asserted that the election of an emperor belonged of right to the electoral princes just as the election of a bishop belonged of right to the chapter or clergy of the diocese, that an election made by the *maior et sanior pars* of the electors was valid providing that the rights of any individual elector had not been contemned and that the person of the elect and the electoral procedure should be subject to scrutiny, the one for his suitability and the other for its regularity. To the pope belonged the right of such examinations. The elect would be examined as to his *idoneitas* for the imperial office and rejected if found wanting — as for instance he would be if he were sacrilegious, excommunicate, tyrannical, mad, heretical, pagan, perjured or an oppressor of the Church. If through default of the electors or unsuitability of the candidate, there was a disputed election, it was for the *iudex superior* to find a remedy, even to making provision of a candidate of his own choice.

The success of this analogy depended on proving that the imperial 'chapter' derived its power from the authority of the pope. It was precisely here that the Translation of the Empire theory played its part. The superior right of the pope had its justification in the historical origins of the empire. Because the then holder of the Roman empire was deficient in his function of providing protection for the Roman Church, he was deprived of his office and the empire conferred on one who was willing and able to afford such protection. The right of the electors, therefore, as a papal charge, was exercised under the papal *ius*; the right of the elect, chosen to perform a papal service

---

[1] Cf. specially, C.C.Bayley, *The Formation of the German College of Electors in the Mid-thirteenth Century* (Toronto 1949); also F. Kempf, *Papsttum und Kaisertum bei Innocenz III: die geistigen und rechtlichen Grundlagen seiner Thronstreitpolitik* (Misc. hist. pont. 19.; Rome 1954).

as *advocatus* and *defensor* of the Roman Church was likewise subject to the pope. Thus *principaliter*, in its historical origins, and *finaliter*, in the sense of the end or function served by an emperor — defence of the Roman Church — the empire pertained to the pope.

From the canonists' point of view, this statement solved the question of whether or not the pope had two swords.[2] Rare was the canonist after *Venerabilem* who attempted to argue that papal right in the empire was confined to conferring a mere title on the elect.[2a] The implications of this change for the canonist understanding of the general principles of papal power in temporal affairs will be discussed later. Here it can be noticed that the 'two swords' argument in its narrower sense, as relating to the empire specifically, was soon given its typical form. From many glosses, that of St. Raymond of Peñafort might be chosen both for its conciseness and as illustrating how even conservative and moderate canonists gave their assent to the principle that the emperor held his power of the pope:

> Sed numquid immediate an mediate habet imperator imperium a Deo Quidam dicunt quod immediate. Pro eis est X di. *Quoniam*, XCVI di.

---

[2] It is clear from the commentaries of such leading early decretalists as Vincentius Hispanus and Laurentius Hispanus that the new doctrine was not received altogether uncritically by canonists. But a good deal more work on the composition and relationships of early decretalist *Apparatus* is necessary before it will be possible to pinpoint with any accuracy the shades of the doubt registered by the critical. For example, it seems that Laurentius was seen by his canonist contemporaries as the least enthusiastic supporter of the doctrine of *Venerabilem* (cf. n. 19 below). But it is extremely difficult to work out what was his true position, which seems to have modified, in default of a critical study of his *Apparatus ad Decretum* and its relationship to the *Glossa Palatina* and the *glossa ordinaria* as well as to his *Apparatus ad Compilationem IIIam*. Yet the critical aspect of the short period of the first canonist commentaries on *Venerabilem* left an abiding mark on the course of development of canonist political doctrines and of medieval political thought generally. The *glossa ordinaria ad Decretum*, a product of this period, a major piece of literary equipment for all disputants in the theoretical disputes concerning the relationship of the two powers, was very reserved in its teaching about papal possession of two swords. In two of the three contexts in which the topic was ventilated, it was entirely noncommital, stating the case *pro* and *contra*, without offering a solution (D. 96 c.6 s.v. *usurpavit* and D. 22 c.1 s.v. *coelestis*). In the third (D. 10 c.8 s.v. *discrevit*) it inclined markedly to a pro-imperial position (the political sympathies of the writer, Joannes Teutonicus, in a different pro-imperial context have been well discussed by G. Post, 'Two Notes on Nationalism' *Traditio* 9[1953] 298-300). There was thus preserved within the canonist tradition and by extension within the medieval tradition as a whole, at least a question mark against the proposition that the pope had two swords.

[2a] One, however, apparently, was the compiler of the *Glossa Palatina*: 'Ego non credo unam [potestatem gladii] ex alia pendere: ar. contra, extra iii, qui filii sint legitimi, Per venerabilem, et romana ecclesia transtulit imperium in occidentem et principibus alemanie dedit potestatem eligendi, extra iii, de electione, Venerabilem': ad D. 10 c.8 s.v. *discrevit* (Durham Cath.MS C.III.8, fol. 4ra). Cf. also Stickler, 'Sacerdotium et Regnum' 18.

Cum ad verum et Authent. preallegata, *Quando oporteat episcopus*, XCIII di. *Legimus*, vers. *exercitus sibi faciat imperatorem*. Alii dicunt quibus assentio quod mediate: papa enim habet a Domino utrumque gladium. Item cum abscindisset auriculam Malco gladio materiali, non dixit ei Dominus: pone gladium, Sed: *converte in vaginam*, ac si aperte diceret: habeas gladium materialem, eius tamen executionem non exercens, sed alii committas, et videtur hoc expressum, XXII di. *Omnes*, Extra III de electione, *Venerabilem*, XV.q. VI, *Alius*.[3]

One major political problem was solved but another one was posed. *Per venerabilem* was the second major contribution made by Innocent III to the canonistic dialectic. This decretal expressed the claim that the pope had the power of legitimizing for temporal purposes as well as for ecclesiastical ones. Thereby canonists were presented with as delicate a point as they could desire around which to debate the respective spheres of spiritual and temporal authorities, and the principle and practice of papal power in temporal affairs.

In 1202, William, count of Montpellier, petitioned Innocent III through the archbishop of Arles for the legitimation of the children born of his mistress. William was anxious to ensure that they would be in line of succession to him, and supported his request by recalling to the pope that he had already performed a similar service for the children of Philip Augustus and Ingeburg.[4] Innocent's lengthy reply made a decretal which the canonists came to know as *capitulum difficile et multum famosum*.[5]

The decretal began with the assertion that the apostolic see did have, 'verisimilius,' full power to grant William's request, namely to legitimize his bastards for purposes of succession.[6] This was based on a variety of considerations drawn from papal exercise of legitimation power in promotion to holy orders. If the pope could dispense not merely natural children but adulterines and sons of priests so that they could become bishops, *multo fortius* it would seem that he could legitimate for secular purposes, especially where no superior with power of legitimizing, other than the pope, existed. Again, if a bishop knowingly ordained a serf, he attained free status, even though the bishop would have to compensate the lord; it would seem monstrous then, if he who was legitimate for spiritual affairs should remain illegitimate for temporal purposes. Whence

---

[3] *Summa iuris* 1.11, *ed. cit.* p. 40.

[4] For a detailed study of Philip's request and Innocent III's attitudes, and the circumstances of William of Montpellier cf. R. Génestal, *Histoire de la légitimation des enfants naturels en droit canonique* (Paris 1905) 182-201.

[5] As the rubric had it. Antonius de Butrio, in the fourteenth century, commented: 'Haec est solemnis decretalis obscure decidens quod principaliter intendit ipsam declarabo iuxta possibilitatem mihi a Deo concessam' (cited by Génestal, *op. cit.* 182).

[6] In addition to the text itself (4.17.6) the very numerous canonist *casus* to it should be consulted.

eo ipso that legitimation was granted in spiritual matters, *consequenter* it held for the temporal sphere.

After these preliminaries, in which power to legitimize in temporal matters was claimed, the letter dealt with the petition itself, especially with William's appeal to the case of Philip Augustus. The pope denied that this was a similar case. For the king of France was separated from his wife by judgment of a papal legate, but William had abandoned his wife. The king of France had contracted with Ingeburg before he received the prohibition against remarrying; William had taken a mistress *in contemptum ecclesiae*. The king of France proved objections of affinity against the marriage; the verdict of the legate had been quashed because of an irregularity of procedure, not because the proof of affinity was defective. William, on the other hand, had no valid reasons for separation. It could fairly be doubted whether the king's children were in fact illegitimate as long as the affinity question was being investigated; once affinity was proved and it was established that there had been no valid marriage, legitimation of the children was unnecessary. Furthermore, since the king had no temporal superior, he could subject himself to the pope *sine iuris alterius laesione* and might have done the legitimation act himself, *non tamquam pater cum filiis, sed tamquam princeps cum subditis*. But William did have a temporal superior.

Innocent passed to the third part of the decretal — an *exposé* of the principles in virtue of which popes had the right and power of exercising temporal jurisdiction (as in the secular legitimation of children by the pope) *certis causis inspectis* .... *casualiter*. The justification of this principle constituted a major statement of the *imperium sacerdotii*. The Mosaic law concerning the authority of priests, completed by the Petrine texts, the vicariate of Christ prefigured by Melchisedech, the *plenitudo potestatis* explained through St. Paul: 'Nescitis quoniam angelos iudicabitis? quanto magis secularia?', were all advanced to explain that recourse ought to be had to the apostolic see in all difficult or ambiguous cases.[7]

---

[7] Particular weight attaches to this formulation: 'medium inter causam et causam (cf. Deut. 17.8), quod ad utrumque refertur tam ecclesiasticum tam ciuile: in quibus cum aliquid fuerit difficile vel ambiguum ad iudicium est sedis apostolice recurrendum, cuius sententiam qui superbiens contempserit observare, mori praecipitur, id est per excommunicationis sententiam velut mortuus a communione fidelium separari. Paulus etiam ut plenitudinem potestatis exponeret, ad Corinthios scribens ait: Nescitis quoniam angelos iudicabitis? quanto magis secularia?' There was here a principle of critical importance for the future development of canonist thought. Innocent III was contending that in any difficult or ambiguous case, ecclesiastical or secular, recourse might be had to the pope whose judgment must be accepted under pain of major excommunication. This principle was linked with the term *plenitudo potestatis*. It was implied that *plenitudo potestatis* over spiritual things included a papal discretionary power over temporal affairs where the spiritual good demanded the exercise of such a power. This was the germ of the later canonists' view of *plenitudo po-*

The contention that the pope had a power to legitimize in temporal affairs ensured that the canonist tradition bore within itself at least one live point of political contention. At any rate to the time of Hostiensis, it was this text which was the focus of the freshest canonist thinking about the principles of the relations of the two powers. The decretal also had important things to say, in its third part, about the principle itself of papal power in temporal affairs.

Solite may be singled out as constituting a third major contribution. It was a restatement of the general principle of sacerdotal superiority.[8] In one sense perhaps, it may be said to have been a contemporary restatement of Gelasius' *Duo sunt* in the form in which Innocent III knew that text from the *Decretum*, and in the way decretists had interpreted it — as an expression of sacerdotal superiority. At any rate, Gelasian language was consciously used at one point[9] and decretalists habitually bracketed *Duo sunt* and *Solite* together,[10] They saw the one as complementary to the other, in an exposition of the bases of the *maioritas* of the *sacerdotium*, the authorities mutually supplementing one another, *ad declarandum prerogatiuam sacerdotis.*

This decretal contained one very characteristic and fundamental Innocentian argument to establish the preeminence of the papacy — a particular exegesis of the *vaticinium Ieremiae* (Jer. 1.10): 'Ecce constitui te hodie super gentes et super regna . . . '

---

testatis in its temporal aspects, which is analyzed in more detail below. It should be noticed that Innocent III had given a marked slant to the standard interpretation of Deut. 17.8, though this did to some extent prepare the way for the Innocentian interpretation; cf. P. Comestor: ' *De appellatione populi ad summum sacerdotem.* Quod si contigeret iudices illos ambigere de sententia aliqua ascenderent ad summum sacerdotem, et quod ille iudicaret, fieret': *Historia scholastica* c.6 (PL 198.1253). This Innocentian penchant for turning Old Testament exegesis to the service of papal power was a marked feature of his thought and was an important aspect of his contribution to the canonist tradition, see below pp. 44-45. The text Deut. 17.8 has been interestingly discussed by B. Tierney, with whose interpretation I am in general agreement, ' "Tria quippe distinguit iudicia . . .": A Note on Innocent III's Decretal *Per Venerabilem,*' *Speculum* 37 (1962) 48-59.

[8] This decretal is not in the Register but figured in *Comp.* III 1.21.2 = X. 1.33.6 and Rainerius' *Collectio* (PL 216.1182-85). It was a reply to the Greek Emperor Alexis III who had apparently contended that the *imperium* was preeminent over the *sacerdotium.* Alexis' reason for ventilating this problem was explained in the *Gesta Innocentii* § 62, as a tactical move in the negotiations concerning Greek participation in a forthcoming general council. PL 214. cxxiii.

[9] In an interpretation of the sun-moon metaphor: ' . . . fecit Deus duo magna luminaria, id est, duas instituit dignitates, que sunt pontificalis auctoritas et regalis potestas.'

[10] When commenting on the same metaphor when the point was being made that the one shone 'maius' than the other; e.g. Joh. Teutonicus ad *loc. cit.* (B.M. MS Roy. 11. C.VII, fol. 132ᵛ); *gl. ord. ad Decretales, loc. cit.*

This text had a long exegetical history in ecclesiastical literature.[11] It had become increasingly prominent in papal letters and the writings of reformers, from the time of Gregory VII, where it did service to underline the pastoral charge incumbent on all prelates — cultivators of the *agricultura Dei*, they were bound to root out vices and to labor for the successful fruition of all Christian seed. It kept this meaning through the twelfth century as a commonplace of the papal chancery, as a public expression of the papacy's pastoral mission in the Church. It was favored especially when papal legates were dispatched. St. Bernard was in the same interpretative stream when with some characteristically vigorous verbal strokes he sought to impress on Eugenius III that his command was a *ministerium* and not a *dominium*. It was quite a natural course of evolution that the text, in these papal pastoral contexts, should be associated with the Petrine texts themselves, as revealing an Old Testament antecedent of the pastoral mission. The style of the twelfth-century chancery in general was given to pointing such parallels between the priestly charge over God's people and the papal solicitude for the Church. It was also perhaps natural, given the linking of Jer. 1.10 with the power of binding and loosing (a judicial power), that it should come to be associated with the right of exercising judicial power over the 'gentes et regna' of Christendom, in particular over those who held political authority. It was this association, not hitherto seemingly made directly by any pope, though it had been by at least one prominent churchman, which Innocent III adopted wholeheartedly.

It became a basic Innocentian text to express the primacy in general, and spiritual power over rulers in particular. It was used in no less than three of his major political decretals. Jeremias prefigured that papal rule over the universal Church which was confirmed *expressius* by the singling out of Peter as the rock on which the Church was founded. Likewise he foreshadowed that papal power over the souls of men, confirmed *excellentius* by the divine charge to bind and loose. Of deepest significance to canonists was the judicial aspect of papal power which Jer. 1.10 revealed *in figura*: as Innocent put it to Philip Augustus in *Novit*:

> quod autem possimus et debeamus etiam *coercere*, patet ex eo quod inquit Dominus ad prophetam . . . Ecce constitui te. . . . .

Solite, Novit and *In Genesi* indicated, by way of Jer. 1.10 anticipating the Petrine commission, that with the ministerial function of the pope went a coercive power, by means of which sacerdotal preeminence was given political significance. In the exercise of the papal office, the two things were held to

---

[11] Excellently traced by Y. M.-J. Congar, 'Ecce constitui te super gentes et regna (Jér. 1.10) "in Geschichte und Gegenwart",' *Theologie in Geschichte und Gegenwart: Michael Schmaus zum sechzigsten Geburtstag dargebracht* . . . (Munich 1957) 671-696.

be inseparable: in the care of souls, the judicial power over rulers was as means to end. *Duo sunt* had yielded the same lesson, but Innocent III restated the principle in scriptural and therefore more fundamental terms. *Solite* expressed more fully and specifically the content of what Gelasius had called the 'gravius pondus sacerdotum' and what Innocent III called (after the Old Testament) the 'imperium sacerdotis.'[12]

Three decretals, *Novit, Licet* and *Per venerabilem*, had important things to say about the reception by the papacy of requests from secular powers for papal action in temporal affairs. The restatement of principles here involved may be considered as the fourth way in which Innocent left his mark on the canonist tradition.

The background of the celebrated decretal *Novit* lay in King John's appeal for Innocent's help against Philip Augustus, then steadily encroaching on his French possessions, already adjudged forfeit by the French king and baronage. John, not recognizing this sentence, claimed that Philip had broken his treaty oath in respect of Poitou, that the king of France was unwilling to listen to his requests for justice, and, on these grounds, laid the matter before the Pope. Innocent took up John's cause enthusiastically and, pricked by Philip's rebuff that the affair being feudal was outside papal jurisdiction, produced a strong state-ment of the *imperium sacerdotis*. It recalled *Solite* in using the same texts, Jer. 1.10 and Matth. 16.18 as the primary justification of an intervention in a moral matter, and substantially recapitulated Huguccio's interpretation of *Duo sunt*: 'nonne dictum est de quolibet nolente satisfacere, dic ecclesie (Matth. 18.17)?'[13]

The claim here expressed was potentially wide in its implications, but in the strict context had reference to the breaking of treaties and to declarations of war. It was thus the basis of the papal claim to arbitrate between contending rulers. War, the breaking of the 'vinculum caritatis,' as a moral matter touching the stability and harmony of Christian order could hardly, in the Innocentian and canonist logic, escape the sway of the Church: 'ad ecclesiam enim spectat pacem servare et servari facere.'[14]

Licet ex suscepto was addressed to the bishop of Vercelli and concerned the problem of whether a particular case should be heard by him, by the pope or by the commune. Innocent ruled that the case should only be heard ecclesiastically if the consuls were unwilling or unable to render justice. If not, or if the judges were shown to be prejudiced ('suspecti'), then recourse might be had to the bishop or to the pope, especially because there being a vacancy

---

[12] Cf. Deut. 17.12

[13] Cf. above p. 17, n. 16.

[14] Tancred, *Comp.* III ad 2.1.2 s.v. *contra pacem* (Durham Cath. MS C.III.4 fol. 131ʳᵃ); J. Teutonicus ad *loc. cit.* (B.M. Roy. 11. C. VII, fol. 142ᵛ); *gl. ord. ad Decretales* 2.1.13 *v.cit.*

at that time in the empire, there was no secular superior from whom redress might be obtained.

In *Per venerabilem*, as has been seen, while rejecting the particular petition in question, Innocent III underlined a general principle about the hearing of requests for papal temporal intervention. If there was no temporal authority to whom recourse might be had by an inferior power for the solution and removal of legal doubts and difficulties, the pope might act, in his capacity of *debitor iustitiae in omnibus*.[15]

The fifth aspect of the Innocentian contribution to canonist thought to be listed, is yet another angle on sacerdotal supremacy. *Excommunicamus* was, in part, a restatement of the principle of the cooperation of the powers — but in terms which made it clear how that principle was determined by that of the superior right of the *sacerdotium*.

The third canon of the Fourth Lateran Council was a code of such legislation, summarizing in definitive form the already existing statutes ordaining the proper punishments for heresy in the various public offices of Christian society. What became for canonists the fourth section of the code, ordained that secular powers should be required and compelled where it was thought necessary, to swear to protect the faith and to expel heretics from their territory. If a secular power neglected to cleanse its lands of heretics when called upon to do so, it should be excommunicated by the metropolitan and bishops of the province concerned. Should satisfaction not be made within a year, this contempt would be certified to the pope who would declare its subjects free of their obedience. The territory would then be open to occupation by the faithful who, with the extermination of the heresy, would enjoy full legal possession. The rights of a suzerain over lands declared open for occupancy were safeguarded unless the suzerain himself placed obstacles in the way of the extermination of the heresy. For canonists, the whole statute *Excommunicamus* and the other laws which preceded it, were important as revealing an aspect of the cooperation of the powers and the conditions and circumstances in which the Church had recourse to the secular arm. Here it is necessary to notice the further strengthening of deposition theory, in such a way that the *imperium sacerdotis*, the removal of rulers for heresy, the deposition of Childeric and the Translation of the Empire were bound together as the most vigorous expression of the papal power to coerce rulers.

---

[15] 'Licet ex suscepto servitutis officio simus omnibus in iustitia debitores, sic tamen in iure suo nos quibusdam convenit providere, ne aliis iniuriam facere videamur, et, quod absit! inde sumatur materia scandali, unde provide debet consideratione sedari.' (PL 215. 892: except for the first three words, this sentence did not appear in the final version of the letter in the *Corpus Iuris*). The expression *debitor iustitiae* was a traditional one and appeared regularly in papal letters at least from the time of Gregory VII (for his usage of it, cf. *Reg.* i.53 ed. Caspar, p. 80; ii.44, p. 180; iv.26, p. 341; iv.28, p. 344; vi.13. p. 416)

Thus far five aspects of the Innocentian contribution to the political stock of the *Corpus Iuris Canonici* have been distinguished: the solution of the two swords question in relation to the empire (*Venerabilem; In Genesi*); the positing of a new and practical problem of the competence of the pope in temporal affairs (*Per venerabilem*); a restatement of the general principles of the judicial nature of sacerdotal supremacy (*Solite, Novit*); the demonstration of a number of practical illustrations of this supremacy (*Novit, Licet, Per venerabilem, Excommunicamus*); a restatement of the nature of secular coopera- tion with the spiritual power (*Excommunicamus*).

These five points all dealt with the *ideas* that Innocent contributed. There must now be added three further contributions which might be expressed as a political *language*, a political *perspective* and a method of political *argument*.

Innocent III gave the seal of official approval to three terms of very great importance for all future examination of papal primacy. None of them did he invent nor were they specifically political. But they came to be used in political contexts soon after their introduction into *Compilatio* III. Of these terms, *Vicarius Christi* and *plenitudo potestatis* had a long history in Christian literature, were in twelfth-century decretist use, had been used by popes before Innocent III, and were not primarily terms wherewith to justify papal supremacy in temporal affairs. [*Papa est*] *iudex ordinarius omnium* was of early decretist coinage and formed with the two foregoing expressions part of the language of papal primacy which was achieving standardization before Innocent III's pontificate. Innocent III had an important place in the history of these three terms since it was he who was responsible in one way or another for their introduction into the common law of the Church. Whilst it is true that the introduction was made largely in contexts which referred to spiritual and ecclesiastical matters, nevertheless he was himself an agent in the process of their adoption into the canonist political vocabulary. These were the key thirteenth-century canonist thoughts about the papacy, concerning either the primacy generally and fundamentally, or that specific part of the primacy which related to temporal affairs. It was Innocent III who had given them their official place in ecclesiastical jurisprudence.

These three expressions were formulae which together summarized all that the canonists knew about papal headship of the Church. As political expres- sions that had reference to papal headship of Christendom, they had their meaning in that part of the canonist logic concerned with the direction of Christian society, of which the pope was the one existing focus of institutional unity. With these terms, the vocabulary of the 'monist' position had been enlarged.

But Innocent III has also to his credit, in the evolution of the terminology in which papal power was analyzed, certain terms which enlarged the vocab- ulary of the 'dualist' position. The antithesis 'non iudicare de feudo sed decernere de peccato' of *Novit* and the formulation of *Per venerabilem*, 'certis causis inspectis *casualiter* exercemus iurisdictionem temporalem' were the essence of a decretalist discussion about the 'indirect' power of the pope in temporal affairs. In the matter of the language used by canonists in the thirteenth century to discuss the relationship of the powers, it is clear that the Innocentian contribution was twofold. It was in words that he had supplied that canonists discussed both the monist and the dualist facets of their problem.

The political perspective that Innocent III altered for canonists concerned the unity of Christian society. Imbued himself with a deep consciousness that the diverse units of the Christian world formed a single *populus Christianus*,[16] something of this sentiment was reflected in his legislation and hence in canonist writing. Innocent III did not of course himself invent the notion that — as Le Bras has put it — 'La Chrétienté est cet ensemble cohérent de terres gouvernées par des princes officiellement soumis à la présidence religieuse du pontife romain, qui exerce sa puissance spirituelle (et peut l'exercer directement) sur tous leurs sujets.'[17] But he did revitalize the idea. And as he renewed the principles that gave the papacy its title-deeds as a supranational jurisdiction, clarified the nature and increased the number of the applications of that power, so the attention of canonists was directed to the framework within which the Innocentian political logic had its meaning. The framework was the nature of Christian society itself. Decretists had been content to assume it, but early decretalists began to draw it into their arguments, though not very extensively. Later decretalists made it their main focus of attention in examining the nature of papal power in temporal affairs. And in this new political perspective, the three terms noted above played a decisive part.

Finally there must be considered the method of political argumentation which Innocent III popularized and made a stock article in the canonist store. The Old Testament yielded a rich harvest of political theology and history. It is true that many an ecclesiastical writer before Innocent had appreciated this, but the canonists, as far as discussing the relations of the powers was concerned, had not regarded the Old Testament as a major source. It was through Innocent III's decretals that canonists were introduced to its significance. The use of Jer. 1.10 has already been noticed. *In Genesi legimus*, as its *incipit* suggests, was a detailed lesson in the relevance of the teachings of the Old Testament to contemporary problems besetting the *sacerdotium*. It laid before the early decretalists a view of the superiority of the priesthood in the Old Testament, of that superiority being continued and indeed enhanced

---

[16] As well brought out by Rupp and Kempf.

[17] *Institutions ecclésiastiques*, p. 24.

in the New Testament, with papal succession historically linked, through Christ, to the priest-kings of the Old Law. *Per venerabilem* had a similar postulate, though it was stated less emphatically. In effect, it made a practical deduction from the principle for the claim to a papal power to hear and solve the legal difficulties and ambiguities of Christendom which was based on Deuteronomic law.

'Les théologiens de 1300 judaïzaient trop,' it has been said.[18] The process began with Innocent III, at any rate as far as the canonists were concerned. Innocent IV and Hostiensis were to place considerable emphasis on Old Testament history when they in their turn were forced to defend papal right to power in temporal affairs. They were using a method introduced into the canonist tradition by Innocent III.

What changes occurred in canonist thought as a result of these eight Innocentian contributions and at what stages did they occur in canonist writings?

Change must be described in relation to some fixed point. Great care must be taken here that the early decretalists are not compared with a decretist fixed point too arbitrarily chosen. For there was a variety of opinion held among decretists, and to choose too narrowly from among them a norm by which to measure later change, would vitiate the whole comparison.

Proceeding cautiously, it is suggested that five changes, all important, but some more so than others, occurred in canonist thought in the Innocentian period itself, or shortly thereafter. These changes will first be examined. Then an attempt will be made to assess their relative importance.

Two of the changes can be related to canonist methodology. It has been noticed earlier that the 'two swords' *quaestio* was the nearest decretists came to a formal political treatise. While it did not contain the totality of their thought on the principles of the relations of the powers, it did constitute their most important single vehicle of political discussion. The same *quaestio* remained equally a feature of early decretalist thought. But standardization of its form was being achieved and its content became more formalized. In the tracing of the change involved here, we are in touch with several different aspects of the changes effected in the canonist tradition by Innocent III.

The second methodological change was the appearance of something like a new literary form, devised by the early decretalists to assemble information on the papal role in temporal affairs. Canonists professed a practical science. They were therefore given to registering the occasions on which a particular principle was operative in practice. They had a strong tendency to list the occasions when a particular jurisdiction was exercised. Decretists had done this very frequently — notably in cataloguing papal *iura reservata*. What

---

[18] By M.D. Chenu, 'Dogme et théologie dans la bulle *Unam Sanctam*', *Mél. J. Lebreton* II (Paris 1952) 314.

appears to be new with the early decretalists was the enumeration of the occasions when the pope acted in the temporal sphere. The new Innocentian literature gave them plenty of material to consider on what basis the pope intervened in the secular order. This question of the *secundum quid*, they tended to answer in the two swords *quaestio*. The questions of *quare* and *quando* were answered by the assembling of the various circumstances of the exercise of temporal power. This new feature became standardized in canonist literature and is a *locus* of very great importance for the right understanding of the thought of Innocent IV and Hostiensis.

It was however not only the methodological framework which the early decretalists assembled. Within it there occurred two broad changes in the materials of political discussion which were to be of great consequence for later thirteenth-century canonist thought.

These two changes can be put as an antithesis. There appeared more developed expositions of both extreme and moderate interpretations of the principles of papal power in temporal affairs. Without going beyond the canonists' own language, it is possible to use what is also modern terminology to express the difference: that between a view positing a direct papal power in temporal affairs and one urging an indirect power. The first was expounded systematically by Alanus Anglicus; the other, rather less systematically, by several of his contemporaries.

The fifth and last change to be noticed concerned what earlier was postulated as being the *primum caput* of ecclesiastical superiority: the claim to the power to order the deposition of secular rulers. With the adoption of the Translation of the Empire theory and the sharpened concept of the duty laid on rulers under sanction of deposition to suppress heresy, there was a new clarity in canonist views about the seating and unseating of temporal authorities.

In none of these five changes, however, was there any very sharp break in the continuity of decretist and decretalist thought.

The two swords *quaestio* or the *argumentum de iurisdictione divisa* — really two separate issues, but considered together both by decretalists and decretists — was revised. Different decretalists, analyzing the full implications of *Venerabilem*, produced different discussions. But the one here selected for examination was the most important of them for it was eventually to find a place in the *glossa ordinaria* on the *Decretales*.[19]

---

[19] The gloss in question was formulated essentially by Tancred and with some minor modifications was accepted in the *glossa ordinaria* by Bernard of Parma. His 'edition' of it does not reveal fully the way the gloss developed from discussion among the early decretalists. Glosses on *Comp.* I however, make the development clear: 'Ar. de iurisdictione distincta, ut de Cons. di.iii. Celebritatem, in fine; x. di. Quoniam; xcvi. di. Cum ad verum; Qui fil.s.leg. Lator, in fine; xxiii.q.v. Regum; viii.di. Quo iure; xxxiii.q.ii. Interfectores. Contra: xxii di. Omnes; v.q.v. Delatori; Qui fil.s.leg. Conquestus; xx.q.iii. Presens; xv.q.vi.

It was compiled by Tancred in his *Apparatus* on *Compilatio* I, from three canonist opinions, those of Huguccio, Laurentius Hispanus, and Alanus Anglicus. It will be recalled that Huguccio had argued that the pope did not confer anything on the emperor except his title. That he had some support among the early decretalists is clear when Tancred made Laurentius Hispanus urge an apparently supporting position. The precise extent of this support is very difficult to determine because of the very difficult textual problems concerning Laurentius's work. The joint position of Huguccio and Laurentius was criticized by Alanus, and as far as canonists were concerned, it was he who won, when his opinion was accepted by Tancred and Bernard of Parma.

Huguccio was overwhelmed with a panoply of arguments professedly drawn from Innocentian sources: the single papal headship of Christian society; the vicariate of Christ; the *rex-sacerdos* postulate that Melchisedech, Moses and Christ had each held two swords; the Translation of the Empire and the power of deposition, all did service to establish the position that the pope had two swords. This gloss reveals better than any other single source that the Innocentian influence early penetrated canonist thought; in language (the political use of 'vicarius Christi'), in perspective ('unum corpus ecclesie'), in method ('Moyses utrumque gladium habuit cuius successor est apostolicus') and idea ('iudex [imperatoris] est dominus papa quia electum confirmat et cassat, ut de elect. venerabilem'). And this, it must be recalled, was not an isolated individual opinion but became the accepted orthodox view, the standard exposition of the constitutional relationship of pope and emperor and of the papal headship of Christendom.

What further than these two questions gave this gloss an important (political) doctrinal significance was its underlining of the deposing power. The Transla-

---

Alius; xxiv.q.i. Loquitur. Solutio: Magister Huguccio dicit, et bene, quod a solo Deo habet potestatem in temporalibus imperator, papa in spiritualibus, et sic divisa est iurisdictio. Prius enim est imperator qui coronam accipit a papa, et gladium ab altari, ut xciii. di. Legimus. Nam ante fuit imperium quam apostolatus. Iau(rentius). Ego dico cum Alano, sicut ipse notavit, de appell. Si duobus, quod imperator habet gladium a papa: est enim unum corpus ecclesie, ergo unum solum caput habere debet. Item Dominus utroque gladio usus est, ut xcvi. di. Cum ad verum, et i.q.iii. Ex multis. Sed solum Petrum vicarium suum constituit in terra, ergo utrumque gladium ei reliquit. Item Moyses utrumque gladium habuit, cuius successor est apostolicus. Preterea, iudex est dominus papa quia electum confirmat et cassat, ut de elect. Venerabilem, lib. iii. et etiam confirmatum deponit, xv.q.vi. Alius. Et hoc totum inuenitur expresse in quodam extrav. Innocentii tertii, In Genesi. Est tamen argumentum contra, Aut. Quo. op. epis. in prin. (*Nov.* 6), sed canon preiudicat legi. t(ancredus)': ad *Comp.* I 4.18.7 [= X.4.17.7] s.v. *ad regem* (MSS B.N. 3930, fol. 54rb, Durh. Cath. C. III. 4, fol. 47ra). The Innocentian decretal cited here has sometimes been misidentified by modern commentators. It is neither X.1.6.55 nor c. 24 of 4 Lateran Council (as stated for example by Mochi Onory, *Fonti canonistiche*, p. 199) but the *In Genesi* of the *Regestum de negotio Romani imperii* (ed. Kempf, no. 18 pp. 45-52) and of Rainerius' collection, PL 216.1179-1182.

tion of the Empire and the substitution of Pepin for Childeric by Pope Zachary were firmly linked, the former confirming the latter. Nor was this
only the opinion of Tancred and Alanus. It was universally accepted by the
early decretalists — even by Laurentius, whose view of the 'two swords'
question had been criticized as too restrained.[20] The coupling together of the
Translation and the existing decretist deposition theory based on *Alius item*
formed the myth of the historical beginnings of the western empire on which
so much of deposition theory in fact depended.

But the canonists did not think that their deposition theory depended essentially on historical arguments. For them, history merely illustrated the practical working of a papal power to coerce rulers, the essence of which was his
power over souls. That a ruler might be deposed for heresy was axiomatic
on their line of argument and the legislation of the Fourth Lateran Council
decreeing that penalty was automatically linked with their other deposition
arguments:

> *Precepimus fieri per potestates et principes seculares:* quod facere potest
> dominus papa obtentu peccati, ut supra, de iud. Novit. Vi(ncentius). Et
> ita potest papa eciam seculares iudices priuare dignitatibus suis non solum
> propter heresim set eciam propter alias iniquitates, ut xv.q.vi. Alius. Nam
> et imperium transfert de loco ad locum, ut supra, de elect. Venerabilem.
> Jo(hannes Teutonicus). Et non solum dominus papa, set eciam quilibet
> ecclesiasticus prelatus per excommunicationem potest quemlibet cogere
> secularem ad faciendam iusticiam de subditis suis, ut xxiii.q.v. Administra-
> tores. t(ancredus).[21]

Sacerdotal superiority was examined from another point of view when
canonists came to list the occasions when an ecclesiastical judge might concern
himself with temporal jurisdiction.

This was the *genre* of political writing introduced by the decretalists and in
many ways it is more revealing than the more abstract discussion of first
principles with which the 'two swords' *quaestio* dealt. At any rate, it was
the type of gloss that kept canonists in the closest contact with actual cases
and contemporary papal practice. Much the most significant section of the
gloss was that giving examples of papal action *ex defectu iustitiae secularis*;

---

[20] Laurentius: 'Nec dico istos gladios equales nam materialis recurrit ad spiritualem
in causis pro iure reddendo ut spiritualis inuocat materialem tanquam instrumentum suum
quantus pro facto supplendo, aliter quomodo posset romana ecclesia transferre imperium ab
una persona ut hic, uel regem deponere, ut xv.q.vi, Alius?' as *Comp.* III 1.6.19, s.v. *a Grecis
transtulit* (B.N.MS 3932, fol. 116ᵛᵇ).

[21] Ad *Comp.* III 5.4.1 [= X.5.7.10] (Caius Coll. MS 17.28 fol. 303ʳ; B.M.MS Roy. 11.C.VII
fol. 197ʳ). Cf. also Johannes Teutonicus: 'Sic ergo papa potest omnes iudices siue duces
siue comites deponere propter heresim, et eciam propter alias iniquitates, xv.q.vi. Alius,
nam et transfert dignitatem de loco ad locum, ex.iii. de elec. Venerabilem': ad *Comp.* IV
5.5.2 s.v. *vasallos* (B.M.MS Roy. 11.C.VII, fol. 236ᵛ).

Vacante imperio. Iste ergo unus casus in quo iudex ecclesiasticus potest se inmiscere seculari iurisdiccioni scilicet, cum superior non inuenitur: alius est cum iudex secularis negligit facere iusticiam ut hic, versi. dummodo etc. et infra capitulo proximo. ar. xxiii.q.iiii. Administratores. Tercius, cum aliquid fuerit ambiguum et difficile et uariatur inter iudices infra, qui filii sint legitimi, Per venerabilem. lau(rentius) . . . . . Septimus, cum per denunciationem racione criminis aliqua causa defertur ad iudicem ecclesiasticum ut supra, titulo proximo, Novit. Octavus, cum iudex secularis est suspectus ut hic in fine, et in auten. ut differentes iudices § i et ii. c. ult. coll. ix . . . . t(ancredus).[22]

Thus would papal authority make good the defects of secular justice whatever their cause. The *debitor iusticiae* was at the call of anyone who was deprived of justice through some obstruction, omission, malice or negligence which blocked the operation of the routine juridical machinery. Or he might intervene on his own initiative to achieve the same result. The listing of cases whereby these points were made was a standard feature of decretalist work from the early thirteenth century on.

The last change to be examined centres round the emergence of clear formulations of the respective principles of the 'direct' and 'indirect' papal power in temporal affairs.

The most radical interpretation of Innocent III's political doctrine was provided by Alanus.[23] He was an extremist and knew himself to be such. The clarity with which he could distinguish how a different line of argument or different consequences followed from adopting his or the more cautious alternative opinion was but one part of his intellectual quality as an analyst of papal power. Only great insensitivity to the individuality of canonist writers would be content to label him extremist and take the matter no further. Alanus wrote with style, great clarity and logic and some not inconsiderable originality. His views deserve examination not because he might appear to be the first of canonist extremists or the precursor of a Boniface VIII, but as one who with Huguccio and Innocent III attempted a comprehensive rethinking of the principles and practices of papal monarchy.

Nevertheless he was an extremist — in the sense that he held a view of papal power which gave it a directness of operation in the temporal order which canonists on the whole, both before and after him, would not admit *in toto*, since it overbore the principle of the distinction of the powers.

Alanus was a literalist. He believed quite simply that if the pope was vicar of Christ, was head of Christian society, was the maker and breaker of emperors

---

[22] Ad *Comp.* III 2.2.1 (Durh. Cath. MS C.III 4, fol. 131ᵛᵇ).

[23] Study of his views has been considerably facilitated by A. M. Stickler's publication of extracts from the two recensions of the *Apparatus 'Ius naturale'* in 'Alanus Anglicus als Verteidiger des monarchischen Papsttums', *Salesianum* 21 (1959) 346-406.

and kings, when it was said that he had 'fulness of power,' it meant that he
had all power, to the extent that he could overrule any temporal power, apparently in any matter whatsoever. He was the 'iudex ordinarius omnium
de omni negocio.'[24] He urged that there was no limitation in principle on
papal action in temporal affairs, though there might be for reasons of expe-
diency.

He was prepared to draw practical deductions from his general principle of
papal absolute power in the temporal order. Thus he held that the pope
had power to legitimize for all temporal purposes,[25] could by his judgment
impose or lift sentence of outlawry from the secular courts,[26] had the sole right
of permitting declarations of war,[27] might depose anyone without reference
to any other authority,[28] could judge de feudo if he thought fit.[29] Alanus took
very literally the concept of the vicariate of Christ — this was an absolute
position and knew no reservations in either spiritual or temporal order. He
allowed that the pope was under obligation not to reserve the power of the
temporal sword for his own use.[30] But there was no limit to be imposed as to
when the pope could act over the head of the secular prince in temporal affairs,
if the pope judged such interventions necessary.

---

[24] A principle he formulated on at least four occasions — App. 'Ius naturale' ad D. 96
c.6 s.v. discrevit (Stickler, 'Alan. Anglicus' 362) and ad C. 23 q.2 c.1 s.v. ex edicto (B.N.MS
15393, fol. 181ᵛᵃ); ad Comp. I 2.20.7 s.v. iuris (Stickler, art. cit. 364); ad c. Per venerabilem
in his collection of Innocent III's decretals, Stickler, 'Sacerdozio e regno' 23.

[25] ' . . . . secundum nos papa super principem est etiam in temporalibus et ideo
habet potestatem legitimandi quoad actus seculares': ad c. Per venerabilem, s.v. seculares
actus (Stickler, art. cit. 23).

[26] 'Secundum illos qui dicunt quod imperator et reges debent a papa iurisdictionem
habere, potest papa infamiam iuris omnino remittere et quoad actus canonicos et quoad
actus legitimos etiam a civili iudice irrogatam. Secundum alios qui hoc non concedunt
non potest remittere nisi quoad actus ecclesiasticos': ad C.2 q.3 c.7 s.v. susceperunt (Stickler,
'Alan. Anglicus' 365-6). That the first of these two views was his own seems a fair deduction from his commentary on D. 96 c.6.

[27] ' . . . . et secundum opinionem nostram quod dominus papa esse iudicem ordinarium
principum quo ad spiritualia et quo ad temporalia, ad eum antequam indicat bellum tenetur
recurrere ut per eum iusticiam consequatur si potest. Secundum aliam opinionem ad ipsum
recurreri non oportet': ad C. 23 q.2 c.1 s.v. ex edicto (B.N.MS 15393, fol. 181ᵛᵃ).

[28] 'Ideo dicatur quod ipsum iure suo potuit deponere et hodie omnes principes terre si
de hoc facto liqueret et status ecclesie nichil illesus permaneret': ad C.15 q.6 c.3 s.v. deposuit (Stickler, 'Alan. Anglicus' 367).

[29] 'Non intendimus iudicare de feudo: quia ad presens, de plenitudine tamen sue potestatis
posset secundum opinionem nostram, qui dicimus quod papa est iudex ordinarius omnium
hominum de omni negotio': ad c. Novit in his collection of decretals, Stickler, 'Sacerdozio e
regno' 23.

[30] 'Set numquid papa posset materialem gladium sibi retinere si vellet? R. Non, quia
dominus gladios divisit, ut hic (D.96 c.6, c. Cum ad verum) et ecclesia ex hoc plurimum tur-
baretur': Stickler, 'Alan. Anglicus' 363.

Of course Alanus did not stand as the sole protagonist of an extreme view. There had been many anticipations of his ideas. Nor (as has been seen in the instance of the two swords *quaestio*) were all his views rejected. But no canonist before or after him pursued in so ruthlessly consistent a way such an unqualified logic of the vicariate of Christ in Christian society. It is significant that Alanus's views became more trenchant as the pontificate of Innocent III went on. If we are to use canonists to explain the political thinking of Innocent III, it might be asked which canonist reflects his mind most nearly — the teacher of his youth, Huguccio, or Alanus, who revised his thinking *coram magistro* as the pontificate progressed?[31] Was not Alanus expounding just that concept into which Innocent had distilled all his thought on papal monarchy,

> ... solus autem Petrus assumptus est in plenitudinem potestatis. Iam ergo videtis quis iste servus, qui super familiam constituitur, profecto vicarius Jesu Christi, successor Petri, Christus domini, Deus Pharaonis: inter Deum et hominem medius constitutus, citra Deum, sed ultra hominem: minor Deo, sed maior homine: qui de omnibus iudicat et a nemine iudicatur.[32] —

a position so uniquely sublime that it was unthinkable that there were any men or affairs not submitted to the quasi-divine jurisdiction? Was not Innocent III's whole political logic based on the premise that the vicar of Christ was charged with the general welfare of Christendom and where that was concerned, there were no theoretical restraints to the comprehensiveness of his jurisdiction? No person, no matter escaped this control, nor was the permission of anyone else needed for any action which the pope considered necessary for the general welfare, nor might anyone sit in judgment of such acts as the pope had thought necessary. And if this was Innocent's basic assumption,[33] did not Alanus go closer to its full articulation than Huguccio?

Whatever answers are given to these questions it remains true that the canonists followed Alanus only partially. He had sought to impose a simple unified pattern on the diverse and complex political material with which the canonists had to deal. Most decretalists continued to believe, in the main, that the problem of the powers was rather more complicated than Alanus

---

[31] The first recension of the *App.* 'Ius naturale' dates from c. 1192, the second, c.1202. Fr. Stickler's article by printing together the two versions clearly demonstrates the development of Alanus from a restrained to a forceful expositor of papal authority. For the unfortunately very scanty biography of Alanus see Stickler, 'Alan. Anglicus' 376-8.

[32] *Sermo II: in consecratione pontificis maximi*, PL 217-658. The immediate sources from which Innocent drew these phrases would appear to be St. Bernard, *De consideratione* 4.7 and the *dictum* of Gratian: 'sola enim Romana ecclesia sua auctoritate valet iudicare de omnibus; de ea vero nulli iudicare permittitur', *ante* C.9 q.3 c.10.

[33] It is suggested below, p. 129, that it was also Boniface VIII's in *Unam sanctam*.

had allowed. They were prepared to consider an opposite tendency which spoke of an indirect papal power, since it gave more emphasis to the principle of the distinction of the powers, and thereby moved towards a more nuanced exposition of the problem.

It is an interesting comment on the contribution of the early thirteenth century decretalists to ecclesiastical scholarship that the one who is now generally accorded the credit of first formulating the modern doctrine of the indirect power, explicitly acknowledged a source for it which went back directly to the thirteenth century.

Robert Bellarmine said that Innocent IV was the author of the term 'indirect power.'[34] Actually Innocent IV was merely reproducing a gloss of one of his canonist predecessors, made in relation to *Novit*. Bellarmine also phrased his theory of the indirect power in relation to *Per venerabilem*. Though he did not mention the name of any decretalist in this context, the deduction he made from it had also been anticipated in the same period. Our concern here is with the decretalists, though Bellarmine helps us to understand what the canonists were saying.

They used the 'indirect' term in two contexts, in ways that were very similar but were not quite identical. There was a third, quite different context, where it was used, which will not concern us here. And there is a fourth context which ought to be considered, though the canonists did not actually use the term in it. Bellarmine did, however, to establish the same point as the early decretalists. They had the substance without the term itself. The object of the examination of these various shades of opinion is not primarily to investigate the origins and meaning of the term 'indirect power.' It does, however, provide the means of analyzing a matter of considerable significance in the understanding of thirteenth-century canonist thought — the nature of the Innocentian contribution to its understanding of the principle of the distinction of the powers. In *Novit* Innocent III declared that 'non enim intendimus iudicare de feudo . . . . sed decernere de peccato.' His distinction gave rise immediately to the view that the pope had direct cognizance of sin and through

---

[34] 'Porro auctorem harum vocum (*scil.* "directe" et "indirecte") habemus Innocentium IV pontificem doctissimum. Is enim explicans cap. Novit, De iudiciis, para. de feudo, dicit pontificem directe non iudicare de feudis, secus autem indirecte ratione peccati': *Tract. de potestate summi pontificis in rebus temporalibus adversus Guilielmum Barclajum* cap. v. Later he acknowledged that Innocent IV's gloss was taken from the *glossa ordinaria* on the *Decretals*, cf. the text cited by S. Tromp, 'De evolutione doctrinae potestatis indirectae Romani Pontificis circa res temporales in controversiis S. Roberti Bellarmini,' *Acta Congressus iuridici intern.* (Rome 1934) 3.106. In fact these 'voces' were used by most of the early decretalists, cf. F. Gillmann, 'Von wem stammen die Ausdrücke "potestas directa" und "potestas indirecta" papae in temporalibus?' *Archiv für kath. Kirchenrecht* 98 (1918) 407-9, and the notes following here.

this jurisdiction had an indirect influence on the temporal issue involved. For if the sin concerned possession of a fief, if theft was proved, there could be no forgiveness of the sin until restitution had been made. Thus the direct jurisdiction over the sin involved a secondary or indirect temporal effect. The distinction was a commonplace among the early decretalists when glossing *Novit* and it was to a certain extent generalized.[35] Thus it could be agreed that while certain crimes, such as perjury, usury, adultery were ecclesiastical because ecclesiastical courts had direct cognizance of them, all crimes were ecclesiastical to some extent in that all 'pertinent indirecte, si agatur ad modum denunciationis ad penitenciam.'[36]

This was the formulation of a theory of papal power indirect in relation to the *means* employed. It was not postulated that the result of affecting the course of temporal affairs would be achieved by the direct hearing of the temporal issue. *Per venerabilem* revealed an indirect power of a not dissimilar type, though it is distinguishable.

The decretalists were unhappy about the contention that the pope had power to legitimize *etiam quoad temporalia*. It provided a test case as to the reality of the principle of the distinction of the powers. Three views are distinguishable among decretalists.

One, the view of Alanus, was complete acceptance of the right in its most literal form.[37] A second, a complete rejection of the right, maintained that

---

[35] Johannes Teutonicus: '*non enim intendimus iudicare de feudo:* directe set tantum racione peccati et inducendo ad penitenciam, ut vi. q. i. Illi qui et xxii.q.i. Predicandum, xxiii.q.iiii. Ecce, et sic per consequenciam cogetur restituere feodum, ut xxiiii.q.vi. Si res aliena. Io.': ad *Comp.* III 2.1.2 (B.M.MS Roy. 11. C.VIII, fol. 142ᵛ; Gillmann, *art. cit.* 408 attributed the gloss to Johannes Galensis. Bernard of Parma reproduced it *in toto* in the *glossa ordinaria* of the *Gregoriana*). Vincentius Hispanus: '*non enim intendimus . . .* directe, set indirecte cognoscendo an peccet et inducendo ad penitenciam, xxii.q.i, Predicandum' (B.N. MS 14611, fol. 43ᵛᵇ; Gillmann, *loc.cit.* printed a contracted version of this gloss). Tancred (?): '*processit*: scilicet amonendo ipsum directe set tamen racione peccati et inducendo ad penitenciam ipsum, ut vi.q.i. Illi qui et xxii.q.i. Predicandum, xxiii.q.iiii. Ecce et sic per consequenciam potest restitui feudum, ut xvii.q.vi. Si res' (Durham Cath. MS C.III.4, fol. 130ᵛᵇ).

[36] Hence it could be stated that 'omnes cause indirecte spectant ad ecclesiam supra eo. Nouit, l. iii' (Johannes Teutonicus, ad *Comp.* IV 2.2.2 [= X. 5.40.26] B.N. MS 3932, fol. 210ᵛᵃ, B.M. MS Roy. 11.C.VIII, fol. 218ʳ) or more fully: 'nota crimen sacrilegii ecclesiasticum esse quod verum est, licet quandoque a iudice seculari punitur, ut C. de sacrosanc. ecc., Si quis in hoc genus. Item crimen usurarum hereseos symonie adulterii ad separacionem thori. Hec directe pertinent ad iudicem ecclesiasticum punienda et omnia alia indirecte, ut est ar. xxiii.q.i.c.ult. ex.iii e.ti. Licet ex suscepto' (unsigned gloss [Damasus?] *Comp.* II 2.2.2 = X. 2.2.6] s.v. *per dominum*, B.M.Roy. 11.C.VIII, fol. 85ᵛ). The quotation in the text above is from the *Apparatus* of Damasus (B.N. MS 3930, fol. 73ʳᵃ). The gloss just cited appears to be substantially the same.

[37] Cf. n. 25 above.

the pope had no power of legitimation *nisi quoad spiritualia.*[38] The other view was a compromise between these two extremes. Stated by Johannes Teutonicus[39] and accepted by Raymond of Peñafort[40] it held that the pope had such a right, though not directly. Legitimation *in temporalibus* followed from legitimation *in spiritualibus,* 'indirecte et per quandam consequentiam.' Many decretalists accepted this view with the important qualification that the 'consequential' temporal legitimation did not hold for purposes of succession to property, though it might for other secular purposes.[41] This compromise view, the representative early decretalist opinion, thus was an attempt to qualify the scope of papal power in temporal affairs.[42] It was a dualistic opinion, as was their use of the indirect power terminology in relation to *Novit.*

But *Per venerabilem* had relevance to the principle of dualism in another way. Innocent III had claimed that *certis causis inspectis* the pope might

---

[38] Maintained apparently by Laurentius Hispanus: '*in patrimonio beati Petri libere potest apostolica sedes* (scil. legitimare in temporalibus): Maxime dixit Io(annes Teutonicus), set l(aurentius) contra, quia eo teste non potest legitimare aliquem quo ad forum seculare ubi non habet temporalem iurisdiccionem nisi princeps hoc ei commiserit ut infra e.c. ult. nisi ordine mediante ut infra notaui in seruo ordinato': ad *Comp.* III 4.12.2 (B.N.MS.3932, fol. 181rb: B.M. MS Roy. 11.C.VII, fol. 191r). But for another view of what was Laurentius' opinion see the interpretation of St. Raymond, n. 40 below.

[39] 'Plenam habet potestatem in hoc quia ex quo legitimat aliquem in spiritualibus per consequens legitimus est in temporalibus ut sequitur: tamen per hoc non probatur quod papa habeat iurisdiccionem in temporalibus nam legitimare spectat ad uoluntariam iurisdiccionem ut ff. de off. procon. l.ii. Item quia ad papam nichil spectat de temporalibus, ut supra, de app. Si duobus, l.i. supra de iud., Nouit, l.e., nisi in casibus ut notaui supra, de foro comp. c.ii, l.e: ad hoc dic quod papa non habet potestatem legitimandi in temporalibus set tamen eo ipso quod quis legitimatus est in spiritualibus intelligitur legitimatus in temporalibus unde per quandam consequenciam legitimat, set non directe: sepe enim dimittitur per consequenciam quod per se non permittitur, ut iiii.q.iii. Servi, ff. de auct. tut. l. i. Io.': ad *Comp.* III 4.12.2 (B.M.Roy.MS *cit.* fol. 191r).

[40] 'Item pone quod aliquis est legitimatus quoad actus ecclesiasticos et spirituales numquid per hoc erit legitimatus etiam quoad actus seculares? Videtur quod non, quia sicut imperator indiget auxilio pontificis in spiritualibus, ita e contra pontifex indiget auxilio principis in secularibus, d.x. Quoniam. Verius dicas quod talis intelligitur vel legitimatus indirecte vel per quandam consequentiam etiam ad actus seculares; monstruosum enim videtur ut qui legitimus ad spirituales fieret actiones, circa seculares actus illegitimus remaneret, extra. iii. qui filii sint legitimi, Per venerabilem: multa enim possumus indirecte que non possumus directe, C. de iudiciis, Quoties, extra. iii. de dote post div. restit. De prudentia. Dicunt tamen Laurentius, Vincentius et fere omnes doctores quod non erit legitimatus quoad successionem licet quoad actus legitimos alias sit legitimus': *Summa iuris* 2.23, *ed. cit.* 96.

[41] Cf. Vincentius: 'Erit legitimus quo ad actus seculares ut possit esse iudex, testis et huius, set quoad habebit hereditatem paternam non credo. vinc.': ad *Comp* III, c. *cit.* (B.M. Roy. MS *cit.* fol. 191r).

[42] The whole discussion was to be reopened by Hostiensis, see below pp. 112-114.

exercise temporal power *casualiter*. The canonists took this adverb as an invitation to list the cases when this power was exercised and, as has been seen, could show a number of different examples. They made little attempt to disentangle the notion of this papal power from the circumstances of the exercise of it which they had carefully compiled. The farthest they would go towards an abstraction was to say that the pope would intervene when his action was needed.[43] It was implicit in the argument that this need was related to a spiritual end, namely the preservation of justice. Bellarmine however, attempted to disentangle the notion from the circumstances and supplied an abstraction which became the classical text of the modern theory of the indirect power.

It was a generalization which expressed an idea of the indirect power different in kind from that which he had learned from *Novit* and the early decretalists. In relation to *Novit* it was not contemplated that any temporal jurisdiction would be exercised by the spiritual power. The matter in question (sin) was a purely spiritual one and was dealt with ecclesiastically. It was the proper fulfilment of the ecclesiastical penalty which had consequential or indirect effects in the temporal order, just as the legitimation of a child had consequential or indirect effects for the purposes of secular law. But when Innocent III and the early decretalists and Bellarmine spoke of temporal jurisdiction being exercised *casualiter* or *in casibus*, they meant that in these cases the ecclesiastical judge acted, in a certain sense, as a temporal judge. There was envisaged a direct hearing of temporal issues by ecclesiastical judges.

The canonists did not call this an indirect power, for in relation to the *means* employed it was not such. Bellarmine did call it an indirect power: it was for him an indirect power in relation to the *end* being pursued.[44] The spiritual power would be exercising a direct temporal power to achieve a spiritual end. The spiritual power had as its proper end, spiritual matters: the fulfilment of that end might demand the exercise of temporal jurisdiction. This was the point being made by Innocent III and the canonists. But Bellarmine wished to consider this an indirect power in the sense that the proper end of

---

[43] '*Certis causis inspectis*: scilicet cum requiritur (requirimur, B.N.3932) et hoc probatur auctoritate deutronomii, cum scilicet variatum est inter iudices. lau(rentius)': ad *Comp. III, c. cit.* (B.M.Roy.MS *cit.* fol. 191ᵛ). This gloss was retained in the *glossa ord.* ad *Decr. Greg.*

[44] '(. . . . . per voces 'directe' et 'indirecte' . . . intelligimus) . . . potestatem pontificiam per se et proprie spiritualem esse, et ideo directe respicere, ut obiectum suum primarium, spiritualia negotia; sed indirecte, id est per ordinem ad spiritualia, reductive et per necessariam consequentiam, ut sic loquamur, respicere temporalia, ut obiectum secundarium, ad quod non convertitur haec spiritualis potestas nisi in casu, ut loquitur Innocentius III in cap. 'per venerabilem', Qui filii sint legitimi: *In aliis*, inquit, *regionibus, certis causis inspectis, temporalem iurisdictionem casualiter exercemus*': Bellarmine, *Tract. de pot. pont. in rebus temp.* c.v.

the spiritual power was in certain cases pursued by means which were not directly proper to it, namely by the exercise of temporal power.

The canonists made no real attempt to formulate an abstraction about this 'adventitious' exercise of temporal power by the pope. Bellarmine's terminology is confusing since he did not distinguish his twofold use of his term. But both were in agreement on the substance: that the preservation of the general welfare of Christendom might occasionally demand the exercise of temporal jurisdiction by the papacy.

The decretalists of the early thirteenth century then, whilst coining the terminology which later theorists were to generalize to try to cover the whole scope of the exercise of papal power in temporal affairs, did not themselves attempt to make a complete interpretative framework of the *potestas indirecta*. Yet *Novit* and *Per venerabilem* did something to develop the principle of dualism as one aspect of canonist thought. It could be maintained that the pope had no power in the temporal sphere *nisi indirecte ratione peccati et in certis causis casualiter* and the *glossa ordinaria* kept this dualist position alive :

> Certis causis: scilicet cum requirimur, et hoc probatur auctoritate Deutero-nomii, scilicet cum variatum est inter iudices sive ambiguum, tunc recurri-tur ad iudicem ecclesiae, ut infra sequitur; et licet ex certis causis, non ideo est ordinarius quo ad temporalia, supra de officio ordinarii, Pastoralis, sed *casualiter*, ut dicit litera, supra, de foro competenti, licet et c. Ex tenore et c. Ex parte. Et ita est hic argumentum de iurisdictione distincta.[45]

Such views of the papal power expressed in such an authoritative source, in the very centre of the canonist tradition, ensured that the dualist position was always a factor of importance in canonist thought. It was a direct rejection of the intellectual excesses of Alanus Anglicus and the upholding of the view that the temporal order had its proper field where the spiritual power might not lightly trespass.

The political analyses of the thirteenth century canonists did not move far from the concepts, terms and methods indicated by Innocent III. He had, so to say, re-equipped the concept of the decretist *imperium spirituale* with restatements of its fundamental bases and clothed it anew by the official adoption of the terms *vicarius Christi, plenitudo potestatis* and *iudex ordinarius omnium*. He had clarified its practical content by a strengthening of deposition theory, in respect of the empire and of heretics, and by various exercises of it to supplement *in defectu iustitiae secularis*. He had urged an interpretation of the history of Christian society which made of Old Testament hierocracy

---

[45] Bernard of Parma was heavily in debt to Laurentius Hispanus for this gloss — see above, n. 43, and Laurentius: '*usurpare*: immo licet ex certis causis, non ideo ordinarius quo ad temporalia, ar. supra, de off. ord. Pastoralis, Ex parte. l(aurentius)': ad c. *cit*. (B.N. MS 3930, fol. 190ra).

a source to justify papal monarchy, its responsibility for the common welfare of the *populus Dei — Christianitas* and its superiority over the emperor specifically and Christian rulers generally. Naturally, the accumulated weight of this reappraisal of sacerdotal superiority shifted the emphasis of canonist thought somewhat further away from dualism.

Perhaps the nature of the shift can be best described in short compass by saying that it was Hugh of St. Victor rather than Stephen of Tournai who was found to have formulated best the general principles of the *ordo Christiana*. Stephen had put his emphasis on dualism: though postulating the unity of the Christian *civitas*, he had nothing to say of its papal headship or of sacerdotal preeminence. Hugh of St. Victor, on the other hand, though accepting the principle of divided jurisdiction, emphasized that in the one society of the *universitas Christianorum*, the spiritual power was preeminent *in dignitate, institutione et auctoritate*.[46] No doubt Stephen of Tournai and Hugh of St. Victor did not differ essentially on the fundamentals of Christian society, but they did differ markedly on what they singled out for emphasis. It was typical of the new attitude of canonist thought that it was Hugh of St. Victor who was remembered by the decretalists.[47]

---

[46] *De sacramentis* 2.2.2-4 (PL 176.416 ff). The influence of this work in the formulation of Innocent III's *In Genesi* has been pointed out by F. Kempf in his edition of the *Regestum super negotio Romani imperii* (Rome 1947); see pp. 409-12 for the draft of this decretal which shows the influence more clearly than the final version. For the citation of *In Genesi* in the decretalists' 'two swords' *quaestio* cf. n. 19 above.

[47] Cf. Hostiensis: 'Unde et secundum fratrem Alexandrum de ordine minorum, ecclesia est multitudo fidelium sive universitas christianorum, quod comprobatur de cons. di.i. Ecclesia, vii.q.i. Novacianus, habens duo latera; dextrum scilicet clericorum qui ea qua ad spiritualem vitam pertinent administrant; item sinistrum, scilicet laicorum qui terrene vite necessaria tractant. Est et duplex potestas spiritualis, scilicet que caput habet summum pontificem, et secularis, que caput habet regem, quod comprobatur xcvi di. Duo sunt, et in eo quod no. infra, qui fil. s. leg., Per venerabilem, Causam que ii. et supra, de eta. et qua., Cum sit ars artium, in prin. Spiritualis prior est terrena in tribus, scilicet in dignitate sive maioritate, in quantum spiritus est maior et dignior quam corpus, supra, de transl. epi. Inter corporalia. Unde Abraham patriarcha tamquam minor obtulit decimas Melchisedech tanquam maiori, Gen. iiii.v. "Benedixit etiam ei Melchisedech tanquam maior" (cf. Gen. 14.19), nam sicut habetur Heb.vii. ubi idem ostenditur, "sine ulla contraditione: quod minus est a maiore benedicitur" (Heb. 7.7), ad idem, xxi.di. Denique, ad finem. Item prior est institutione, quod patet per sacerdotium Melchisedech, de quo promissum est quod precessit legem scriptam, ut no. de const. Translato, et per hoc intellige quod sacerdotium a Deo primum institutum est, Exo. xxviii. v. "Legitimum sempiternum erit Aaron et semini eius post eum sed et hoc facies ut mihi in sacerdotio consecretur" (cf. Exod. 27.21 and 38.1). Demum per sacerdotium iubente Domino, regalis potestas est ordinata, i. Reg. viii. v. "Dixit Dominus ad Samuelem, audi vocem eorum et constitue super eos regem" (I Kings, 8.22) quod et fecit de Saule cui ait I Regum x. v. "Ecce unxit te Dominus super hereditatem suam in principem" etc. (I Kings. 10.1). Sed et prior est in potestate sive auctoritate, nam spiritualis auctoritas terrenam potestatem instituere habet ut sit iudicare autem si bona non fuerit, i.

Yet when this has been said, it remains true that the majority of canonists refused to agree that the pope, by virtue of his spiritual authority, had an unqualified right to legitimize for all temporal purposes. *Duplex potestas*, within the one Christian body, had a real meaning. Innocent III had done something to recall it by apparently claiming a right which violated it. He had, however, also contributed something positive to the principle, in *Novit*, from which canonists deduced a more accurate understanding of the principles and practice of ecclesiastical jurisdiction, *indirecte ratione peccati*. There was a field of action proper to the temporal order and it was a violation of justice to override it.

Canonist thought emerged from its Innocentian phase with an enhanced understanding of the superiority of the spiritual power; it had not lost its awareness that the distinction of the powers was a principle of divine law. In examining early decretist writings, the reader often has the impression that, as a whole, canonists in that period were most interested in establishing the principle of divided jurisdiction, and that the theme of sacerdotal superiority, though always present and occasionally strongly proclaimed, was, on the whole, muted. From decretalist writings, on the other hand, an exactly reverse impression is to be gained. It is thus apparent that the Innocentian period has opened a new chapter — but not a new book. Canonist thought preserved an essential continuity on its two levels of upholding both the *imperium sacerdotii* and *duplex ordo iurisdictionis*. Innocent III had fostered the former without quite suffocating the latter. It remains to be seen if and how Innocent IV altered this state of affairs.

3. *Innocent IV, the Decretalist*

It is not difficult to find firm and forceful judgments expressed by historians about Innocent IV's political principles. Many of them are naturally enough based more on considerations of his political actions than of his political theories, in being concerned more with evaluating his political sagacity and integrity as a ruler than with his place in an academic intellectual tradition. Often it seems that historians in their anxiety to condemn his political conduct have neglected to give careful study to his more academic work and have

---

Cor. vi. "Nescitis quoniam angelos iudicabimus: quanto magis secularia? (I Cor.6.3). Ipsa tamen spiritualis etsi deviet a nemine iudicatur i. Cor. ii.v." "Spiritualis iudicat omnia et ipse spiritualis a nemine iudicatur" (I Cor.2.15) quod de papa omnino verum est, ix. q. iii. Nemo et c. Aliorum, excepto crimine heresis, xl. di. Si papa': *Apparatus* 1.15.1 s.v. *potestatem*. Hostiensis said he was drawing on the doctrine of Alexander of Hales, but Alexander himself, in this context, was merely reproducing Hugh of St. Victor's teaching. — The mark of this line of argument is very clearly written into *Unam sanctam*.

hurried to label his principles as extreme as they found his practice to be imprudent. Innocent IV has never enjoyed a good press: the political and intellectual sins of the medieval papacy have generally been seen writ large in his career.

The case against Innocent IV as a political theorist may best be presented by two very fair and cautious critics whose authority among expositors of medieval thought is such that their views have become universally accepted: Carlyle and Rivière. To both, Innocent IV was the source from which developed the extremism so marked among papal apologists at the end of the century. This was accomplished especially by the novelty of his canonistic theory. For Carlyle, 'the canonical theory of the temporal authority had been profoundly modified by Innocent IV;'[1] for Rivière, 'comme canoniste, il avait interprété dans le sens le plus maximiste les textes du *Corpus Iuris*.'[2] Thus Innocent IV could be allotted his place in the evolution of canonist views: he created a *system* of hierocracy from 'the incidental phrases and suggestions of Innocent III,'[3] on whose work later extremists could 'élever l'édifice dont [il] avait posé les bases et dessiné le plan.'[4] Most interpretations of Innocent IV's opinions as a canonist political thinker derive from one or another of these judgments. Others have even gone beyond them and have seen Innocent's work as marking a real break with what had gone before, where an existing note of prudent realism was rejected in favor of an unrestrained insistence on papal absolutism in the temporal order. According to a recent expositor, with Innocent IV hierocracy reached its 'final stage' and he was the real creator of that extremism which Boniface VIII personified: *Unam sanctam* 'répète en fait les théories d'Innocent IV.'[5]

There are difficulties in the way of accepting these conclusions *tout court*. They are of two sorts: one of historical perspective, when Innocent IV is measured against his predecessors and successors; the other is methodological.

It is difficult to effect a proper comparison of Innocent III and Innocent IV if it is postulated that Innocent III had only 'incidental phrases and suggestions' to offer about the relations of the powers. This is an impermissible deflation of Innocent's significance in the evolution of canonist thought. He was in a real sense, as Hostiensis considered him, 'pater iuris canonici, divini et humani,' a major theorist of papal authority, and it was he who more than any other pope who 'established the foundations and designed the plan'

---

[1] R. W. and A. J. Carlyle, *A History of Mediaeval Political Thought in the West* V (Edinburgh and London 1928) 324.

[2] J. Rivière, *Le problème de l'Église et de l'État au temps de Philippe le Bel* (Louvain 1926) 39.

[3] Carlyle, *op. cit.* 324.   [4] Rivière *op. cit.* 46.

[5] M. Pacaut, 'L'autorité pontificale selon Innocent IV', *Le Moyen Age* 66 (1960) 85-119 at 88.

of canonist thinking about the exercise of papal power in temporal affairs. To appreciate properly Innocent IV's place in the mainstream of canonist thought, it is quite essential to begin by acknowledging the central place of Innocent III in the making of the canonist tradition. There was nothing 'incidental' about the theory behind *Venerabilem, In Genesi, Per venerabilem, Solite, Novit, Licet, Vergentis* and *Excommunicamus.* They were together a synthesis of the principles of the relations of the powers.

There is a second difficulty: the relationship posited between Innocent IV and Boniface VIII. It is not nearly accurate enough to say that *Unam sanctam* 'repeated' the theories of Innocent IV. No direct textual link can be established between Innocent's writing and this decretal; there is no evidence that Boniface VIII drew directly on any Innocentian document. But there is clear evidence that he drew on two twelfth-century writers, St. Bernard and Hugh of St. Victor, to make his major points about the subjection of the temporal power.[6] If then *Unam sanctam* is to be regarded as an extreme statement of papal power in temporal affairs and Boniface VIII was using these twelfth-century statements in the same sense as their authors, there is another error of perspective in making Innocent IV primarily responsible for developing extremism.

If the case against Innocent IV is to be made by comparing him with Innocent III and Boniface VIII, then it should be established, firstly, that his contribution to the stock of canonist political thinking was more farreaching than Innocent III's and, secondly, that he was the true inspirer of *Unam sanctam* and Bonifacian thought. It does not seem possible to demonstrate either of these propositions.

The third difficulty is of a different type and is the fundamental one. It is axiomatic that the accurate placing of Innocent IV in the canonist tradition depends on a comprehensive knowledge of that tradition itself. To put the matter bluntly, neither Carlyle nor Rivière had read sufficient canonist literature to be in a position to make judgments about Innocent IV's contribution to the evolution of canonist thought. Carlyle himself showed some awareness that interpretations of canonist thought were likely to be deficient if based entirely on the material in print in his day, and he did not use all of that. Thus he wrote of Innocent IV without using any decretist material later than *c.* 1160, no decretalist before Goffredus de Trano and neither of the *glossae ordinariae.* His interpretation, therefore, rested on a textual basis which took account neither of mature decretist scholarship nor of the glossators of the *Quinque Compilationes Antiquae* — the literature *par excellence* of the formative period of the canonist tradition, the indispensable background to any study of later thirteenth-century canonist work.

---

[6] Cf. Rivière, *op. cit.* 397-400, 406-7.

That Innocent IV has not had fair treatment from the historians of medieval political thought can be demonstrated by way of one test case. It has been shown above how *Per venerabilem* provided the major focus of decretalist discussions about the relations of the powers and the balancing of the principle of sacerdotal superiority with that of the distinction of the powers. A highly controversial document, it is the best touchstone in canonist literature for estimating the extremist or moderate tendencies of an individual writer. Recently it has been given particular importance in making a comparison between Innocent III and Innocent IV: '(Innocent IV) pense qu'en théorie, le Saint Siège peut se mêler du temporel quand il le veut. La différence entre les deux pontifes se décèle facilement à propos de la légitimation des bâtards; alors que, dans la décrétale *Per venerabilem*, Innocent III renvoie cette décision à la compétence du pouvoir royal, Innocent IV . . . estime que l'Église romaine n'est pas entièrement incompétente.'[7]

Innocent III's view of his power of legitimation was set out on two occasions. On the first, to Philip Augustus, he stated categorically and emphatically.

> Cum igitur maior idoneitas in spiritualibus quam in secularibus requiratur, *dubitari non debet quin ipsa tales ad actus legitimare valeat seculares*, praesertim ad petitionem eorum qui praeter Romanum pontificem alium inter homines superiorem minime recognoscunt habentem huiusmodi potestatem.[8]

On the second occasion, to Count William of Montpellier, he was rather less definite, but nevertheless still claimed that a papal legitimation was valid in the secular order:

> *verisimilius creditur et probabilius reputatur ut eos ad actus legitimare* (*apostolica sedes*) *valeat seculares*, praesertim si praeter Romanos pontifices inter homines superiorem alium non cognoscant qui legitimandi habeat potestatem.[9]

Innocent IV commented on this claim that the pope had power to legitimize *in temporalibus*, and rejected it decisively as a breach of the principle of the distinction of the powers:

> *verisimilius creditur* etc. Non tamen verum est: nam temporalia et spiritualia diuersa sunt et diuersos iudices habent: nec unus iudex habet se intromittere de pertinentibus ad alium, licet se ad inuicem adiuuare debeat, xcvi. di. Cum ad verum, supra, eo.tit. Lator (4.17.5.), supra, de iudi. Nouit (2.1.13).[10]

As his commentary went on to show, Innocent was indebted to his canonist predecessors for his understanding of this aspect of papal power. He was

---

[7] Pacaut, *art. cit.* 111.   [8] PL 214.1193.

[9] X.4.17.13 (*Per venerabilem*).

[10] *Apparatus* ad 4.17.13 s.v. *verisimilius*.

thus neither making a break with the canonist tradition nor interpreting *Per venerabilem* in its 'sens le plus maximiste' (though Alanus had shown that this could be done very easily) nor twisting the canonist tradition to the needs of hierocratic doctrine. Innocent IV's clearly dualist principle was an authentic expression of the mainstream of canonist thought. As his citations of sources indicate, it was based on tradition (*Cum ad verum*) and on the most important of recent papal reformulations of Gelasius (*Novit*). Innocent took account of the canonist work of nearly a century to form his opinion: it was a fully representative, thoroughly orthodox canonist view. Certainly it did 'profoundly modify' Innocent III's thought. But it was not to do so in an extremist direction.

So much by way of preliminary. For, as was seen earlier when analysing twelfth-century decretists, the positing of the dualist principle by the canonists did not conclude their discussion of the relations of the powers but rather began it. The real examination of the problem could only develop when the dualist principle was balanced with that which conditioned it, the principle of the supremacy of the spiritual.

How did Innocent IV analyse sacerdotal superiority? How far was it a new analysis? Did it differ essentially from earlier thirteenth-century papal and canonist analyses? The area of investigation within which to find the answers to these questions chooses itself. The struggle with Frederick II was the major political event of this pontificate, if not, from the papal point of view, of the whole thirteenth century. It was this conflict which led Innocent IV to marshal the data relevant to papal superiority amassed by his canonist forbears. This he did on the one hand for offensive purposes — in preparing and justifying Frederick's deposition — and on the other for defensive purposes — in repelling the Frederician charge that the assumption of a papal power in temporal affairs was a usurpation unfounded in divine or human law.[11]

Politically speaking, Innocent IV's special monument in the canonist tradition was his own commentary on his decree *Ad apostolice sedis* which recited

---

[11] 'Sed dicet aliquis hoc summi pontifices statuere per se: unde cum non sine culpa sacrilegii loquatur . . . ' (*App.* ad 2.2.10 s.v. *vacante;* full text printed below, n. 22). I take this to be a reference to the position Frederick II formulated: 'Nam etsi nos nostre catholice fidei debito suggerente manifestissime fateamur, collatam a Domino sacrosancte Romane sedis antistiti plenariam potestatem in spiritualibus, quantumcumque quod absit sit ipse peccator, ut quod in terra ligaverit sit ligatum in celis, et quod solverit sit solutum, nusquam tamen legitur divina sibi vel humana lege concessum, quod transferre pro libito possit imperia aut de puniendis temporaliter in privacione regnorum regibus aut terre principum iudicare': MGH *Const.* 2.362 (July-September 1245). Frederick's position has been fully analyzed by W. Ullmann, 'Some Reflections on the Opposition of Frederick II to the Papacy,' *Archivio Storico Pugliese* 13 (1960) 3-26.

the charges against Frederick and pronounced his deposition. His deposition theory was a compound of three themes. One went back to Gregory VII through *Alius item* and the decretist tradition and was strengthened by *Venerabilem*. The second was the basis of the *imperium sacerdotis*, the power of binding and loosing. The third was a consideration of the political implications of the papal position of *vicarius Christi*. There was no real novelty of principle in this theory, though the emphasis on *vicarius Christi* was characteristically Innocentian, and runs throughout all his statements on the exercise of papal power in temporal affairs.

The commentary on *Ad apostolice sedis* began with the point being made that the sentence of deposition, though promulgated in general council, did not acquire its legal force from the council. It was for the pope to judge and the sentence could have been issued by him alone — as Pope Zachary had chosen to act in deposing Childeric. This action was referred to again in the commentary. Though cited with characteristic Innocentian terseness, it was clearly intended to express one of the main justifications of Innocent's own action against Frederick.[12]

A fuller statement of the thought which, at the Council of Lyons, lay behind the by now classical *Alius item* text was given in a memorandum written at the Council. Innocent had asked for the discussion of two points — the principle of the deposing power as such, and whether or not Frederick II had merited the penalty of deposition. The author of this memorandum (possibly Hostiensis) asserted as an axiom of canonist thought that an emperor could be deposed if he proved incorrigible in his sinful behavior and if because of it the unity of Christendom was sundered. Childeric was deposed: but he was only a king and his fault was incompetence. How much more therefore did the pope have power to depose one whose fault was the greater (sin) and who, as emperor, was more closely subject to the pope than any king, since the pope was the judge of an emperor's suitability for office? The removal of an emperor for incorrigible misconduct was the inescapable conclusion, then, of the papal power of binding and loosing and of the special constitutional relationship of pope and emperor.[13]

---

[12] 'Presentia concilii est ad solemnitatem tamen: quia etiam sine concilio solius pape sententia sufficeret ad damnationem imperatoris, xv.q.vi. Alius, xi.q.ult. Patet et c. seq. Ipse solus habet plenitudinem potestatis, ii.q.vi. Decreto ... *privamus:* nota quod papa deponit imperatorem, xv.q.vi. Alius, et est hoc de iure': *App.* ad *De sent. et re iud.* c. *Ad apostolice sedis* (= *Sext.* 2.14.2).

[13] This document constitutes a source for the history of the Council of Lyons which has often been overlooked. Reproduced by Hostiensis in both his *Summa* and *Apparatus*, it is a juristic appreciation of the problems on which Innocent IV had asked for the advice of the Fathers in the interval between the second (5 July) and third (17 July) sessions of the Council, cf. Hefele-Leclercq, *Histoire des Conciles* V 2.1642, (though this document makes it clear

This double theme (basically the interpretation of *Alius item* and *Venerabilem* together) was again expounded after the Council when Frederick II challenged the right of the pope to depose him. The emperor admitted both the power of binding and loosing and the papal right to crown him. But he denied the canonists' deduction from these two powers, that the pope could 'transfer empires at will or punish kings temporally by depriving them of their kingdoms or judge the princes of the world.' The reply to this case, in *Aeger cui levia*,[14] was a strong defence of the canonists' inference and the document gave a revealing *exposé* of the deposition logic.

This was not of course the first time in the history of papal - imperial relations that a pope had been led to defend an interpretation of the *Quodcumque ligaveris* . . . text, which permitted the deposition of a ruler. It would be strange if the arguments used by Gregory VII against Henry IV were not paralleled or reflected in the Frederician contest. There are in fact firm lines of affinity between the decrees of deposition levelled at Henry, with the justificatory letters addressed to Bishop Hermann of Metz, and Innocent's attempt to vindicate his own action. *Alius item* is one of them, but it is not the only one. Likewise, it would be strange if those trenchant reformulations of the

---

that Innocent IV sought guidance on a wider range of questions than is here suggested). 'Ideo consultus apud Lugd. in concilio generali quidam episcopus, primo, super potentia deponendi; secundo, super contemptu clavium; tertio, super captione, depredatione et interfectione prelatorum; quarto, super fractione pacis, per ecclesiam firmate: in quibus omnibus, sicut pro firmo tenebat curia, peccauerat Federicus, et iuxta proposita sic respondit: Secundum opiniones maiorum meorum imperator pro quolibet mortali peccato deponi potest, quod intelligas de gravibus et si incorrigibilis sit, maxime quando ecclesia universalis inde scandalizatur et concutitur, ut in isto. De hoc no(tatur) per Ioan(nem Teutonicum), 40 dist. Si papa, in glo. que incipit, 'quod intelligitur,' in fin., sup. verbo 'a fide devius,' (This gloss reads: 'Sed pro quo peccato potest imperator deponi? pro quolibet, si est incorrigibilis unde deponitur si est minus utile, ut xv.q.vi. Alius.') et in summa Hug(uccionis). Si enim Zacharias papa regem Francorum, qui a Romano pontifice coronam non recipit, nec per eum examinatur, nec ab eo comprobatur vel reprobatur, non tam pro suis iniquitatibus, quam pro eo quod tante potestati erat inutilis, a regno deposuit, et alium loco ipsius substituit, xv. q. vi. Alius, multo fortius imperatorem qui specialius quoddammodo subest ei, pro suis iniquitatibus, poterit removere, ut infra eodem, Venerabilem, et 96 dist., Duo sunt, et cap. Si imperator': *Summa* 1.6. § 10 (Cambridge, Trinity Coll. MS B. 16. 46, fol. 17ᵛ). I have edited this text with commentary in an article to appear in *Studies in Church History*, vol. 2, 'Medieval Deposition Theory: A Neglected Canonist *Consultatio* from the First Council of Lyons.'

[14] There is some controversy as to whether this document, which is not in Innocent IV's Register, is to be accepted as Innocent's work or not, cf. E. Amann DThC s.v. *Innocent IV;* Rivière, *op.cit.* 40; Pacaut, *art. cit.* 93; J. A. Cantini, DDC 7.1031-32 s.v. *Sinibalde dei Fieschi.* I have accepted the view of Ptolomy of Lucca who referred to this letter 'licet non sit in corpore iuris, sed est quedam epistola apologetica ad Fredericum imperatorem' (*Determinatio compendiosa de iurisdictione imperii* ed. Krammer, 59) and which Innocent 'per universum mundum transmisit' (*ed. cit.* 60).

imperium sacerdotis which Innocent III had given to ecclesiastical jurisprudence were not strongly in evidence.

The papal defence rested essentially on a single consideration; nothing 'de rebus aut negotiis' fell outside the apostolic jurisdiction in moral matters. The argument developed along lines of exegesis of Matth. 16.18 established by Gregory VII — 'nichil ab eius potestate subtraxit' — and Innocent III — 'nichil excipiens qui dicit quodcumque.'[15] For both Innocent III and Innocent IV, Jer.1.10 reinforced this interpretation. The logic was finally established with a text whose political interpretation both these popes had confirmed: 'An nescitis quoniam angelos iudicabimus? Quanto magis secularia!' For Gregory VII, Innocent III and Innocent IV the argument of the Pauline text was the same: he who may judge the higher (spiritual) necessarily had jurisdiction over the lower (temporal). The conclusion that emerged echoed Innocent III and the early decretalists:

> Relinquitur ergo Romanum pontificem posse saltem casualiter suum exercere pontificale iudicium in quolibet christiano cuiuscunque conditionis existit, presertim si de ipso alius iusticie debitum nolit reddere vel non possit, maxime ratione peccati . . .[16]

Judgment of sin, excommunication if guilty, loss of temporal jurisdiction 'saltem per consequens' was thus the basic argument. *Aeger cui levia* stated it in unusually vigorous language (it was a document of apologia) but it was essentially the position of Gregory VII.

What had changed since Gregory VII's day, however, was papal understanding of the constitutional relationship of pope and emperor. That there

[15] For texts of Leo I, Gelasius I, Nicholas I etc. proclaiming the comprehensiveness of papal judicial power, see W. Ullmann, 'Some Reflections . . . on Frederick II . . . ' 13 n.24.

[16] 'Generali namque legatione in terris fungimur regis regum, qui non solum quemcumque sed, ne quid de rebus aut negociis intelligeretur exceptum, sub neutro genere generalius universa complectens, etiam quodcunque ligandi super terram pariter et solvendi apostolorum principi nobisque in ipso plenitudinem tribuit potestatis, etiam ut doctor gentium huiusmodi plenitudinem non restringendum ostenderet, dicens: 'An nescitis quoniam angelos iudicabimus? Quanto magis secularia!' (cf. Gregory VII, *Reg.* viii 21 and Innocent III in *Per venerabilem*; further references in Ullmann, 'Some Reflections on . . . Frederick II . . . ' 18 n.23). 'Nonne ad temporalia quoque porrectam exposuit datam eidem in angelos potestatem, ut hiis intelligantur minora subesse, quibus subdita sunt maiora? Non minoris quidem, immo longe maioris potestatis esse credendum est eternum Christi pontificium in fundatissima Petri sede sub gratia ordinatum, quam inveteratum illud, quod figuris legalibus temporaliter serviebat, et tamen dictum est a Deo illius temporis pontificatu fungenti: "Ecce constitui te super gentes et regna ut evellas et plantes," non solum utique super gentes sed etiam super regna, ut potestas eiusdem innotesceret tradita de utrisque. Hac potestate usi leguntur plerique pontifices veteris Testamenti qui a nonnullis regibus, qui se indignos fecerant principatu, regni solium auctoritate sibi divinitus tradita transtulerunt. Relinquitur ergo . . . ': ed. E. Winkelmann, *Acta imperii inedita s. XIII et XIV*, II (Innsbruck 1885) 677-8.

was a bond between pope and emperor different in quality from the bond
between pope and other rulers was certainly Gregorian doctrine. But the
exact nature of the bond had itself not been defined officially before Innocent
III. The papal right to deprive the emperor of his office was held to be the
corollary of the right of confirming an emperor-elect. For confirmation was
a scrutiny of the candidate's fitness for the imperial office. It was meaningless,
therefore, if it did not carry with it the right to reject the unsuitable, whether
his unsuitability was apparent before or after coronation. *Aeger cui levia*
drew out the full logic of Innocent III's view of the relationship of pope and
emperor as expressed in both *Venerabilem* and his revision of the ceremony
of imperial coronation.[17]

'Two swords' doctrine was established by familiar arguments — Luke 22.38,
Peter Damian's exegesis of Matth. 16.19 from D. 22 c.1 of the *Decretum*, the
Translation of the Empire, coronation symbolism, the imperial oath of fidelity
to the pope. All this added up to what Innocent IV in his *Apparatus* called
the 'specialis coniunctio' of pope and emperor.[18] Since it was the pope who
controlled the making of this union, it followed that he had the power to
judge when it had been broken. When it was so adjudged, the emperor lost
his office.

The *mélange* of canonist thought about imperial subjection to the pope
which was *Aeger cui levia* bore one impress which was characteristically Innocentian: the emphasis placed on the political meaning of the vicariate of
Christ. The pope was vicar to continue the 'eternum Christi pontificium,'
the providential ordering of the world under God, outside of whose rule 'omnia
edificant ad gehennam.' His function was to discharge that 'generalis legatio'
of the King of Kings whose reign through representatives on earth was obser-
vable throughout history — primordially 'in figuris legalibus' (Jeremias,
Melchisedech), and onwards from the time of the fulfilment of the Old Law
when the vicariate of Christ was established in the Roman see.

This was the theme which Innocent IV developed as the central point of
his commentary on the decree of deposition. He was concerned above all
with the 'regimen unius persone.' The Creator of mankind, he argued, had
left his work in the charge of a single ruler, His vicar, divinely charged with
the preservation of the tranquillity of order. As no power was withheld from
Christ Himself, who could, had He wished, have deposed rulers should the
harmony of the Christian world have demanded it, so with His vicar.[19] There

---

[17] Cf. W. Ullmann, *Growth of Papal Government* 431, 461-2.

[18] 'Nam specialis coniunctio est inter papam et imperatorem, quia papa eum consecrat
et examinat et est imperator eius advocatus et iurat ei: et ab eo imperium tenet, supra,
de elec. Venerabilem, lxiii di. Ego, Tibi domino': *App.* ad 2.2.10 s.v. *vacante.*

[19] 'Nota quod papa deponit imperatorem, ut xv. q.vi. Alius, et est hóc de iure, nam cum

is here, as indeed throughout Innocent's political writing, an interpretation
of the kingship of Christ certainly from the theologian's point of view a crude
one, but nevertheless one which for Innocent contained a great truth about
the structure of Christian society.[20] *Unum corpus, unum caput:* the head, as
vicar of Christ, was uniquely responsible for the general welfare of the one
Christian body politic; this was the plan whereby the Creator 'sicut diligens
paterfamilias'[21] provided for the common good of His people.

Innocent IV amplified this notion of the *regale sacerdotium* in a second
Frederician context. Frederick had alleged that the exercise of papal power
in temporal affairs had no other warrant than that which popes had defined
without scriptural justification, for themselves. Innocent set out to show that
on the contrary the possession and use of such power was a fundamental principle of divine law, part of the divine plan for mankind, the last term in an exercise of the divine providence which began with the very creation of man.

Innocent thought the charge sacrilegious because it amounted to a repudia-
tion of the divine wisdom. His premise was that the *populus Dei* had a continuous history from the Fall to the thirteenth century; the *ecclesia universalis*
was the prolongation and fulfilment of what had come into existence in the
Old Testament. If the *populus Dei* had such a continuous history, the law
of subjection of God's people to His priesthood holds as true in the New Dispensation as in the Old. The rule of the papacy over Christendom, therefore,
was a direct continuation of the rule of the Jewish priests over the people
of Israel. This interpretation of history as a justification for the papal guardianship of Christendom was expounded by Innocent IV (and by Hostiensis) in
the context of the by now classical decretalist list of the occasions on which
the pope might intervene in the temporal order. They fitted that list into
a framework, an interpretation of Christian history designed to show the lesson

---

Christus filius Dei dum fuit in hoc seculo, et etiam ab eterno dominus naturalis fuit et de
iure naturali in imperatores et quoscunque alios sententias depositionis ferre potuisset et
damnationis et quascunque alias: ut pote in personas quas creaverat; et donis naturalibus
et gratuitis donaverat et in esse conservarerat; et eadem ratione et vicarius eius potest hic.
Nam non videtur discretus dominus fuisse ut cum reverentia eius loquitur, nisi unicum
post se talem vicarium reliquisset qui hec omnia posset. Fuit autem iste vicarius eius Petrus,
Math. xvi. ultra medium, et idem dicendum est de successoribus Petri cum eadem absurditas
sequeretur si post mortem petri humanam naturam a se creatam sine regimine unius persone
reliquisset, et ar. ad hoc supra, qui fil. sint leg. Per venerabilem ultra med., de hoc nota
supra, de fo. comp. Licet': *App.* ad *c. Ad apostolicae sedis* s.v. *privamus* (= *Sext* 2.14.2).
See n. 22 below for the development of this theme of the vicariate.

[20] Innocent IV's view of the kingship of Christ should be seen in relation to thirteenth-
century papal doctrine as a whole, cf. J. Leclercq, *L'idée de la royauté du Christ au moyen
âge* (Paris 1959) 40-64, especially the very perceptive summary at 62-4.

[21] Cf. *App.* ad 3.34.8 s.v. *pro defensione.*

of a perpetual vicariate of God exercised to preserve the harmony and tranquillity of God's chosen people.

Universal Christian history presented the uninterrupted feature of government under God by His vicar. Nothing falls outside the designs of His providence which has always encompassed the supreme direction of His people as it strives to attain the promised land. Though God always ruled the world, from the time of the Flood He chose to rule His creatures through ministers, of whom the first was Noah himself, entrusted as 'rector populi' with the functions of both priest and lawgiver. This divine vicariate was handed on through the succession of patriarchs, judges, kings, who, at one time or another, filled the office of *rector*. At the Incarnation, the Saviour, 'naturalis dominus et rex noster' resumed this office for Himself and in its thus completed form passed it to Peter and his successors. As the inchoate priesthood of the Old Law was completed and translated through Christ to Peter, so the direction and control of the *populus Dei* passed to Peter. The pope, as vicar of Christ, continued to exercise in that *populus*, the *ecclesia universalis*, that power over mankind which Christ Himself exercised, kingship: *Dominus iudex noster, dominus legifer noster, dominus rex noster.*[22]

Innocent IV did not add substantially to the practical content of the exercise of this kingship. He did not add further to the list of occasions when the pope intervened in the temporal order that had been drawn up by the early decretalists; his exposition of the *eternum Christi pontificium* was a framework put round a list which itself remained very much as it had been.[23] He

---

[22] 'Nota quod deus creavit in principio celum et terram et omnia quae in eis sunt, angelicam et humanam naturam, spiritualia et temporalia: ipsaque per seipsum rexit sicut factor suam rem gubernat et homini quem fecit precepta dedit et transgredienti penam imposuit per seipsum, scil. Ade et Eve, Gen. iii, mulieri quoque dixit etc., et ibi Ade vero dixit etc. Qualiter autem Chain per seipsum puniverit et Lamech et Cham et quosdam alios, in eo. lib. Gen. iii et v, c. legitur; et sic recto mundo per ipsum Deum usque ad Noe, ex tempore Noe cepit Deus creaturas suas regere per ministros quorum primus fuit Noe: de quo qui fuit rector populi ex eo apparet quod sibi Dominus gubernationem arche per quam ecclesia significavit promisit, Gen.v et vi. Item quia etiam Dominus Noe et filiis rectoriam et legem sibi dedit, Gen. ix; de Noe autem, licet non legatur sacerdos fuisse, officium tamen exercuit sacerdotis statim post ingressum arche antequam leges daret, Gen. viii, quod officium sacerdotis simul Abel et Chain, primo fecerant. In hac autem vicaria, successerunt patriarche, iudices, reges, sacerdotes, et alii qui pro tempore fuerunt in regimine populi Iudaeorum et sic duravit usque ad Christum, qui fuit naturalis dominus et rex noster, de quo dicitur in psalmis, Deus iudicium tuum regi da etc. (here Hostiensis professedly quoting Innocent, added: et Esaie xxxiii, Dominus iudex noster, dominus legifer noster, dominus rex noster). Ipse vero Dominus noster Jesus Christus vicarium suum constituit Petrum et successores suos quando dedit claves regni celorum et quando dixit eis: pasce oves meas, licet in multis distincta sunt . . . (as cited below, p. 70) *App.* ad 2.2.10 s.v. *imperio;* Hostiensis, *App. ibid.*

[23] Hostiensis reproduced substantially the list given by Innocent IV and acknowledged that he was drawing on the work of Innocent whom he invariably referred to as 'dominus

had, however, a generalization to draw from it. Looking at the list with its strong emphasis on interventions in cases of doubt, negligence and other obstacles to the fulfilment of secular justice, he concluded that,

> quae per inferiores ratione iurisdictionis humanae terminari non possunt, ad ecclesiam pertinent.[24]

In other words, there was never lacking the possibility of recourse in difficulties to the highest tribunal of Christian society:

> in omnibus et in singulis specialibus que occurrunt necesse fuit saltem per unum reipublice provideri . . . officii nobis commissi debitum non debemus alicui petenti denegare: hoc autem pertinet ad officium nostrum etiam in temporalibus ubicunque super dubio quoque requirimur.[25]

---

noster.' In this instance Hostiensis' version is somewhat more clear than the master's and it is given here in preference. The list preceded the outline of history given in the preceding note. 'Iste est ergo unus casus in quo iudex ecclesiasticus potest se intromittere de iurisdictione seculari: quando scilicet iudex secularis non invenitur, ut hic et alius in aut. ut dif. iud. § in civitatibus, coll.ix. Secundus cum secularis negligit iustitiam facere, ut supra eo.cap. v. dummodo, et c. Ex transmissa, in fine, et infra c.i, in fine, in quo potest etiam ipsum eundem iudicem ad reddendam iustitiam per censuram ecclesiasticam cohercere, xxiii.q.v, Administratores, et nota supra eod. Cum sit generale v.i. super verbis, sunt remissi. Tertius cum super dubio inter seculares iudices variatur, quod dic ut plene no. infra, qui fil. sint legi. Per venerabilem § rationibus v. sed quia sicut, et preced. Quartus quando agitur de terra supposita iurisdictioni ecclesie, infra de appel. Si duobus et no. supra prox. Quintus si est de consuetudine speciali, supra eo. Si clericus. Sextus si sic est de privilegio speciali, supra tit.i. Novit. Septimus de consuetudine generali contra malefactores ecclesie, supra eo. Cum sit generale. Octavus ratione peccati denunciati iuramenti vel pacis, supra ti. i. Novit. Nonus cum secularis iudex est suspectus, ut hic et in fi. et melius in aut. ut diffe. iudi. § si vero contigerit, col. ix. Decimus ratione connexitatis, infra de dona. inter vi. et uxo. De prudentia. Undecimus ratione cuiuslibet criminis et negotii ecclesiastici, vi. q.ii.c.i, infra, de usur. Quia, et iste casus multos habet sub se, ut no. infra eo. Ex tenore et supra eo. Cum sit generale, et supra, tit. i. Novit. Duodecimus ratione mortuariorum a defunctis relictorum, in quo etiam secundum legem si episcopus negligens fuerit, devolvitur potestas ad metropolitanum, in aut. de eccle. ti. § si autem pro redemptione et seq. coll. ix. infra de rebus eccle. non alie. c.fi.; transeunt enim hec omnino sub iurisdictione ecclesiastica, xxii.q.fi. Secundum canonicam et § seq.': *App. loc. cit.* It is to be noticed that this list does not differ essentially from that compiled by Tancred, as cited above, p. 49.

[24] 'Nota quod ecclesiastica libertas consistit in privilegiis super spiritualibus et privilegia super temporalibus. Item consistit in privilegiis generaliter ecclesie concessis et etiam in privilegiis singularibus cuiuscunque ecclesie. Primo ergo dicimus de spiritualibus quod non potest concedere nisi solus deus vel eius vicarius: quale est, quodcunque ligaveris super terram etc.; hoc enim privilegium Christus Petro in persona ecclesie concessit; tale est etiam privilegium quod in omnibus dubiis iuris que per inferiores ratione iurisdictionis humane terminari non possunt, ad ecclesiam recurratur, supra, qui fil. s. leg., Per venerabilem, prope finem . . . ': *App.* ad 5.39.49 s.v. *libertatem.* The whole gloss is of considerable interest as an analysis of the important but often somewhat amorphous concept of *libertas ecclesiae.*

[25] Hostiensis, *App.* ad 4.17.13 (*Per venerabilem*) s.v. *casualiter.*

The Christian *respublica* had its focus of institutional unity in the pope, empowered by his kingship to take such governmental action as would supplement the shortcomings of all political powers:

> Licet in multis distincta sunt officia et regimina mundi, tamen quan-
> docunque necesse est, ad papam recurrendum est, sive sit necessitas
> iuris quia iudex dubius est quam sententiam de iure proferre debeat,
> vel necessitas facti quia alius non sit iudex superior, sive facti puta
> quia de facto minores iudices non possunt suas sententias exequi vel
> nolunt ut debent iusticiam exercere.[26]

It must be noticed here that this concept of a papal prerogative power
whereby the *vicarius Christi* made provision to remedy defects, negligences,
ambiguities, and emergencies lies at the heart of the meaning of the term
plenitudo potestatis. Innocent IV's exposition of the power of the *vicarius
Christi* was also an exposition of the *plenitudo potestatis*.[27] But before turning
to a more detailed examination of this point, some observations on the relationship of Innocent IV's thought to earlier canonist work are necessary. Did
he actually do, or set out to do, anything distinctively new in regard to the
practical working of papal power in temporal affairs?

The deposition of Frederick II, the major political decision of Innocent
IV's pontificate, may have been a rash and arrogant act (as has often been
suggested by historians) but it was certainly not an unprecedented one. The
controversies of Gregory VII and Henry IV, Innocent III and Otto IV, Gregory IX and Frederick II had shown the way all too clearly. There was
assuredly nothing novel about this application in practice of the power of
binding and loosing, where Innocent IV followed closely the path of Gregory VII, reinforced with the various considerations amounting to a 'specialis coniunctio' between pope and emperor. Innocent IV had nothing to add
to *In Genesi* and *Venerabilem* and his view of the constitutional relationship
of pope and emperor was, in all its essentials, that of Innocent III.

There runs through the registers of Innocent III's letters the ever-recurring,
insistent theme that it was for the apostolic 'sedes iustitiae' to make provision
for 'uniuscuiuscunque iura,' to have charge of the 'communis Christiani
populi utilitas.' In its most directly political context, the thought behind
these phrases was best known to canonists from the decretal *Per venerabilem*.
It was especially in relation to this formulation that Innocent IV phrased
his generalization concerning the *recursus ad papam in necessitatibus iuris et
facti*. It can hardly be doubted that his interpretation of the decretal corres-
ponded exactly to the mind of the legislator, for it is Innocent III's letters which show most clearly in the routine practice of papal government

---

[26] Innocent IV, *App.* ad 2.2.10, for the text of which this is the generalized summary, see
n. 22 above.

[27] The argument is developed below, pp. 97-99.

the validity of Innocent IV's theory concerning the exercise of papal power. Innocent IV, spurred by the challenge of Frederick II, produced a formal statement of the principle on which the papacy had long been working: that it was the responsibility of the papacy to ensure the *utilitas* and to make provision for the *necessitas* of the *populus Christianus*. It was this thought of Innocent III, formulated in its diverse aspects in relation to practical cases, in *Novit*, *Licet* and especially, *Per venerabilem*, which Innocent IV faithfully and directly expounded.

He sounded a more personal note when setting this view of papal prerogative in a biblical-historical background. This would seem to have been the fruit of Innocent's own reflections on the course of sacred history. But there was nothing very new, in itself, in the exploitation of the Old Testament to demonstrate sacerdotal superiority. Honorius Augustodonensis and Hugh of St. Victor were but the major exponents of what was a regular enough feature of twelfth century political writing.[28] But it was the enthusiastic acceptance of this type of political argument by Innocent III which was decisive for the canonist tradition: the *eternum Christi pontificium* itself, epitomized especially in Jeremias and Melchisedech; the supremacy of the priesthood 'tempore, institutione, auctoritate'; the origins of kingship; the symbolism of royal coronation rites; the appeal to priests for the resolution of doubts in the Mosaic law. The Innocentian treatment of these basic issues announced a new segment of political argumentation to the canonists. As through Innocent III's *Regestum super negotio romani imperii*, so through the correspondence of Gregory IX with Frederick II after the final breach, runs the argument of the continuity through all history of the *imperium sacerdotii*, completed and translated through Christ to Peter. Innocent IV's interpretation of the same theme was new in its language and in its fulness of treatment, but the method by which his case was to be proved had both figured prominently in two major papal-imperial crises and was also an accepted part of decretalist thought.

Vicarius Christi was not however the only term to encompass Innocentian thinking about the papal power in temporal affairs. It had a corollary: *plenitudo potestatis*. The one expressed the office, the other expressed the jurisdiction — both had their terms of reference in a concept of a single united Christian society over which the vicar of Christ exercised authority. Innocent IV's understanding of *vicarius Christi* has been examined and *plenitudo potestatis* should not logically be separated from it. There are practical reasons of presentation, however, which demand that the examination of this term be done separately and postponed until a brief summary of this broad survey of canonist thought from Gratian to Innocent IV has been attempted.

---

[28] There is perhaps an echo of Innocent IV's sentiments in Grosseteste's statements concerning the pope, who as 'princeps super omnem populum suum Israeliticum, plenitudinem habet potestatis . . .' (*Ep.* 127, R.S. 364).

The broad survey of canonist thought from Gratian to Innocent IV reveals the critical importance of the pontificate of Innocent III in the formation of canonist doctrines of papal power in temporal affairs. One of the major tasks of the decretalists was to absorb the lessons he taught concerning sacerdotal and papal supremacy; this task was virtually completed by Innocent IV and Hostiensis. In particular, attention had been turned to the unitary concept of Christian society. The decretists, on the whole, unlike other twelfth-century writers, had not given much attention to this aspect of ecclesiastical thought. Though this traditional postulate was a premise of their thinking, decretists were content to assume it, not apparently considering it necessary to discuss it in itself. It was Innocent III, the great refurbisher of tradition, who reclaimed it for ecclesiastical jurisprudence and gave it a regular place in canonist commentaries. With Innocent IV, the canonist tradition received its first major systematic exposition of what had always been its first assumption: the unity of Christian society, one because the papacy existed as the principle of unity; the pope, 'antonomastice iudex'; the Roman curia, 'communis omnium Christiani populi nationum.' The power of punishing rulers, even of deposing them, the exercise of temporal jurisdiction to remedy defects of secular justice were the practical applications of this principle.

The discussion of the 'regimen unius persone' occupied a comparatively large proportion of Innocent IV's writing — not surprisingly since in the controversy with Frederick II, the need was felt for a defence of sacerdotal superiority. But it did not follow from this concentration on the unitary concept that canonist thought, in his pontificate, lost sight of the principle of the distinction of the powers. The *Glossa ordinaria* on the Decretals by Bernard of Parma was completed in this period and the *Glossa ordinaria* on the *Decretum* was revised. Both these central texts, the groundwork of canonist teaching, showed that canonists had retained a realistic view of the duality of jurisdictions in the actual practice of Christendom.[29] There were to be very many instances in the conduct of papal business showing that the full force of the principle of sacerdotal surperiority had to be tempered before the claims of

---

[29] On Johannes Teutonicus and the *Glossa ordinaria super Decretum*, see above, p. 48, n. 21. But it should be noted that a certain patriotic feeling for the independence of the empire did not extend as far as denying a papal power to depose emperors, see the texts given above, p. 48, and n. 21.

On Bernard of Parma and the *Glossa ordinaria super Decretales* see the texts on 4.17.3 s.v. *certis causis inspectis* cited on p. 55 above; his *notabilia* on 2.1.13, 2.28.7, 4.17.7 and 5.33.2; and his glosses 2.1.13 s.v. *iurisdictionem nostram*, 2.28.7 s.v. *credimus*. But this careful registration of the texts *de iurisdictione distincta* did not prevent Bernard from holding the 'two swords' theory as expressing the relationship of pope and emperor, the papal headship of Christendom (cf. 4.17.7 s.v. *ad regem* cited above, p. 46 n. 19) and the deposing power (cf. 5.7.10 s.v. *precipimus:* this gloss is substantially that of J. Teutonicus *et alii* printed above, p. 48 n. 21).

secular powers. On the level of pure theory, however, nothing is more significant of the vitality in canonist thought of the principle of divided jurisdiction
than the rejection by Innocent IV himself of the claim that the pope could,
by virtue of his spiritual superiority, legitimize *suo iure* in temporal affairs.[30]
His thought, as with the canonist tradition generally, knew two levels of
argumentation — one, more prominent in controversies, where the unity of
Christendom under its supreme monarch the vicar of Christ was emphasized,
and a second, paying due regard to the existing political structure of Christendom, which recognized the validity of divided jurisdictions. Both trends have
to be taken into account to understand the canonist contribution to medieval
political thought.

---

[30] See also his view on the role of kings in episcopal elections, below p. 123-124. Since this
study was written, J. A. Cantini has examined very carefully the 'mens dualistica' of Innocent IV, 'De autonomia judicis saecularis et de Romani pontificis plenitudine potestatis in
temporalibus secundum Innocentium IV,' *Salesianum* 23 (1961) 407-80. But it is clearly
going too far to argue that Innocent IV believed in a 'paritas' of the powers (cf. p.448).

PART II

THE LANGUAGE
OF SOVEREIGNTY

The study of the concept of papal authority in the thirteenth century cannot proceed very far without encountering the term *plenitudo potestatis*. In papal letters expounding the subject to schismatics, heretics, rebels, infidels and the newly converted, in the legislation of general councils, in the routine exercise of papal headship, in papal sermons, in the analyses of canonists and theologians, in the political treatises of apologists, the received term to express papal sovereignty was *plenitudo potestatis*. It occurs so frequently in so many contexts of the papal thought of the thirteenth century that there is almost an *embarras de richesse* in choosing a representative text with which to begin an analysis of it.

One text, however, selects itself before all others for such a consideration because of the authority of its pronouncement. This is the Profession of Faith which served as the basis of the ephemeral union between the Latin and Greek Churches arranged between Gregory X and Michael VIII Palaiologos at the Second Council of Lyons in 1274.[1] The statement in this Creed concerning papal primacy is without doubt the most authoritative thirteenth-century formulation of the principle, since it must rank as a formal definition of the doctrine of the primacy.

The term *plenitudo potestatis* occurs twice in the Lyons formulation. It was used the first time,

> Ipsa quoque sancta Romana ecclesia summum et plenum principatum
> super universam ecclesiam catholicam obtinet, quem se ab ipso Domino

---

[1] The full text may be consulted in Hefele-Leclercq, *Histoire des Conciles* VI.1.176; Mansi 24.70 or DThC 9.1384-86, where it is analyzed briefly by F. Vernet. The Creed itself was first sent to the Greeks by Clement IV in March 1267 (Potthast no. 19951; Raynaldus, *a.* 1267 §§72-79); for a discussion of the immediate circumstances of the despatch of the Confession cf. D.J. Geanakoplos, *Emperor Michael Palaeologus and the West, 1258-1282* (Harvard 1959) 200-04. Part of this Creed, including the sentence 'Ipsa quoque . . . ' quoted in the text was incorporated in c. 4 *De Romani Pontificis infallibili magisterio* of the First Vatican Council.

> in beato Petro apostolorum principe sive vertice, cuius Romanus Pontifex
> est successor, cum potestatis plenitudine recepisse veraciter et humiliter
> recognoscit.

to give the essentials of papal primacy its specifically juristic form: supreme
monarchical jurisdictional authority. The second usage,

> Ad hanc autem sic potestatis plenitudo consistit, quod ecclesias ceteras
> ad sollicitudinis partem admittit . . .

served to emphasize one aspect of the supreme power; that all other ecclesiastical powers derived their jurisdiction from the Roman Church.

There can be no doubt that the ultimate origins of this juristic exegesis
of the Petrine texts and of the 'derivational' thesis whereby lesser ecclesiastical
jurisdictions receive their power from the highest go back to Leo I.[2] The term
plenitudo potestatis itself, whereby the pope, entrusted with *cura communis*
of all Christians, admits prelates to a 'pars sollicitudinis' was fashioned by
Leo as one aspect of his 'juristic construction of the monarchic function of
St. Peter and its continuance in his heir (the pope).'[3] He did not, however, give
the term especial emphasis, using it, it seems, only once. But that one occasion
became a classical formulation, for it was taken up by the compilers of canonical
collections. Under the impetus of the Gregorian reform, it became more
widely known through the treatises and collections of the period. In due
course, it appeared four times in the *Decretum* — in three canons[4] and once
used in a *dictum* by Gratian himself.[5]

His personal use of the term was restricted. He did not attach it to the
pope at all, but used the *plenitudo potestatis — pars sollicitudinis* antithesis
to contrast the respective positions of metropolitan and suffragan. He was
using it, therefore, in the sense of 'fulness of office,' the same sense in which
contemporary papal letters were beginning to use it in speaking of what the

---

[2] 'Vices nostras ita tuae credidimus charitati, ut in partem sis vocatus sollicitudinis, non
in plenitudinem potestatis'. *Ep.* 14 (PL 54.671). Cf. J. Rivière, 'In partem sollicitudinis
. . . Évolution d'une formule pontificale', *Recherches des sciences religieuses* 5 (1925) 210-31
and especially, W. Ullmann, 'Leo I and the Theme of Papal Primacy', *Journal of Theological
Studies* 11 (1960) 25-51.

[3] Ullmann, *art. cit.* 44, demonstrating how 'within the precincts of the theme of papal
primacy Leo's theology appeared in the garb of Roman jurisprudence.'

[4] The original Leonine text was given in C.3 q.6 c.8; in a text of Pseudo-Gregory IV's in
C.2 q.6 c.11: ' . . . vices suas ita aliis inpertivit ecclesiis, ut in partem sint vocatae sollicitudinis, non in plenitudinem potestatis'; and in a Pseudo-Isidorian one, C.2 q.6 c.12: 'Ipsa
namque ecclesia, quae prima est, ita reliquis ecclesiis vices suas credidit largiendas, ut in
partem sint vocatae sollicitudinis, non in plenitudinem potestatis. Unde omnium appellan-
tium apostolicam sedem episcoporum iudicia, et cuncta maiorum negotia causarum, eidem
sanctae reservata esse liquet.'

[5] Pr. C.9 q.3: 'Vocantur enim episcopi a metropolitano in partem sollicitudinis, non
in plenitudinem potestatis.'

conferring of the *pallium* gave to a bishop, or what papal delegation gave to a legate.[6] The earliest decretists were not apparently much attracted by the potentialities of the term of an expression denoting the totality of papal sovereignty, though Rufinus, Stephen of Tournai and others found it apposite when contrasting the dispensatory powers of pope and bishop.[7] Already the canonists were analyzing the content of papal legislative, administrative and judicial supremacy — the promulgation, dispensation and interpretation of law, the right to cite any Christian to the papal court, the right to make changes in ecclesiastical organization. But while they were discussing the occasions of the exercise of papal authority and also discussing the Petrine texts themselves, they had not yet chosen *plenitudo potestatis* as the technical term which would summarize both the essential juristic principle of the Petrine commission and include the circumstances of its exercise. They were content with such phrases as *plena potestas, superlativa auctoritas, plenaria potestas,*[8] *plena auctoritas,*[9] *summa potestas.*[10] In this respect the canonists were con-

---

[6] Cf. G.B. Ladner, 'The Concepts of "ecclesia" and "christianitas" and their Relation to the Idea of Papal "plenitudo potestatis" from Gregory VII to Boniface VIII', *Misc. hist. pont.* 18 (Rome 1954) 63-4.

[7] Cf. Rufinus, C.25 proem. *ed.cit.* 421 and J. Brys, *De dispensatione in iure canonico praesertim apud decretistas et decretalistas usque ad medium saeculum XIV* (Bruges 1925) 143.

[8] As for instance in the *Summa 'Elegantius in iure'* (1169-70): 'Ipsi (*scil.* summi pontifices)... canones abrogare eisque derogare et novos condere et privilegia dare dataque tollere plenam habent potestatem dum tamen in his omnibus nichil contra fidem presumant vel in quo universalem ecclesiam offendant. . . . Mater nostra Romana ecclesia que superlativam in omnibus auctoritatem gerit . . . itaque prima sedes ex cause cognicione corrigendorum causa vitiorum maxime privilegia et imminuendi et immutandi nunc personaliter, nunc generaliter plenariam potestatem habet': B.N. MS lat. 14997, fol. 8ʳᵛ.

[9] Which decretists discussed in terms of papal legislative authority following Roman law and civilian analyses. Cf. Rufinus: 'Plena auctoritas illa dicitur que in se continet preceptum et generalitatem' (ad D.11 c.2 *ed.cit.* 27); similarly, Joannes Faventinus, B.M. MS Roy.9.E.VII fo. 7ʳᵃ; *Summa 'Tractaturus Magister'*: 'qui habet potestatem condendi, necessaria, generalis est in scriptis pape vel imperatoris': ad dict. Grat. post c.30, C.11 q.1 (B.N. MS 15594, fol. 51ʳᵇ); anon. gloss (Durham Cath. MS C.I.7): 'solus papa plenam habet auctoritatem que tria in se continet, preceptum, generalitatem, necessitatem observancie': ad D.11 c.2; anon. gloss (Durham Cath. MS C. II.1): '*ille solus habet ius interpretandi canones:* est auctoritas generalis et necessaria, [et] principis: huius est interpretari et condere, et continet in se necessitatem, generalitatem, preceptum: nec generalis, nec necessaria magistri: huius nec est interpretari nec condere et tamen in se preceptum continet; non generalis set necessaria, iudicis: huius non est condere set interpretari et continet in se preceptum et necessitatem': ad dict. Grat. post c.30, C.11 q.1 (fol. 157ʳᵇ). Civilian parallels to this type of analysis may be studied in *Quaestiones de iuris subtilitatibus* ed. H. Fitting (Berlin 1864) 57 col.2; Hugolinus, in *Dissensiones Dominorum sive controversiae veterum iuris romani interpretum*, ed. G. Haenel (Leipzig 1834) 330; Rogerius, *Summa Codicis*, in *Bibliotheca iuridica medii aevi: Scripta anecdota Glossatorum* I, ed. A. Gaudenzi (Bologna 1888) 14-15.

[10] As with Rufinus, when in introducing C.9 he stated he intended to show 'quomodo

servative; St. Bernard, professedly basing himself on the canons, had already indicated the aptness of the term to cover the substance of the primacy.[11]

It is difficult to pinpoint exactly when the recognition occurred, but it had certainly begun when Simon of Bisignano wrote his *Summa* (1177-79), was almost complete when Huguccio wrote his, and was finally rounded off in the pontificate of Innocent III. The evolution of the term in this period reveals in microcosm a whole process of the formation of canonist doctrines.

The course of development of the term and notion of *plenitudo potestatis* was determined by three broad interconnecting factors — the achievement of a comprehensive coverage of all the material assembled in the *Decretum*, the harnessing of the legal principles and procedure of the *Corpus Iuris Civilis* to ecclesiastical usage, and the refertilization of those two monuments of *ius antiquum* by contemporary papal legislation. Each of these had its part to play before *plenitudo potestatis* emerged as the fully fledged technical term for the expression of the primacy of jurisdiction.

By Huguccio's time, the *Decretum* had been scoured for material relating to papal primacy. The traditional exegesis of the Petrine texts, recurring so frequently in the canons of many popes of many centuries had been refurbished by decretist effort. A second stream of tradition had likewise been tapped. In the whole history of the organization of the Roman Church as a composite juridical entity, the model of the structure of the Roman Empire had always been a powerful conditioning feature. From the adoption in the fourth century of the administrative divisions of the Empire as the basis of provincial and diocesan divisions down to the thirteenth century, when the integration of Roman law with canon law was virtually completed, the influence of imperial Rome on papal Rome was profound and far reaching.[11a]

Romanus pontifex omnium ecclesiarum et clericorum summam potestatem teneat' (*ed. cit.* 298); J. Faventinus, similarly (MS *cit.* fo. 87b).

[11] De consid. 2.8.16 (PL 182.752), 3.4.14 (*ibid.* 766): *Ep.* 131, 132 (*ibid.* 286-7). For analyses of St. Bernard's theology of the primacy and detailed discussion of his use of *plenitudo potestatis*, cf. Y. Congar, 'L'ecclésiologie de S. Bernard,' *S. Bernard théologien* (*Anal. Sacr. Ord. Cist.* 9 [1953] 136-190 at 159-165 and 181-190; also, B. Jacqueline, 'Bernard et l'expression "plenitudo potestatis",' *Bernard de Clairvaux* (Paris 1952) 345-48.

[11a] Alongside Hobbes's famous gibe: 'And if a man consider the original of this great ecclesiastical dominion, he will easily perceive that the Papacy is no other than the *ghost* of the deceased *Roman empire*, sitting crowned on the grave thereof' (*Leviathan*, chap. 47, ed. M. Oakeshott, p. 457) should be placed the more measured judgment of a recent historian: 'Le droit romain permit à la communauté chrétienne de s'organiser en société. Ce service se poursuivra pendant des siècles. Il fera dans un certain sens, de l'Église catholique la plus authentique héritière de l'Empire romain': A. Boon, review of J. Gaudemet, *La formation du droit séculier et du droit de l'Église*, in *Bull. de théol. ancienne et médiév.* 8 (1958) 178. Various aspects of this theme as it developed from mid-eleventh century onwards, have been examined by K. Jordan, 'Die Enstehung der römischen Kurie,' ZRG *Kan. Abt.* 59 (1939) 97-152; P.S. Leicht, 'Il Pontefice S. Gregorio VII ed il diritto romano,'

It was of course essentially a legal and organizational influence. Roman law offered the most developed techniques whereby unity under the sovereignty of central authority might be ensured; the papacy was the first monarchy to exploit its services, and its lawyers the first to develop a jurisprudence under its guidance. Already by the end of the eleventh century this process of *imitatio imperii* by popes and ecclesiastical lawyers had progressed far — by mid-twelfth century, too far in some aspects to the mind of St. Bernard.[11b] But even as the note of warning was being sounded, the imitative process was about to enter its last and decisive phase. Ecclesiastical jurisprudence achieved its autonomy as a branch of *sapientia Christiana*, distinguishable from theology, with its own proper methods and ends, its separate schools and texts. The study and teaching of Roman law gave maturity of form to this newly independent discipline, whose intellectual triumph was its assimilation of Roman-imperial thought into Roman-papal thought and practice.

One stream of tradition, then, brought to the decretists the exegesis of the Petrine texts and with it, from Leo I, the term *plenitudo potestatis*. The second, that of Roman law, brought to them an analysis of the substance of monarchical authority. When the two streams coalesced, the canonist concept of papal jurisdictional primacy was complete and the term *plenitudo potestatis* established as its shorthand expression, its formula of summary. For its evolution to run its full course, there remained only to have it confirmed in some contemporary official papal statement and to be incorporated, in its new form, in the *Corpus Iuris Canonici*.

It has been seen that the Lyons Profession of Faith used the term *plenitudo potestatis* in two senses: one, the more general, to summarize the totality of papal jurisdiction and the other, to express the relationship between lesser ecclesiastical jurisdictions and the papacy. It was this latter, more restricted use of the term, whereby the fulness of the power of a pope was contrasted with the limited power of a bishop, which was logically the first to engage the decretists' attention, for it was in this sense that they first encountered the phrase *plenitudo potestatis* in the *Decretum*. By the time of Huguccio's *Summa* there was a very clear teaching attaching to the traditional Leonine formula. *Plenitudo potestatis — in partem sollicitudinis* did not merely express the difference between the universal and the local. It indicated that a subor-

---

Studi Gregoriani 1 (1947) 93-110; P.E. Schramm, 'Sacerdotium und Regnum im Austausch ihrer Vorrechte,' *ibid.* 2 (1947) 403-457; A. Hof, 'Plenitudo potestatis und Imitatio imperii zur Zeit Innocenz' III,' *Zeitschr. f. Kirchengesch.* 66 (1954-5) 39-71; above all, G. Le Bras, 'Le droit romain au service de la domination pontificale,' *Rev. hist. de droit franç.*[4] 27(1949) 377-98.

[11b] St. Bernard's well-known invective is discussed by Le Bras, *Institutions ecclésiastiques* 72 and the progressive penetration of Roman law into canon law summarized into its principal stages, 73, 77-8.

dinate jurisdiction derived its power from the sovereign. All the weight of the exegesis of the Petrine texts supported this conclusion, and the analysis of the nature of jurisdiction provided by the civil law underlined it.

As is to be expected, the bulk of decretist exegesis about papal primacy was from the common stock of Roman orthodoxy. From traditional texts[12] decretists reproduced a traditional exegesis[13] presenting Peter as the 'saxum immobile' on which the Church rested, exercising *ministerialiter* the power of Christ and therefore one head with Him, charged with supreme responsibility for its *regimen* and therefore given supreme power to discharge the task; surety for the Church's abiding indefectibility of faith.[14] Such doctrine was summarized and compressed into the formulae of the canonist idiom of which the most important was to become *plenitudo potestatis*. The whole amounted to the emphatic restatement of the traditional principle of the uniquely divinely-ordained quality of papal monarchy.[15]

It is not necessary for present purposes to go into the detail of this exegesis. Sufficient here to notice that among the many practical purposes for which decretists had recourse to the Petrine texts was in order to distinguish the several gradations of the ecclesiastical hierarchy. Gratian did this by recounting the history of the development of priestly orders from their 'institutio inchoata' in the Old Testament to their fulfilment in the New. In this history the conferring of the keys on Peter was the central event. His selection 'quasi summus sacerdos' was to single him out 'prae omnibus et pro omnibus.'[16]

---

[12] A handy compendium of the individual canons of the *Decretum* which were the bases of decretist discussion may be consulted in the *Margarita Decreti seu Tabula Martiniana*, compiled by Martinus Polonus († 1279) printed in many of the early editions of the *Decretum s.vv. Apostolica, Ecclesia, Roma, Sedes, Petrus, Papa.*

[13] Decretist exegesis found its chief originality in its discussion of the possible limitations of a personal papal power especially with respect to the definition of the faith in relation to the college of cardinals and a general council. Cf. B. Tierney, *Foundations of Conciliar Theory* (Cambridge 1955) 23-67; J. A. Watt, 'The Early Medieval Canonists and the Formation of Conciliar Theory,' *Irish Theological Quarterly* 24 (1957) 13-31; B. Tierney, 'Pope and Council: Some New Decretist Texts,' *Mediaeval Studies* 19 (1957) 197-218.

[14] Cf. the texts, especially those of Huguccio, printed by F. Gillmann, 'Zur scholastischen Auslegung von Mt.xvi, 18,' AKKR 104 (1924) 40-53.

[15] Put succinctly and strikingly by the decretist Rufinus when as bishop of Assisi he preached at the opening of the Third Lateran Council: 'Sacrosancta Romana ecclesia cum sit apex omnium cathedrarum, cum sit mater ecclesiarum omnium, magistra quoque omnium, dignissime ipsa sola omnium ecclesiarum obtinere meruit monarchiam': *Le discours* ... (above, p. 1 n. 2) 118. Huguccio gave a classic summary of the reasons why the Roman Church was *mater omnium ecclesiarum*: 'racione principii, racione institutionis, racione prelacionis': D. 11 c.1 s.v. *sit mater* (Pembroke Coll. MS 72, fol. 124ᵛᵃ). The formulation was still in use at the end of the thirteenth century, cf. Guido de Baysio, *Rosarium, ibid.*

[16] 'Petrum vero quasi in summum sacerdotem elegit, dum ei prae omnibus et pro omnibus claves regni coelorum tribuit: et a se petra, Petri nomen sibi imposuit: atque pro eius fide

Gratian clearly attached importance to this phrase for he was to repeat it later in the *Decretum*.[17] It was intended to convey two notions: that Peter was the constitutive principle of the unity of the Church, with particular reference to the unity of her governmental order; and that within this order, though not in the sacramental one, Peter was superior to the Apostles. Gratian was arguing in the spirit of a canon which he included in the same *distinctio*:

> In novo testamento post Christum dominum *a Petro* sacerdotalis coepit ordo.[18]

Certainly the decretists interpreted in this sense. For Huguccio (here representing common opinion), the superiority of the *prelacio* of Peter began with his despatching the other Apostles on their work of evangelization. Thus the distinction between Petrine *prelacio* and the Apostolic was that the former was directly divinely instituted, while the latter was instituted by Peter.[19] Thus on the axiom that whatever had been given to Peter 'racione papatus' had been given to each of his successors,[20] it was deduced that the Roman Church,

---

se specialiter rogasse testatus est; et ut ipse caeteros confirmaret, subiunxit dicens: Ego pro te rogavi Petre, ut non deficiat fides tua; et tu aliquando conversus confirma fratres tuos': dict. pr. D. 21.

[17] 'Unde cum omnibus discipulis parem ligandi atque solvendi potestatem dominus daret, Petro pro omnibus et prae omnibus claves regni coelorum': dict. post c.4 C.24 q.1. The *apparatus* of the *glossa ordinaria* period interpreted in agreement:'pro omnibus ut notetur unitas; pre omnibus ut notetur prelacio': *Gloss. Pal.* ad *loc. cit.* (Durham Cath. MS C.III.8, fol. 70ᵛ); Alanus (B.N.15393, fol. 198ᵛᵇ); Joannes Teutonicus (ed. Paris 1561, col. 1447)

[18] D.21 c.2 (Ps.-Isid.).

[19] Huguccio stated the position generally in relation to D.21 c.2 which he summarized: 'In hoc capitulo ostenditur quod ecclesia romana prima est et prelata omnibus aliis; ipsa enim instituit omnes alias set ipsa a solo Christo instituta est, et omnibus aliis prelata est, et qui talem prelacionem vult auferre a romana ecclesia esse hereticus censeatur.' He developed the theme of Roman *prelacio* (in discussing the words of the text 'Hic ergo ligandi solvendique potestatem primus accepit a domino: primusque ad fidem populum sue predicationis virtute adduxit verboque instituit. Ceteri vero apostoli cum eodem pari consortio honorem et potestatem acceperunt: ipsumque principem eorum esse voluerunt'): '*primus* id est maximus et precipuus, id est, precipue: hic dicitur quia totum videbatur fieri ab illo quia habebant ab eo confirmacionem et auctoritatem predicandi et convertendi populum ... *pari consorcio*, illi pares fuerunt quo ad ordinem quia quamcunque ordinem habuit Petrus, habuit et quilibet aliorum, set Petrus prefuit illis in dignitate prelacionis, in amministracione, in iurisdiccione; ipse enim de aliis disponebat et eos ad predicandum mittebat. Item prefuit in appellacione quia ipse solus cephas, id est caput apostolorum dictus est' (MS *cit.* fol. 130ʳᵇ).

[20] Huguccio: '(papa) qui locum in dignitate Petri obtinet, et quantam dignitatem et potestatem habuit Petrus racione papatus tantam habet eius successor': ad D. 19 c.2 (MS *cit.* fol. 128ʳᵃ).

instituit omnes prelatos quocumque sint in ecclesiastica dignitate vel offi-cio.[21]

It was in the light of this derivational principle that the decretists interpreted the *plenitudo potestatis — in partem sollicitudinis* formula. As Huguccio, following Simon of Bisignano, put it:

omnes uocantur *ab eo* (papa) in partem sollicitudinis non in plenitudinem potestatis.[22]

Thus a bishop was seen, so to say, as an individual unit of jurisdiction in the body politic of the Church. The relationship of that unit to the central authority, the holder of sovereignty, might be expressed according to the model supplied by the body politic of the Empire. An imperial magistrate exercised his jurisdiction only in virtue of the authority granted to him by the one who alone held *iurisdictio plenissima*. A bishop then, wielding a simi-larly local jurisdiction was seen as deriving his power from him who alone held *plenitudo potestatis*.[23] That it was the pope who *called* a bishop *in partem sollicitudinis* became decretist common opinion. It was a doctrine to which the major theologians[24] and canonists[25] of the thirteenth century gave their

---

[21] Ad D.21 c.2 (MS *cit.* fol. 130rb) Cf. also the text quoted n. 19.

[22] Simon of Bisignano: '*vices vos sedis apostolice sedis*: quia forte summus pontifex hunc archiepiscopum legatum suum fecit (vel?) quia omnes vocantur ab eo in partem sollicitudinis non in plenitudinem potestatis' (ad D. 100 c.10, Lambeth Pal. MS 141, fol. 16vb); Huguccio, similarly (Lincoln Cath. MS 2, fol. 176rb); Joannes Teutonicus: '*vices:* per privilegium fecerat eum legatum suum, sicut suus praedecessor fuerat. Vel ideo dicit, quia omnes vocantur ab eo in partem sollicitudinis, non in plenitudinem potestatis, ut ii. q. vi. Decreto' (*ed. cit.*, col. 513).

[23] Code 3.7 (*de iurisdictione omnium iudicum*) was the Roman law source suggesting parallels for the decretists. The civilian Azo, whose definition of jurisdiction still obtained in canonist thought at the time of Hostiensis (see *Summa*, 2.2. § 15, col. 409) had this sug-gestive formulation: . . . dividitur autem iurisdictio, quia alia plenissima est et ea est in solo principe, alia est minus plena et ea est in ceteris magistratibus . . . plenam ergo vel plenissimam iurisdictionem soli principi competere dico: cum lege Hortensia populus ei et in eum omne imperium et omnem potestatem transtulerit' (text printed by S. Mochi Onory, *Fonti canonistiche* 67 n.2). Rogerius distinguished between 'iurisdictio communis et plena' and 'semiplena': *Summa Codicis tit. eod.* (*ed. cit.* p. 41). Compare Huguccio: 'auctoritas pape dicitur plena quia plenitudinem habet potestatis, aliorum auctoritas dicitur semiplena quia vocati sunt in partem sollicitudinis': ad D.11 c.2 s.v. *plena auctoritate*. There was therefore a juristic tradition behind St. Thomas' well-known analogy: 'Papa habet plenitu-dinem potestatis pontificalis quasi rex in regno, episcopi vero assumuntur in partem sollici-tudinis quasi iudices singulis civitatibus propositi . . . ': *In IV Sent.* IV dist. 20.q.1, a.4, § 33.

[24] Cf. e.g. St. Bonaventure: 'Christi vicarius fons, origo et regula omnium principatuum ecclesiasticorum, a quo tanquam a summo derivatur ordinata potestas usque ad infima ecclesiae membra': *Breviloquium* 6.12.

[25] Hostiensis: 'Nam ab illo (papa) omnis dignitas ecclesiastica originem sumit, 22 di. c.1': *Summa* 1.15.8, 32.3. Guilelmus Durantis: ' . . . et summus pontifex, quia caput est omnium pontificum a quo illi tanquam a capite descendunt et de cuius plenitudine omnes accipiunt,

assent and which was solemnized in the Lyons Profession of Faith. Behind the view there lay primarily a particular view of the origin of the *ordo sacerdotalis* and the relationship of Peter to the other Apostles based on an exegesis of Matth. 16.18. But Roman administration, suggesting parallels, had added its confirmation of the principle.

Even as *plenitudo potestatis* was becoming a vital term in the restricted context of *prelacio*, it was becoming in decretist thought the recognized term to express the generalized concept of papal sovereignty as such. Roman law had much to do with this development as decretists analysed *iurisdictio* according to imperial norms and examples and expressed the jurisdiction of the papal monarch in the readily available Roman juristic terminology. Along with very numerous particular applications of Romanist models to ecclesiastical procedures went a marked tendency towards expressing the principle of papal power of command in association with that of imperial authority. The *lex animata* was paralleled by the *canon vivus*;[26] as Rome for the empire had been *communis patria omnium*[27] so it was for Christendom — it became again the common general forum;[28] the '*omnis potestas* est in principe collata' of Roman law was paralleled by the *plenitudo potestatis* of canon law.[29] Each monarch enjoyed in his appropriate sphere sovereignty — complete legislative and judicial discretion and unaccountability to any higher human authority; each, as has been seen, was the ultimate source of any jurisdiction exercised in the body politic. It was exactly in accordance with the logic of such a parallelism of sovereigns that Huguccio could consider that both pope and emperor, in their different fields of operation, held a *plenitudo potestatis*.[30] The term was

---

quos ipse vocat in partem sollicitudinis, non in plenitudinem potestatis': *Rationale divinorum officiorum* 2.1.17.

[26] E.g. Huguccio: 'Tocius iuris canonici noticia sit in pectore domine pape, et tocius iuris legalis noticia sit in pectore imperatoris': D. 18 c.7 s.v. *regula* (Pembroke Coll. MS 72 fol. 127vb); Alanus, *Apparatus 'Ius naturale'*: 'ius enim omne habet vel habere presumitur princeps vel papa in pectore suo, ut C. De testibus l. Omnibus': ad *loc. cit* (B.N. MS 15393 fol. 13va). On the future development of this idea, cf. F. Gillmann, 'Romanus pontifex iura omnia in scrinio pectoris sui censetur habere,' AKKR 106 (1926) 156-174.

[27] Dig. 49.3.1; 50.1.3.

[28] The dictum and the principle behind it was important in the development of the notion of the pope as *iudex ordinarius omnium* discussed below. Cf. Huguccio: 'quolibet medio pretermisso potest fieri appellacio ad papam quod in aliis non obtinet . . . et hoc videndum est quia romana ecclesia est commune et generale forum omnium clericorum et omnium ecclesiarum et dominus papa est iudex ordinarius omnium': ad C.2 q.6 c.4 (B.N. MS 15396, fol. 115vb).

[29] Cf. Huguccio: 'Set nonne clerici uel populi possent compelli ut impleant quod papa uel princeps vult, cum papa habeat plenitudinem potestatis et omnis potestas sit in principem collata?': ad dict. Grat. ante D.4 c.4 s.v. *moribus utentium* (Pembroke Coll. MS 72, fol. 119va).

[30] 'Unde intelligitur uterque plenitudinem potestatis habere quoad hoc' (scil. ius condendi leges vel canones): *loc. cit.* s.v. *leges*.

the juristic expression of supreme authority whether in Church or State and
was characteristically associated with what was to Bodin the *primum et
praecipuum caput* of sovereignty: 'la puissance de donner et casser la loy.'[31]

It was also associated with a listing of the various occasions on which supreme
authority was exercised. If the principle of the absolute power of command
was highlighted in the term *plenitudo potestatis*, it could also be described
in terms of the *maiores causae* which were the concern of the sovereign alone.
Civilians as well as canonists used this method of listing the matters in which
the exercise of sovereign power alone was appropriate. Recitals of such occasions, often put into verse as a mnemonic, became a standard feature of
canonist writing, with the actual number of the known occasions increasing
with the extension of papal legislation. The list drawn up by Huguccio, an
early and representative example of the *genre*, was limited by the standards
of the decretists, but was a fairly comprehensive description of the practical
content of papal administrative, legislative and judicial supremacy:

> *Huic soli sedi concessa:* hec autem multa sunt, scilicet episcoporum depo-
> sitio, ut iii.q.vi. Quamuis (c.7): episcoporum abrenunciatio, ut vii. q.i. De-
> nique (c.9): episcoporum mutacio, ut vii.q.i. Mutaciones (c.34): episcopo-
> rum exempcio a potestate alterius, ut xvi.q.i. Frater noster (c.52): episcopo-
> rum restitucio, ut ii.q.vi. Ideo (c.10): questio fidei, ut xxiiii.q.i. Quoties
> (c.12): dispensacio in consanguinitate vel affinitate, ut xxxv.q.viii. De
> gradibus (c.1.): difficultas negocii, et iudicium dissensio, ut infra eadem,
> Multis (c.5) et di.xii, Preceptis (c.2): restitucio hereticorum, cognicio eorum,
> ut xii.q.ii. De viro (c.17): sacrilegorum absolucio, qui violentas manus
> iniecerint in clericos ut xvii.q.iv. Si quis suadente (c.29): privilegium ap-
> pellandi ad ipsum a quocunque iudice omnibus pretermissis mediis, ar.ii.
> q.vi. Ad romanam (c.8): et auctoritas congregandi concilia, ut in hac
> distinccione aperte continetur.[32]

Other decretists would fill the gaps in this list, by adding, for example,
the power of interpreting the canons, approving a new religious order, can-
onizing saints.[33]

Thus when *plenitudo potestatis* had come to be the received technical term
to denote papal sovereignty, three strata, so to say, lay beneath it: the scrip-

---

[31] *La République* cited by P. Mesnard, *L'Essor de la philosophie politique au XVIe siècle*
(Paris 1951) 494.

[32] Ad D. 17 c.3 (MS *cit.* fol. 126va).

[33] Cf. e.g. anon. gloss MS Caius 676 ad C.2 q.6 c.4 s.v. *ad caput* (fol. 80ra) The early decretalists introduced the practice, which became regular, of summarizing these cases in verse:
'Restituit papa, solus deponit et ipse/Dividit sic unit, eximit atque probat/ Articulos saluat
synodumque facit generalem./ Transfert et mutat, appellat nullus ab illo': gloss. ad *Comp.*
II 5.13.4 s.v. *unire* (B.M. MS Roy. 11.C.VII fol. 109^v). Cf. Raymond of Peñafort, *Summa
Iuris* (*ed. cit.* 49); Hostiensis, *Summa* 1.32. § 3 col.280 (with an additional twenty-eight
lines added to the four cited above).

tural foundations of the Petrine primacy, the principle of juristic supremacy clothed in garments taken from the wardrobe of Roman law, and a catalogue of the sovereign's *iura reservata*. With Innocent III the term acquired its final standing: it was he who set the formal seal of official approval on it.[34] He was to give it a more regular place in the conventional language of the papal chancery, as well as its official juristic form for the *Corpus Iuris Canonici* and to use it sonorously when in his *Sermones* he declaimed of the majesty of the Roman Church.

There was little, if anything, however, about his use of the term which was intrinsically new. By the end of the early decretist phase of canonist literature, after an initial hesitation, the old Leonine formula had been vigorously revived. It retained its traditional form in expressing the simple distinction between the completeness of papal authority and the more restricted power of bishops. It was used further to emphasize what the face value of Pope Leo's text did not indicate: that the lesser jurisdictions derived their power from the highest. Going further still, the term *plenitudo potestatis* was detached from its adjunct *in partem sollicitudinis*. In this form, it was used most typically in the context of papal legislative omnipotence. And by logical extension from the specific to the general, it came to represent the power of absolute command in all aspects of the exercise of papal power. It was thus the generic term to express the principle of the primacy of papal jurisdiction. And in this usage it was beginning to be coupled with *vicarius Christi*.[35] All of these elements provided the first major exposition of the term and its themes to come from the pen of a pope.

The major theme of the *Sermones* as far as the primacy was concerned was an exposition of the scriptural groundwork of the commission to Peter and each of his heirs in order to reveal the absoluteness of his power. His position, foreshadowed in the Old Testament, was that of 'primus et summus magister et princeps ecclesiae'[36] who was called in 'altitudine supremae praelationis.' Other

---

[34] This is not of course to say that Innocent III was the first pope to use the term since Leo I. But it was not generally in use in papal letters of the twelfth century, though it was used occasionally by Lucius III (PL 201.1245, 1288). Its more regular usage by the papal chancery seems to date from the pontificate of Celestine III, cf. the examples cited by P. Zerbi, *Papato, impero e 'respublica christiana' dal 1187 al 1198* (Milan 1955) 170-73.

[35] Cf. M. Maccarrone, *Vicarius Christi: Storia del titolo papale* (Rome 1952) 106, citing Huguccio.

[36] 'Inter quos (apostolos) beatissimus Petrus primus et praecipuus cui singulariter a Domino dicitur: "Tu vocaberis Cephas." Cephas enim licet secundum unam linguam interpretatur Petrus, secundum aliam tamen dicitur caput (cp. Huguccio on D.22 c.2, note 19 above, as the possible immediate source of this terminology). Quia sicut plenitudo sensuum consistit in capite, in caeteris autem membris pars est aliqua plenitudinis; ita caeteri vocati sunt in partem sollicitudinis, solus autem Petrus assumptus est in plenitudinem potestatis. Unde cum Dominus omnibus simul apostolis loqueretur, universaliter ait: "Quorum remiseri-

prelates were as the members of a body of which he was the head;[37] the members
derived their powers from the head where was the 'plenitudo sensuum.'[38]
Peter alone held the plenitude of power; he was vicar of Christ, the *medius*
between God and man who might judge all, but who himself had no superior
after God; who could bind all but be bound by none, without whom no one
could act but who might himself act alone 'de plenitudine potestatis:'

> Mihi namque dicitur in Propheta: 'constitui te super gentes et regna . . . '
> (Jer.1.10). Mihi quoque dicitur in Apostolo: 'Tibi dabo claves regni coelo-
> rum. . . . ' (Matth. 16.18). Cum omnibus loqueretur, particulariter dixit:
> 'Quorum remiseritis peccata . . . (John 20.23). Cum autem soli Petro
> loqueretur, universaliter ait: 'Quodcunque ligaveris . . . . ' (Matth. 16.18)
> quia Petrus ligare caeteros, sed ligari non potest a caeteris. 'Tu, inquit,
> vocaberis Cephas' (John 1.42), quod exponitur caput; quia sicut in capite
> consistit omnium sensuum plenitudo, in caeteris autem membris pars est
> aliqua plenitudinis: ita caeteri vocati sunt in partem sollicitudinis, solus
> autem Petrus assumptus est in plenitudinem potestatis. Iam ergo videtis
> quis iste servus, qui super familiam constituitur, profecto vicarius Iesu
> Christi, successor Petri, Christus Domini, Deus Pharaonis: inter Deum et
> hominem medius constitutus, citra Deum, sed ultra hominem: minor Deo,
> sed maior homine: qui de omnibus iudicat, et a nemine iudicatur: Apostoli
> voce pronuntians, 'qui me iudicat, Dominus est' (1 Cor. 4.4).[39]

Thus did *plenitudo potestatis* receive its first major exposition in papal writing.[40]
A distillation of this exposition filtered into the *Corpus Iuris Canonici*.[41] Several Innocentian decretals alleged the term *plenitudo potestatis* in association

---

tis peccata, remittuntur eis." Cum autem soli Petro locutus est, particulariter dixit: "Quodcunque ligaveris super terram, erit ligatum et in celis"; quia Petrus potest ligare caeteros,
sed non ligari potest a caeteris, ut pote primus et summus magister et princeps Ecclesiae.
Quod etsi omnibus apostolis simul dictum fuisse legatur, non tamen aliis sine ipso, sed ipsi
sine aliis legitur dictum esse; ut quod non alii sine ipso, sed ipse sine aliis intelligatur hoc
posse de plenitudine potestatis': *Sermo* 21, *In solemnitate D. Apostolorum Petri et Pauli*
(PL 217.552).

[37] *Ibid.* 557.

[38] The typically Innocentian simile to express the derivational thesis: in addition to the
example quoted above and in the text, cf. *Sermo* 7, *In festo S. D. Silvestri Pontificis Maximi*
(PL *cit.* 482) and n. 41 below; *Sermo* 13, *In festo D. Gregorii Papae* (PL *cit.* 518).

[39] *Sermo* 2, *In consecratione Pontificis Maximi* (PL *cit.* 657-58). This exegesis of I Cor. 4.4
had been anticipated by Simon of Bisignano (Juncker, *Die Summa des Simon von Bisignano
und seine Glossen* 489) and by Huguccio, ad C.2 q.7 c.41 s.v. *iudicio*. For the passages 'Cum
omnibus loqueretur . . . ' and 'Quia sicut in capite . . . ' compare also *Sermo* 21, note 36
above.

[40] Chancery usage may be studied in any of the Registers of Innocent III. For *Reg.* 1
cf. PL 214.77, 106, 218-9, 286, 319, 324, 394, 456, 458-9.

[41] I have published the eleven decretal usages of the term by Innocent III in my paper
given to the Second International Congress of Medieval Canon Law (Boston 1963), 'The
use of the term plenitudo potestatis by Hostiensis,' Appendix A, to be published in the
Subsidia series of the *Monumenta iuris canonici*.

Decretalists

with the term *vicarius Christi*. Naturally enough, for the purposes of ecclesiastical jurisprudence, the sovereign papal power was expressed particularly in terms of law. It was entirely characteristic of canonist and Innocentian thought with its strong inclination to an *imitatio imperii* that *plenitudo potestatis* in the form in which it reentered the *Corpus Iuris Canonici* was the principle of legislative supremacy expressed in terms drawn from Roman Law. Tancred, the leading early decretalist, wrote a commentary on the vicariate of Christ and the papal plenitude of power which became classical in the canonist tradition, since in expanded form it became part of the *glossa ordinaria* on the *Gregoriana*. Its service was to reduce the principle of supreme papal legislative authority in promulgating new law and changing the old, and of papal unaccountability to any man for his governmental actions, to a number of formulas of summary. This was typical canonist method — to compress an idea into a tag or axiom — and in this case the jargon was derived largely from Roman law:

> *Veri Dei vicem*. Unde dicitur habere coeleste arbitrium, C. de summa trin. l. i, in fine, et ideo etiam naturam rerum immutat, substantialia unius rei applicando alii, arg. C. communia de leg., l.ii. in prin.; et de nullo potest aliquid facere, C. de rei uxo. act. l.i. in prin. et de cons. d.ii, Revera; et sentenciam que nulla est facit aliquam, iii.q.vi. Hec quippe; quia in his que vult, ei est pro racione voluntas, instit. de iur. nat. § set quod principi; nec est qui ei dicat, cur ita facis? de poen. di. iii. § ex persona, alias est c. Quamvis; ipse enim potest supra ius dispensare, infra, de concess. preb. c. Proposuit. Item, de iniusticia facere iusticiam, corrigendo iura et mutando, infra, de app. c. Ut debitus et infra, de consang. et affin. c. Non debet et plenitudinem obtinet potestatis, ii.q.vi. c. Placuit, in fi.[42]

---

[42] Bernard of Parma ad X.1.7.3. Tancred's text on which he had based his gloss reads: '*dei uicem.* In hoc gerit uicem dei quia sedet in loco Iesu Christi qui est uerus deus et uerus homo, ut in instit. innoc. iii. Firmiter credimus. Item de nichilo fecit aliud ut deus, ar. iii. q. vi. Hec quippe et C. de rei uxo. act. l. una, in princ. Item in hoc gerit uicem dei quia plenitudinem potestatis habet in rebus ecclesiasticis, ut ii.q. vi. Decreto, infra, de usu pallii c. ii. Item quia de iusticia potest facere iniusticiam (*sic*) corrigendo ius et mutando, ut in const. innoc. iii. Ut debitus et c. Non debet. Nec est qui dicat ei cur ita facis, ut de pe. di. iii. § Personam. t.' (Durham Cath. MS C.III.4, fol. 103va). An unsigned gloss in B.M.Roy. 11.C.VII on the same text reads: 'In hoc gerit uicem dei quia de nichilo facit aliquid ut iii. q. vi. Hec quippe.C. de rei uxo. ac. l. una, in prin. Item in hoc quod plenitudinem potestatis habet in rebus ecclesiasticis, ii.q.vi. Decreto. Item in hoc quod supra ius dispensat, ut infra de con.preb. non vac. c.i. ut ibi dixi. Alibi tamen appellatur successor piscatoris, xxiiii.q.i. Quoniam uetus' (fo. 120^r). The actual meaning of some of these tags is not immediately obvious — as the *correctores Romani* in the standard edition of the *Gregoriana* pointed out somewhat caustically. But their explanation is useful: 'Tota haec glossa vix aliquid explicat propriis verbis; quod si bene intelligatur, vera astruit, nam de nihilo aliquid facere est ius novum condere et de iniustitia iustitiam, intellige per constitutionem iuris; et immutare substantiam rerum accipi debet in his quae sunt iuris positivi, et ita loquuntur iura, quae citantur' (col.217).

Thus did the term *plenitudo potestatis*, in direct connection with another, *vicarius Christi*, become the received canonist term to express papal jurisdictional preeminence.

Not all canonist writing in this period about the *plenitudo potestatis* was so clumsily expressed nor related exclusively to legislative supremacy.[43] St. Raymond of Peñafort used it more generally — in connection with its scriptural basis and its comprehensive practical content — and more clearly. His commentary, from the pen of one so eminent in the ecclesiastical world of his day, may be taken as marking the typical understanding of the term shortly after the pontificate of Innocent III.[44] So too does the writing and legislation of Innocent's successor, Honorius III, show him the faithful *pedissequus* of his predecessor.[45] And since the medieval intellectual disciplines did not work

---

[43] Nor was it necessarily prolix. Vincentius Hispanus managed to reveal much about the background of the term without in fact offering a personal word, simply by attaching four texts to it: '*plenitudo ecclesiastice iurisdiccionis*: s.ii.q.vi. Decreto: s.ix.q.iii. Per principalem; D. de leg. et const. Digna (*recte* Cod.1.17.4): s. De transla. Inter corporalia, lib. eo. vinc' (*Comp.* III 3.8.2. B.M.Roy. 11.C.VII, fo. 168ᵛ). The first two of the texts cited gave the traditional background: *Decreto* contains the actual term itself and *Per principalem* is a strong statement of the papacy's position, of what Innocent III would call the 'totius ecclesiasticae disciplinae magistratus' (PL 216.1265); the Roman law citation models papal sovereignty on the imperial, and the decretal cited, one of Innocent III's, links the term with the papal position as *vicarius Christi*.

[44] Cf. *Summa Iuris* (1218-1221): 'Papa est summus inter omnes. Ipse enim habet plenitudinem potestatis, alii partem sollicitudinis, ii.q.vi, Decreto, Qui se scit (cc.11, 12). Item licet aliis apostolis dixerit Dominus ut laxarent retia, soli tamen Petro dixit: *duc in altum*, et ei soli dixit ut piscaretur hamo per que preeminens iurisdiccio designatur, xxiiii.q.i, Non turbatur, Est aliud (cc.7,8). Item quia ipse est vicarius Christi et maior homine, minor Deo, extra iii, de translacione episcoporum, Inter (*Comp.* IIIa. 1.5.2). Et ei soli dictum est: *tu es Petrus*, etc, xxi di. Quamvis (c.3). Et ut melius intelligas preeminenciam eius nota quod quedam adeo inherant pape et sedi apostolice quod non possunt per alios expediri nec transeunt etiam cum generali mandato nisi specialiter demandentur . . .' (there follows a long list of such cases; *ed. cit.* 47-49).

[45] Cf. e.g. in his *Sermones de Sanctis: in festo S. Silvestri:* 'Quum autem (dominus) soli Petro locutus est, dixit: *Quodcunque . . . ligaveris* et addidit: *et tibi dabo claves regni coelorum,* ostendit quod caeteri vocati sunt in partem sollicitudinis. Solus autem Petrus assumptus est in plenitudinem potestatis, quia solus potest ligare caeteros, sed non potest ligari a caeteris. Quia successor Petri videlicet summus pontifex, principatum cathedrae Romanae ecclesiae possidet et gubernat, qui plenitudinem honoris sui et amplissimam dignitatem caeteris ecclesiis per universum mundum in Domino constitutis distribuit et dispensat, ordinans in eis patriarchas, primates, episcopos, abbatos, priores caeterosque praelatos': *Honorii III Opera omnia*, ed. Horoy, *Bibl. Patristica* II (Paris 1879) 100. Cf. also his *Sermo in cathedra S. Petri* (col. 134) for a restatement of the same view. One of Honorius' decretals (*Comp.* V. 3.9.1) made use of the term. The canonist interpretation of this usage is well brought out in James of Albenga's *Apparatus* on *Compilatio* V: 'de plenitudine potestatis: ipse enim solus uocatus in plenitudinem potestatis, et alii episcopi in partem sollicitudinis, ut supra, de usu pallii, Ad honorem, et ix.q.iii.c.ult. et penult. et ii.q.vi. Decreto et c.seq. tamen dicit

in parallel, with theologians unaware of how popes were writing and legislating and canonists commenting, it is no surprise to find Alexander of Hales and theologians after him, using the expression *plenitudo potestatis* as the ordinary one for denoting papal primacy.[46] If there was anything distinctive about the theologians' handling of the term by comparison with the canonists' — there was, of course, considerable overlapping — it rested in this. Whereas the canonists emphasized practical legislative and judicial consequences of the plenitude of power, the theologians were concerned with it as a principle of order in the ecclesiastical hierarchy. 'Unum centrum ecclesiae,' said St. Bonaventure, 'cum plenitudine potestatis'[47] and in the same vein, Albertus Magnus, 'in unitate ordinis ecclesiae unus est, qui accipit in plenitudine potestatis.'[48]

By mid-century the term was fully established in both canonical and theological opinion, as well as in official papal chancery usage. One new context in which it figured in the next quarter century should be noticed as it formed part of the immediate background to the framing of the Lyons definition.

So firmly established was the term that it was inevitable that, when a new branch of theology — or at any rate of theological polemic — was developed 'contra Graecos,' *plenitudo potestatis* would figure largely in it. Without attempting an exhaustive examination of this literature,[49] the main lines of exposition of the term can be indicated.

---

cum papa sit uocatus in plenitudinem potestatis, ut iii.q.vii; et uicem ueri dei teneat in terris, ut supra de transl. ep. Quanto l.iii, ubi dicitur (I have here corrected the defective word order of the MS) quod in omnibus potest dispensare, ar. iii.q.vi. Hec quippe et C. de rei uxor. acc. circa prin. et de con. di. ii. Reuera: <intelligitur> sermo igitur preterquam in articulis fidei et preterquam in hiis a quibus pendet generalis status ecclesie quia illa debet usque ad effusionem sanguinis defendere, xxv.q.i. Sunt quidam, et si contra illa faceret posset accusari tanquam hereticus, ut xl.di. Si papa' (B.M.Roy. 11.C.VII, fol. 262ʳ-263ᵛ).

[46] For some examples of Alexander's use of the term, cf. *In IV Sent.* 4.24 (Bibliotheca Franciscana Scholastica Medii Aevi 15; Quaracchi 1957) pp. 406, 425, 426; and 4.38, p.562.

[47] *In IV Sent.* 4.19. art. 3.q.1: *Opera omnia* IV Quaracchi (1889) 508; further examples pp. 532, 539, 635 and in 1.11 art.1 q.1: *Opp.* I (1882) 212.

[48] '*Dabo autem tibi:* singulariter, non quod singulariter acceperit Petrus: sed quia in unitate ordinis ecclesiae unus est, qui accipit in plenitudine potestatis, qui est successor Petri, et Petrus in potestate. Alii autem in eadem unitate accipiunt in parte potestatis, eo quod vocantur in partem sollicitudinis': *Comm. in evang. D. Matth.* c. 16 (*Opera Omnia* 9; Lyons 1651 fol. 308ᵇ)

[49] Three works, all of Dominican origin, are considered here: (1) an anonymous *Tractatus contra Graecos* written probably in 1252 by a member of the Dominican house in Constantinople. It has been printed, somewhat defectively by P. Stevartius (Stevart), *Tomus singularis insignium auctorum tam Graecorum quam Latinorum* ... (Ingolstadt 1616) 535-631. The fourth distinction (pp. 578-592) is entitled (distinctio) *In qua ostenditur quod papa est caput ecclesiae.* (2) The *Libellus de fide sanctae Trinitatis* of Nicholas, bishop of Cotrone, which in its Greek version was presented to Michael Palaiologos and in its Latin version to Urban

The first work of this type, written in 1252 by an anonymous Dominican, contained a *distinctio* 'in qua ostenditur quod papa est caput ecclesiae.' The burden of the argument centered on *plenitudo potestatis* and, to a somewhat lesser extent, *vicarius Christi*. There was nothing particularly original about the treatment of this theme; it was fashioned as the circumstances of debate dictated, especially to establish the universal *praelatio* of Peter as against the local jurisdictions of the other Apostles.[50] Greek sources were used (or were thought to be used) in support of the contention that Peter was the 'caput vel vertex Apostolorum vel apex' — language which perhaps had its influence on the phrasing of the Lyons Profession of Faith.[51] Nicholas of Cotrone, without specifically using the term *plenitudo potestatis*, used similar texts to establish similar conclusions, with especial reference to the subordinate positions of the other patriarchates. The section of St. Thomas's treatise concerned with the primacy, however, made significant use of the term. It was made to underpin what was essentially an analysis of the Petrine texts.

St. Thomas' declared aim was to establish on the authority of the Greek Fathers the proposition: 'Christi vicarium in totam ecclesiam Christi potestatis plenitudinem obtinere.'[52] If his attempt to base the proposition on the

---

IV in 1264. Urban sent the work to Aquinas for his comment, which took the form of (3) *Contra errores Graecorum* (1264), a much improved version of the *Libellus*. Nicholas' treatise has been printed by P.A.Uccelli, *Anonymus liber de fide sanctissimae Trinitatis* ... (Rome 1880) 377-442 and by E.H.Reusch, 'Die Fälschungen in dem Tractat des Thomas von Aquin gegen die Griechen: Opusculum contra errores Graecorum ad Urbanum IV,' *Abh. Akad. Munich* 18 (1889) 673-742: cf. 681-89 for the section *de primatu Romanae ecclesiae*. The treatises of Nicholas and Aquinas have been reprinted with commentary by P. Glorieux, *S. Thomas d'Aquin: Contra errores Graecorum* (Monumenta christiana selecta, Paris 1957). On this branch of literature generally, cf. A. Dondaine, ' "Contra Graecos": Premiers écrits polémiques des Dominicains d'Orient,' *Archivum Fratr. Praed.* 21 (1951) 320-446.

[50] A typical example of the method is afforded in Stervatius' edition on p. 579. One of the Petrine texts is selected, and its exegesis is illustrated with several quotations of John Chrysostom, and the proposition asserted firmly: 'Petrus autem habuit praerogativam dignitatis super Apostolos et plenitudinem potestatis super omnes homines,' and again, 'Commisit quidem Petro praelationem omnium fidelium. Quia etsi Iacobus Hierolymitanam suscepit, Petrus tamen totius orbis: quasi dicat: Sanctus vocatus est Iacobus in partibus Hierosolymitanis sed Petrus in plenitudine potestatis.'

[51] *Ed. cit.* 580. The use of the word 'vertex' is interesting. It was not in the usual vocabulary of canonists and others in the thirteenth century who discussed papal primacy. That it entered the Lyons Creed demonstrates that the literature *contra Graecos* played a significant part in the formulation of the Creed. It was allegedly drawn from the same exegesis of John Chrysostom on John 21.15-17 (cf. *In Ioannem homil.* 88 n.1: PG 59.478) as cited by the anonymous writer of 1252, Nicholas of Cotrone (ed. Glorieux 104), and Aquinas (*ed. cit.* 171; cf. also, Aquinas, *Catena aurea* on John 21, ed. Paris 1611, col. 1589: '*Petrus*: eximius enim apostolorum erat Petrus, et os discipulorum et vertex collegii: unde et negatione delata committit ei prelationem fratrum').

[52] *Ed. cit.* 167.

sources he chose was not altogether successful, he did at any rate give a remarkably comprehensive and succinct exegesis of the Petrine texts. His argumentation developed in five stages, each built round one such text, with commentaries adduced from Greek sources. The rubrics of each section[53] indicate the logic of the argument:

> Quod pontifex Romanus est primus et maximus inter omnes episcopos;
> Quod idem pontifex in totam ecclesiam Christi universalem praelationem habet;
> Quod idem habet in ecclesia potestatis plenitudinem;
> Quod in eadem potestate quae collata est Petro a Christo;
> Quod ad eum pertinet determinare quae sunt fidei.

This progression might well have served as a model for the framing of the Lyons definition which follows a similar order of postulates.[54] But however that may be, it is to be noticed here that the originality of St. Thomas' concept of the *plenitudo potestatis* lay less in the interpretation itself, which accords exactly with existing interpretations, than in the attempt to show it accorded with the teaching of authorities acknowledged by the Greeks. St. Thomas had already acquired some familiarity with the interpretations put by some of the Greek Fathers on the Petrine texts when compiling his *Catena aurea super Evangelia*. In the *Contra Graecos* six different authorities were alleged in the context of papal primacy, of whom St. John Chrysostom (seven citations) and St. Cyril of Alexandria (eight citations) were the most important. But these sources were defective: the *Liber thesaurorum* of St. Cyril which St. Thomas thought he was using was not authentic.[55] The language of this work — 'plenissima potestas' committed 'plenissime' to Peter,[56] 'cui

---

[53] That is, the rubrics given in Edit.Rom.I in *Opuscula philosophica et theologica*, ed. M. de Maria, III (Rome 1886).

[54] As Reusch argued, *art. cit.* 712-13.

[55] Nicholas of Cotrone reproduced a long extract from a source he described as figuring 'in tertio libro Thesaurorum, de Passione Domini' (*ed. cit.* 100). It was from this extract, which has not been identified, that Aquinas drew his Cyrillian quotations. It is noteworthy that almost the same extract as that of Nicholas appeared later in the *De regimine christiano* of James of Viterbo, who also attributed it to Cyril 'in libro Thesaurorum': ed. H.X.Arquillière, *Le plus ancien traité de l'église: Jacques de Viterbe, De regimine christiano (1301-1302)* (Paris 1926) 274-6. It is perhaps not without interest that both Aquinas and James of Viterbo associated this text with the conclusion 'quod subesse romano pontifici sit de necessitate salutis' (Aquinas, *ed. cit.* 171; James of Viterbo: ' . . . et quod ei subesse de necessitate salutis est' *ed. cit.* 276) — suggestive of the literary background to the well known definition of *Unam sanctam*.

[56] Nicholas' text reads (italics indicate the part used by Aquinas): ' . . . a Filio qui ei dedit plene et perfecte claves regni celorum quoniam ('quantum,' James of Viterbo *ed.cit.* 275) *sicut ipse accepit a Patre dux et sceptrum ecclesiae gentium ex Israel, egrediens super omnem principatum et potestatem et super omne quodcumque est, ut ei genu cuncta curventur, plenissimam potestatem; sic et Petro et eius* diadochis id est *successoribus* vel vicariis ('non

omnes iure divino inclinant, et primates mundi tanquam ipsi Domino Iesu obediunt'[57] — was that of the West, not of the East. Nevertheless the Lyons definition was phrased apparently in the general belief that something very near to the term *plenitudo potestatis* had the authority of a leading Greek Father. This belief could not have been the decisive factor in its adoption at Lyons, since the term and its understanding were so well established in Latin thought from very different sources. But no doubt the seeming Greek confirmation was a prized addition to its official acceptability, the addition of the final detail to the evolution of *plenitudo potestatis*.

In the light of the consistency of interpretation of the term by the popes, canonists and theologians of the thirteenth century, it is hardly surprising that the Lyons Profession of Faith gave it its most solemn acceptance. Withal, the definition was on the conservative side, since it did not contain *vicarius Christi*, so generally used in association with *plenitudo potestatis*. Nevertheless the Lyons Creed in its double usage — the principle of papal sovereignty, in its universality and comprehensiveness, and the derivation of episcopal jurisdiction from papal — was an exact reflection of the prominence the expression *plenitudo potestatis* had come to have in Latin thought over the preceding century.

2. *Papa est iudex ordinarius omnium*

There was a second way in which the Lyons definition might be thought to be conservative judged by the terminology generally received by all canonists and some theologians by that time. The Profession of Faith included a statement concerning appeals to the Roman Church;

> Ad quam potest gravatus quilibet super negotiis ad ecclesiasticum forum pertinentibus appellare, et in omnibus causis ad examen ecclesiasticum spectantibus ad ipsius potest iudicium recurri . . . .

The canonists had a technical term to cover this papal prerogative — *papa est iudex ordinarius omnium* — which was used in close association with *plenitudo potestatis*, sometimes indeed almost as a synonym for it. An examination of this term is an essential corollary to the examination of *plenitudo potestatis*, for in canonist thought they were rarely far apart and were developed *pari passu*.

Something of the general origins and meaning of the term was sketched in one of F. W. Maitland's brilliant essays written under the stimulus of Bishop Stubbs' contention that papal canon law had not fully authoritative standing

---

minus sed' takes the place of 'vel vicariis' in James of Viterbo) *plenissime commisit* (ed. Glorieux 100).

[57] Nicholas, *ed.cit.* 101: Aquinas, *ed. cit.* 170.

in the medieval English Church.[58] Maitland gave a magisterial account of the form the judicial machinery of Christendom was assuming in the twelfth century. Development was twofold. On the one hand, under papal initiative, there was the elaboration of a 'centripetal, Romipetal jurisprudence.'[59] On the other, in all parts of the Christian world, there was growing 'the settled practical habit of looking to Rome for declarations of the common law of the Church.'[60] In the context of the controversy, Maitland was more concerned with the second aspect in so far as it applied in England. Nevertheless he pointed out the key concept and its formula which marked the Roman side of the development. The papal curia was striving to give practical content to its claim to be the 'omnicompetent court of first instance for the whole of Christendom.'[61] And the claim itself was expressed most typically in a phrase found in canonist use in the early thirteenth century: 'dominus papa est ordinarius singulorum.'[62]

It was outside the scope of Maitland's essay to deal with the specific origins of the term. But he was so exactly right in his felicitous phrasing of the meaning of the term. More detailed examination of canonist writing and the tracing of its first use by decretists only confirms Maitland's view. *Iudex ordinarius omnium*, as a canonist term, betokened the claim that the holder of the plenitude of power enjoyed an 'omnicompetent court of first instance for the whole of Christendom.'

'Iudex ordinarius' was a term of Roman law. It was adopted by the decretists and developed by them, especially by Huguccio, in a particular context of the *Decretum*; was accepted by Innocent III, who gave it officially to the *Corpus Iuris*, whence it became a received decretalist formula. This development has many points of similarity with that of *plenitudo potestatis*, and the fortunes of both expressions were made in much the same process of the analysis of papal jurisdictional power. An ordinary judge, according to Roman law, was one who exercised his function *suo iure* and not by delegation.[63] It was entirely appropriate, therefore, for a bishop to be known as

---

[58] 'William of Drogheda and the Universal Ordinary,' in *Roman Canon Law in the Church of England* (London 1898) 100-131.

[59] *Op. cit.* 105. Cf. *Decretum* C.24 q.3 c.23 (*Si quis Romipetas*).

[60] *Op. cit.* 129.   [61] *Op. cit.* 104.

[62] Tancred, *Ordo iudiciarius* (1214-16), cited from Caius College MS 85 fol.7. The treatise is in print, F. Bergmann, *Pillii, Tancredi, Gratiae libri de iudiciorum ordine* (Göttingen 1842) 87-316.

[63] As stated, for example, by Johannes Bassianus:: 'Et in summa ordinarius iudex est qui dignitatis nomine gaudet, cuius ratione potest aliquam causam cognoscere, ut archidiaconus, episcopus, preses, pretor, consul': *Libellus de ordine iudiciorum* § 3, in *Bibl. Iurid. Med. Aev.* ed. Gaudenzi II (Bologna 1892) 213a, or by Boncompagni: 'Iudex ordinarius est qui sine speciali mandato potest causas gregis vel populi sibi commissi audire': *Rhetorica novissima* 2, *ibid.* 258b.

an 'ordinarius' but of course his jurisdiction was essentially local (*in partem sollicitudinis*). The holder of *plenitudo potestatis* was universal ordinary.[64]

Decretists first used the term 'papa est iudex ordinarius omnium' with relation to a particularly vigorous statement of papal primacy from the pen of Gelasius I.[65] The Roman Church had the right of judging all: from its sentences there was no appeal; no one might judge it; all had the right of appealing to its judgment. These Gelasian texts did not include the actual term itself but they expressed for decretists, all its content.

We need not, for present purposes, go into the earliest decretist work to try to establish which canonist had the honor of employing the term for the very first time. It suffices here to say that when Huguccio's great *Summa* brought to an end the first phase of decretist glossatorial activity, the term was well established as an integral part of the decretist concept of the plenitude of power. The pope, 'antonomastice iudex',[66] had unimpeded access to all ranks of the Christian hierarchy. His jurisdiction was immediate: he might act over the heads of any intermediate jurisdiction to summon the lowliest cleric to his court: 'obedience to God and the pope always constituted an exception to the bond between a cleric and his bishop.'[67] This absolute power of summons and revocation had an essential corollary. The lowliest cleric himself had the right of unimpeded access to the pope. He might appeal to him without need of intermediate hearing: it was this aspect of the primacy that had an especial significance in the meaning of the term *iudex ordinarius omnium*. As Huguccio put it, with a strong Roman law reminiscence:

> Romana ecclesia est commune et generale forum omnium clericorum et omnium ecclesiarum, et dominus papa est iudex ordinarius omnium quasi nullo existente medio, et ideo quolibet medio pretermisso potest appellari ad eum.[68]

Among Huguccio's followers, the formulation was considered important enough to head the catalogue of papal prerogatives:

---

[64] Wielding the 'ordinariae potestatis principatus' as Innocent III put it in 4 Lat. Council c.5 = X.5.33.23.

[65] C.9 q.3 cc.17,18.

[66] Huguccio: '*iudex*. scilicet summus, id est papa qui antonomastice dicitur iudex': ad C.9 q.3 c.13 (B.N. MS 15396, fol. 157rb).

[67] Ad C.9 q.3 c.21 (B.N. MS 15396 fol. 167va).

[68] The full text reads: 'Ex omnibus his capitulis aperte colligitur quod quolibet medio pretermisso potest fieri appellacio ad papam, quod in aliis non obtinet, ut infra ead. Decreto (c.11), Quisquis (c.19), et q.vii. Metropolitanum (c.45) et viiii. q.iii. Conquestus (c.8), et hoc videndum est quia romana ecclesia . . . (as text above) . . . appellari ad eum, ut in his quinque capitulis dicitur, et viiii.q.iii. Cuncta (c.17), Nunc vero (c.30), Per principalem (c.21)': ad C.2 q.6 c.4 (B.N. MS 15396 fol. 115vb)

Papa vero omnium fidelium ordinarius iudex est, ut infra, ix.q.iii, Ipsi, Cuncta, et ita pretermisso quolibet medio appellatur ad eum.[69]

Thus the early decretist formula *iudex ordinarius omnium* had its birth in the general context of the jurisdictional omnicompetence of the pope over the whole hierarchy, was therefore associated with the plenitude of power and had particular reference to the principle that appeals might be made immediately to the pope, with intervening, subordinate jurisdictions by-passed. This was the context of its first (seemingly) official papal usage, by Innocent III in a decretal which found its way into *Compilatio* III.[70] At very much the same time, the whole notion was stated comprehensively by Alanus Anglicus:

Ex his quinque capitulis (scil. C.2.q.6 cc.19-23) manifestum est quod a quocunque iudice ecclesiastico potest ad papam appellari, nullo medio pretermisso: habet enim plenitudinem potestatis, ix.q.iii. c. Conquestus.

Est enim papa iudex ordinarius omnium, ar. ix.q.iii. c. Cuncta, Nunc vero, Per principalem: ab aliis autem nullo medio pretermisso debet appellari.[71]

Firmly established by the early decretists, adopted officially by Innocent III, the expression was the orthodox terminology of the primacy with thirteenth century canonists. Associated occasionally with wider questions of papal authority, its customary interpretation was the specifically canonist reading of that provision in the Gelasian canon *Cuncta* which spoke in a general way of appeals to the papacy. Thus is it to be found in the *glossa ordinaria* on the Decretals,[72] and in the commentaries of the leading decretalists, Goffredus de Trano,[73] Innocent IV,[74] Hostiensis[75] and Guilelmus Durantis.[76] One

---

[69] Gloss. anon. (Caius 676) ad C.2 q.6 c.4, fol. 216[vb].

[70] 'Praeterea cum sedes apostolica caput omnium ecclesiarum existat, et Romanus pontifex iudex sit ordinarius singulorum': *Comp.* III 1.6.4 = X.1.6.19 (where, however, this passage was omitted). But the point had been registered by the early decretalists: Paulus Hungarus: 'Nota papa est ordinarius omnium': *Notabilia super Comp.* III (B.N. MS 14320, fol. 140[vb]) and Tancred, above, n. 64. Hence its place in later decretalist writing was established and this decretal was generally cited when *iudex ordinarius omnium* was being discussed.

[71] Ad C.2 q.6 c.19 (B.N. MS 15393 fol. 97[a]).

[72] Bernard of Parma: 'Illud generale est quod ad papam potest appellari omisso medio propter plenitudinem potestatis, ii.q.vi. Quoties ad Romanum (c.26) et in pluribus aliis capitulis ibidem: quia per simplicem querelam potest papa adiri, cum ipse sit iudex ordinarius singulorum, ix.q.iii. Cuncta et c. Per principalem': ad 2.28.66 s.v. *post huiusmodi;* cf. also the *Notabilia* to 5.33.23.

[73] *Summa super tit. Decr.* (Venice 1586) *De appellationibus,* fol. 109[vb].

[74] *Apparatus* ad 2.2.17. Carlyle, *History* V 320 gives this text a political significance though the context of the decretal and commentary is purely ecclesiastical.

[75] *Summa, de appell.* 2.28 § 4.

[76] *Speculum iudiciale* 2.3 *de appell.* § 4 *Nunc tractemus* (ed. Frankfurt 1592), fol. 481[b].

rather striking formulation, from an anonymous French procedural work of the second part of the century, will illustrate how the term had penetrated into the analysis of the primacy;

> *Qui dicuntur iudices ordinarii.* Et quod dominus papa sit iudex ordinarius istud habetur in illa constitutione c. Cuncta per orbem (C.9 q.3 c.17). Ibi enim legitur quod ad dominum papam qui iudex est ordinarius singulorum, appellatur ab omnibus, ab ipso autem ad neminem. Quare ipsum superiorem concludimus esse. Praeterea cum Romana ecclesia aliarum ecclesiarum sit genetrix et magistra, et summus rector eiusdem aliorum quorumlibet ministrorum erit ordinarius et magister[77]

In canonist thought the notion that the pope, *iudex ordinarius omnium*, exercised a *principatus ordinarie iurisdictionis* was only slightly less significant as a definition of papal sovereignty than *plenitudo potestatis* itself.

So the canonists had devised the language in which to express their notion of the primacy in its jurisdictional features. Together these two terms which we have been considering were an expression of the translation of the Petrine texts into juristic forms, into a notion of supreme governmental authority, into a concept of sovereignty. It is important to appreciate that this view was the specifically constitutional reading of a basic notion of ecclesiology which contemporary theologians were beginning to formulate. Theologians argued that it was axiomatic that Christ, who so loved His church that He shed His blood for her, had left her equipped with all the means necessary for the achievement of her end, eternal salvation:

> quicquid necessarium est ad vitam spiritualem invenitur in ea.[78]

The theologian was naturally inclined to consider this truism about the nature of the Church in relation to the sacramental order. Christ had put at the

---

[77] *Curialis* (1251-70) ed. L. Wahrmund, *Quellen zur Geschichte des römisch-kanonischen Processes im Mittelalter* 1.3 (Innsbruck 1905) p. 1. The term was not of course confined to the canonists though they had coined and developed it; cf. Albertus Magnus 'Ad id quod queritur de potestate superioris et inferioris, dicendum per distinctionem. Quia superior aut habet potestatem limitatam, aut potestatis plenitudinem, sicut papa qui est ordinarius cuiuslibet. Si primo modo: tunc non habet potestatem in subditos sine inferioris voluntate. Si secundo modo: tunc habet: quia papa est ordinarius omnium hominum . . . ': *Summa Theologiae* 2.24.141 (*Opera omnia* 18 [Lyons 1651] fol. 596ᵇ).

[78] This was to formulate, after Aristotle, the notion of the Church as a *communitas perfecta* = 'ordinata per se ad sufficientiam' (Aquinas, *In Pol.* 1 proem. c.1). Aquinas phrased the idea very clearly, *In Ps.* 45.v.3: *Gloriosa dicta sunt de te civitas Dei:* tria sunt in ista civitate . . . secundum est quod habeat sufficientiam per se: in vico enim non inveniuntur omnia necessaria vitae humanae, sanis et infirmis; sed in civitate oportet invenire omnia necessaria ad vitam: quia quicquid necessarium est ad vitam spiritualem, invenitur in ea.' The canonists were slower to speak of the Aristotelian notion of self-sufficiency as applied to the Church. Joannes Monachus, however, commenting on the citation in *Unam sanctam* of Cant.6.8, wrote: 'nam secundum Philosophum totum et perfectum idem . . . nam illud est perfectum quod totum habet et nihil ei deficit, et illud etiam totum est quod omnia habet': *Extrav. Comm.* 1.8.1. s.v. *sponso.*

disposal of priest and faithful the means of grace by which salvation was to be achieved. The notion was paralleled in terms of the governmental order. It was equally a truism that the Church as a juridical society had not been left deficient in what was necessary for the government of the Church. Thus it was argued that when Christ withdrew His bodily presence, a replacement was necessary to take complete charge of the governmental order. Both Innocent IV, representing the canonists,[79] and St. Thomas Aquinas, representing the theologians, shared this view.[80]

Plenitudo potestatis thus derived from the fundamental postulate that whatever power was necessary for the salvation of the faithful had been given to the Church generally and specifically and *in toto* to the vicar of Christ. Theologians examined the implications of this in terms of the Church's *thesaurarius*: canonists, in terms of *principatus*. Thus both had the particular slant of their respective disciplines whilst sharing the general principle that all things necessary for the salvation, right ordering, and general welfare of the Church had been granted immediately to its visible head. It was the comprehensive control by the pope of all the means which had been put at the disposal of the Church by her founder whereby spiritual life was to be preserved and promoted which constituted the *plenitudo potestatis*.[81] The constitution of the Church was one such means and it was *plenitudo potestatis* in relation to the juridical order that was the special concern of the canonists.

3. *Plenitudo potestatis, iudex ordinarius omnium, and the Secular Order*

The above examination of the origin and development of the two canonist terms fashioned to summarize the concept of papal monarchy has not at any point touched on that aspect of the primacy which related to temporal affairs. The terms arose and were shaped with a view to the purely spiritual and ec-

---

[79] ' . . . nam non videretur discretus dominus fuisse ut cum reverentia eius loquitur, nisi unicum post se talem vicarium reliquisset qui haec omnia posset . . . ': *App* ad *de sent. et re iud.* c. *Ad apostolice* (= in VI° 2.14.2) s.v. *privamus* (ed. Venice 1491 fol. 118ᵛᵇ).

[80] 'Manifestum est autem quod Christus ecclesiae in necessariis non deficit quam dilexit et pro ea sanguinem fudit . . . non est dubitandum quia ex ordinatione Christus unus toti ecclesiae praesit . . . Eadem igitur ratione, quia praesentiam corporalem erat ecclesiae subtracturus, oportuit ut alicui committeret qui loco sui universalis ecclesiae gereret curam': *Contra Gentiles* 4.76. The same language was used by later writers, e.g. Humbert de Romanis, *Opusculum tripartitum* 2.4, ed. E. Brown, *Fasciculus rerum expetendarum* II (London 1640) 209, 210: James of Viterbo, *De regimine christiano*, ed. Arquillière 167, 212; John of Paris, *De potestate regia et populi*, ed. J. Leclercq (Paris 1942) 179.

[81] There was therefore much canonical and theological opinion behind the succinct formualtion of James of Viterbo: 'Verumtamen dicitur Christi vicarius habere plenitudinem potestatis . . . Tanta vero potestas communicata est ecclesiae quanta erat opportuna ad salutem fidelium; quare in vicario Christi tota illa potentia est, que ad hominum salutem procurandum requiritur': *ed. cit.* 272.

clesiastical order. They envisaged jurisdictional relationships within the ecclesiastical hierarchy: the *plenitudo potestatis* of Peter contrasted with the
pars sollicitudinis of the other Apostles; the Roman Church the common
forum *omnium clericorum et omnium ecclesiarum.* In their essence, then,
these terms were quite independent of any claim for the exercise of power
in temporal affairs and they were first coined and developed without explicit
reference to the relationship of popes and princes.

Yet these terms were designed specifically to emphasize the comprehensive
and all-embracing nature of the papal primacy, to express its totality. Since
the claim to exercise a power at least *quodam modo in temporalibus* by virtue
of the *imperium sacerdotis* — the power of binding and loosing — was an
integral part of the primatial authority, our terms were bound to have some
relevance to it. The problem now is to determine what was that precise relevance.

Both terms were in fact applied to the position of the pope in respect of
temporal affairs from the end of the twelfth century. There is some evidence
that some decretists towards the end of the century were arguing that by
virtue of the *plenitudo potestatis* the pope might exercise direct temporal
jurisdiction.[82] Innocent III himself went very near to this doctrine when
in *Per venerabilem* he claimed that he could legitimize in the temporal order
as well as the spiritual. And a leading canonist of this pontificate, Alanus
Anglicus, committed himself to the very trenchant position that because of
the *plenitudo potestatis* the pope could even judge 'de feudo'[83] and that he
was 'iudex ordinarius omnium quoad spiritualia et quoad temporalia.'[84]

These opinions do not serve well as an introduction to an examination of the
typical canonist view of the *plenitudo potestatis* and temporal affairs. For
Per venerabilem was from its first appearance in *Compilatio* III, and remained,
a controversial document among canonists and its doctrine concerning papal
legitimation in temporal affairs, as has been seen, was flatly rejected in the

---

[82] As reported, for example, by Richardus Anglicus, *Summa questionum*: 'Hii enim, qui
summum pontificem utrumque gladium habere (affirmant), alterum tantum auctoritate
alterum auctoritate et administratione, dicunt imperatorem habere gladium a summo pontifice et secundum hoc summus pontifex quemlibet potest restituere infamatum ut ille, qui
habet plenitudinem potestatis': ed. Stickler, *Sacerdotium et Regnum* 42. Somewhat later
Alanus reported the same view: 'Secundum illos qui dicunt quod imperator et reges terre
debent a papa iurisdictionem habere, potest papa infamiam iuris omnino remittere et quoad
actus canonicos et quoad actus legitimos etiam a civili iudice irrogatam. Secundum alios qui
hoc non concedunt non potest remittere nisi quoad actus ecclesiasticos': ad C.2 q.3 c.7, ed.
Stickler, *Alanus Anglicus* 365-66.

[83] Text at p. 50 n. 29 above.

[84] This phrase had particular relevance in Alanus's thought to the deposing power, as
analyzed above p. 50.

glossa ordinaria ad Decretales.[85] Similarly the views of Alanus Anglicus were exceptional among the canonists of his own time and not all of them commanded acceptance from his successors.[86]

Instead of beginning with the first introduction of the term when many of the arguments surrounding it were disputed, it is perhaps better to examine the position more towards the end of our period when there had been time for further discussion and reflection and it is easier to separate the received opinion of canonists generally from the opinions of individual popes and canonists.

What, by the end of the period, had become the keystone of the structure of canonists' political thinking? It has been argued above that the major development in canonist thought about the papal role in temporal affairs was associated with a particular view of the practical implications for the affairs of Christendom of the vicariate of Christ.[87] Innocent IV had been presented with the problem of demonstrating by some principle of divine law that the papacy had a legitimate title for its various interventions in the temporal order. He had taken the standard canonist list of the occasions known to the law when such interventions had been made and fitted it into an interpretation of Christian history. A theology of history proved a juridical doctrine of necessity, of prerogative. Divine providence had ordered the government of the *populus Dei* from its first beginnings in the Old Dispensation. Government by God's representatives was a feature of universal history and had reached its full consummation in the New Dispensation, when the *vicarius Christi* exercised his authority over Christendom. Innocent had looked particularly at the practical consequences of this *regimen* and concluded that it provided the justification for the legality of the deposition of Frederick II, the punishment of negligent rulers and the recourse of anyone to the papal tribunal for justice when for any reason the normal machinery for providing justice was not functioning. In short, this was a claim to be something very like that which Maitland described as the 'omnicompetent court of first instance for the whole of Christendom.' Innocent IV did claim that in judging Frederick II he had acted as 'iudex ordinarius' of the case. He also associated

---

[85] '. . . quo ad forum seculare non potest legitimare, nisi princeps ei permitteret': ad 4.17.13 s. v. *beati Petri*. Cf. also the gloss s. v. *habeat potestatem*.

[86] Thus Bernard of Parma did not accept Alanus's term *iudex ordinarius quoad spiritualia et quoad temporalia*: '(*constitutio papae*) *omnes astringit*: cum sit iudex ordinarius omnium Christianorum et mater [*sic*] omnium ecclesiarum, ut ix.q.iii. Cuncta per mundum, et si etiam aliquid graue praecipiat, faciendum est, xix. dist. In memoriam (c.3), et c.dist. Contra morem (c.8). Et dic 'omnes,' scilicet de sua iurisdictione, quoniam potestates distinctae sunt, x. dist. Quoniam, et infra de appell. Si duobus (2.28.7), nisi forte ratione peccati, infra de iud. Novit (2.1.13)': *Glossa ord.* X. 1.2.13. See also a similar text, p. 56 above.

[87] See above pp. 67-71.

his vicariate with the exercise of *plenitudo potestatis* in the affairs of kings and kingdoms.

The context of this association concerned the right of the pope to fill a vacancy of kingship should it arise. He argued on the basis of *Venerabilem* that there was little problem of principle as far as the Empire was concerned. If the electors were negligent, then the pope would choose an emperor; if there was a divided election, the pope would make a definitive choice. Whilst the Empire was vacant, its jurisdiction devolved on the pope. All this was justified, following *Venerabilem*, on the 'specialis coniunctio' between pope and emperor forged by the Translation of the Empire, the papal rights of examination and consecration which followed from it and the acknowledgement by the emperor of his status in his coronation oath. But there was a problem of principle in relation to other rulers where no such special bond obtained. Innocent formulated the problem and solved it:

> Sed quid si alius rex est negligens, vel alius princeps qui superiorem non habet? Dicimus idem, scilicet, quod succedit in iurisdictione eius . . . sed hoc non facit quia ab eo teneat regnum, *sed de plenitudine potestatis quam habet quia uicarius est Christi.*[88]

If, then, there was no other superior to whom recourse might be had in this crisis, the pope would act as that superior in an act of prerogative power held in virtue of his *plenitudo potestatis* as vicar of Christ. He would supply this deficiency, just as he would any other defect of law if for lack of a higher authority justice would be denied anyone or peace endangered.

This was a way of regarding the plenitude of power as if it constituted a reserve of power in the constitution of society from which the deficiencies

---

[88] '*Vacante*: hoc est propter defectum imperii; in iure enim imperii papa succedit. Unde si alius rector alii superiori quam imperatori subditus negligens esset in reddenda ratione vel non esset rector in aliqua terra, tunc non devolvetur iurisdictio ad papam sed ad proximum superiorem. Nam specialis coniunctio est inter papam et imperatorem, quia papa eum consecrat et examinat et est imperator eius advocatus, et iurat ei, et ab eo imperium tenet, supra de elec. Venerabilem, lxiii di. Ego, Tibi domino, et inde est quod in iure quod ab ecclesia romana tenet, succedit papa imperio vacante. Sed quid si non sit negligens sed subditi sunt sic inobedientes quod non possunt facere iusticiam? Tunc non credo quod succedat in iurisdictionem eius, sed debet eum iuvare et domare rebellionem subditorum, ar. xcvi di. Cum ad verum. Sed quid si alius rex est negligens vel alius princeps qui superiorem non habet? Dicimus idem, scilicet quod succedit in iurisdictione eius, ar. xv. q. vi. Item alius, et supra de elec. Cum inter universas, in fi. Sed hoc non facit quia ab eo teneat regnum, sed de plenitudine potestatis quam habet quia vicarius est Christi supra tit. prox., Novit ver. Non enim. Vel dic quod vacantibus regnis non poterit se intromittere nisi quando peteret in modum denunciationis, ut predicto c. Novit': *App.* ad 2.2.10. — Guilelmus Durantis agreed with this contention, but justified it on the principle that the pope was 'ordinarius omnium fidelium' — a very clear illustration of how closely the terms *plenitudo potestatis* and *iudex ordinarius omnium* were related (cf. *Speculum iudiciale* 2.1. *de comp. iudicis adit.* n. 29).

of lower jurisdictions could be supplemented and provision be made for emergencies. It must be emphasized that popes had been using language of this sort, in relation to ecclesiastical matters, when they were acting outside the regular processes of law, since the time of Innocent III. The line of thought can be simply illustrated with reference to episcopal elections.

Normal electoral machinery in the thirteenth century was capitular election followed by the canonical examination of the election and the elect, performed by the metropolitan.[89] If all went according to the accepted procedure the pope had no part in the proceedings. But if the electors were negligent or there was a divided election or for any other reason due procedure was not working regularly, then the pope, 'supplens ex plenitudine potestatis,' would act to ensure that a bishop was duly appointed. He might do this in a number of ways depending on circumstances: decide as to which of contending candidates was properly elected, provide the chapter's nominee to the see even though the election had been irregular, make a provision of someone else, or even make the chapters' proctors who had come to the curia act as the electors, and so on. But though the manner in which the defect might be remedied could vary, the principle underlying the papal action remained the same. His plenitude of power existed to make good deficiencies and negligences in men's actions and legal procedures. That reserve of power in the constitution of the Church which he held precisely to supplement defect by acting outside the compass of existing law was drawn upon and he acted on his discretionary power, *ex plenitudine potestatis*. The power was one to act *supra* or *praeter solitum cursum legis* and was generally exercised in practice to remove obstacles to the proper functioning of judicial and administrative machinery in ways that he alone could decide were appropriate. For if the function of the pope was to provide for the 'communibus utilitatibus,[90]' it was necessary to postulate for him an unfettered discretionary power to decide how such provision should best be made. 'Plenitudo potestatis omnia supplet.'[91]

Papal letters illustrate this process in action in a number of ecclesiastical matters as a routine feature of thirteenth-century papal government.[92] When

---

[89] The authoritative study of the canon law of episcopal elections is that of G. Barraclough, 'The Making of a Bishop in the Middle Ages,' *Catholic Historical Review* 19 (1933-4) 275-319. F.M. Powicke, *Henry III and the Lord Edward* I (Oxford 1947) 258-74, is a valuable study of the role of the papacy in thirteenth-century English episcopal appointments. I have studied the question in relation to Ireland and have presented a summary of findings in 'The Papacy and Episcopal Appointments in Thirteenth Century Ireland,' *Proceedings of the Irish Catholic Historical Committee* (1960) 1-9.

[90] Hostiensis: '(Romanus pontifex) cuius interest communibus utilitatibus providere': *Apparatus* ad 3.38.17 s.v. *Romano pontifici*.

[91] Hostiensis, *Summa*, 1.44 § 4, col. 373.

[92] The principle was expressed as one whereby provision for *necessitas* or *evidens utilitas* was made *de plenitudine potestatis*. The plenitude of power was thus seen as a reservoir of

the language in which such exercises of the discretionary power was already established in the formulae of the papal chancery, canonists took note of it to clarify their understanding of the terminology. Hostiensis distinguished between the papal *plenitudo officii* and the papal *plenitudo potestatis*. The former applied when the pope exercised his authority in the ways which canon law already prescribed for him, namely, in all the circumstances canonists listed as 'maiores causae' reserved to the pope alone. The latter applied when the pope by exercising his absolute power, acted outside the normal course of law — either *supra ius* because he had decided to set existing law aside (dispensation was the best example of this) or because existing law was inadequate for the particular circumstances in question. 'Plenitudo potestatis' thus stood for a theory of prerogative, in that sense of the word which sees its essence as an indefinite power to act out of the ordinary course of the law.[93]

This was the meaning of 'plenitudo potestatis' which Innocent IV had applied to the political order. The pope, he was arguing, had a prerogative power in Christendom. He was not merely head of the purely clerical and ecclesiastical order. He was head of the Christian world which comprehended all Christians, not merely as private individuals, but as organized in political societies and as holders of public office. He was, as Innocent III has stressed, the 'fundamentum totius Christianitatis'[94] charged to provide for the 'necessitas et utilitas totius populi Christiani.'[95] Power was committed to the pope sufficiently for him to have charge of the whole governmental order. Since

---

power which was drawn upon to supply defect, amend the law or dispense from it according as the general welfare demanded such 'extraordinary' action. Cf. e.g. Honorius III: ' . . . cum urgens necessitas exigit vel evidens utilitas maxime publica persuadet, sic laxat provide circa quosdam de suae plenitudine potestatis': MGH *Epp.s.XIII*, I no. 234, p. 163. Gregory IX: 'Indulte nobis a Domino plenitudinem potestatis secundum diversitatem accidentium experiri nos convenit in necessitatibus subiectorum . . . ' *ibid.* no. 637, p.350. Innocent IV: ' . . . quoniam ad hoc Deus in apostolica sede constituit plenitudinem potestatis, ut Romanus pontifex, qui claves in beato Petro potestatis et discretionis accepit, nunc statuta vallet rigoribus, ea dispensative relaxet, prout necessitatis articulis interpellat': *ibid.* II no. 8, p. 8. Naturally this way of thinking left its impress on the *Corpus iuris.* Hostiensis wrote of it: 'Suppletque scilicet defectum si quis est, infra de transac. cap. 1 (1.36.1); ideo tota die in confirmationibus beneficiorum apponitur haec clausula: supplentes defectum, si qua est, de plenitudine potestatis, et comprobatus supra, de elect. Illa quotidiana instantia (1.6.39), nam secundum ipsam potest de iure supra ius dispensare, ut infra de concess. praeb. et eccl. non vacan. Proposuit § ult. (3.8.4)': *Summa* 1.32 § 3, col. 281.

[93] Hostiensis: ' . . . tunc potest dici papam uti plenitudine officii quando secundum iura ius reddit, ut ibi (scil. 6.44 § Caeterum); quando vero transcendit iura, tunc utitur plenitudine potestatis, de quo habes multa exempla infra de offic. leg. § quid pertinet ad officium, vers. quid ergo et seq.': *Summa* 1.8 § 2, col. 135.

[94] Cf. RNRI no. 44 (ed. Kempf 125 lines 3-12); PL 215.1231.

[95] Cf. e.g. PL 214.386,470,979; 215.957; 216.36.

he had the *tota potentia gubernativa*,[96] every contingency of the legislative, judicial and executive order was related to his office. Plenitude of power in Christian society as a whole, not merely in the purely ecclesiastical order, 'omnia supplet.'

Thus the basic assumption underlying Innocent IV's claim that he might as vicar of Christ make provision for a vacancy in a kingdom 'ex plenitudine potestatis' was that the society of all Christians in their political groupings constituted a unity of one Christian people, a community of western kingdoms and nations unified in a common allegiance to the papacy. That on the level of practical affairs, the allegiance was sometimes shadowy and that sometimes the terms in which the papacy demanded recognition of that allegiance were rejected, does not diminish the importance this concept holds in papal and canonist theories in the thirteenth century. Indeed it may well have been the more insisted on according as it was felt to be increasingly under attack and its hold on the minds of Christian emperors, kings and subjects weakening.

For assuredly this was not a new concept of papal thinking about the primacy. A wealth of terms — *Christianitas, populus Christianus, gens* or *societas Christiana*, typically — all in use before ever Gratian compiled his *Decretum*, testifies that the canonists did not invent the idea that Christian society formed a supranational entity. For some centuries the papacy had consciously fostered the idea among the nations of the West, that they constituted a single *communitas*, united through their common Christian 'citizenship,' directed through a common allegiance to itself, informed by a common political ethic, of which the papacy was the guardian, interpreter and judge, susceptible of pursuing a good common to the whole, transcending the individual goods of particular parts. It is a nice point in the history of early papal political ideas as to whether the concept of this society was distinguished from that of the Church — whether there was a distinction between *ecclesia* and *christianitas* or between *ecclesia universalis* and *populus christianus* — or whether it was merely included in the notion of the Church as such. But whatever view is taken on that point, the fact remains that the papacy saw itself and demanded recognition of itself, as the head of an international society composed of the *ensemble* of Christian kingdoms and cities.

There was a certain practical reality behind this ideal. It was not merely one of the pious platitudes of the age without real meaning in the world of affairs. It contributed, for example, to the crusading sentiment, for the holy war was the supreme manifestation of the common Christian civic spirit. It had a certain part to play in European diplomacy for papal intervention or approval of an action or arbitration sometimes might be a help, or be thought to offer a possibility of help, to politicians to gain their ends, or to their victims

---

[96] A phrase of James of Viterbo, *De regimine christiano*, ed.cit. 272.

to thwart them. It was not only the ecclesiastics of the twelfth and thirteenth centuries who had developed, and had been encouraged to develop, the practice of looking to Rome for guidance in the conduct of their affairs. Kings, barons and communes too, looked for papal help when they thought it would serve their interests. It was not an altogether empty boast that Rome was the *communis omnium Christiani populi nationum curia*[97] in the thirteenth century.

Though the concept and reality of Christendom was not new in the thirteenth century, it was nonetheless particularly the period when ecclesiastical writers, of different disciplines, became articulate about it. One might speculate on the reasons for this, though it is not easy to give a wholly satisfactory explanation.

In the practical order, the vigorous political activity of Innocent III, stemming from his own deeply felt and forcefully expressed view of the papal leadership of Christendom was clearly a very important influence in directing men's minds to reexpress traditional ideas about the nature of the unity of Christian society. Also significant, through renewing consciousness of the existence of a common good for Christendom as a whole was the urgent propagandizing of the Crusade, against the twin foes of Christian society, infidel and heretic, initiated by Innocent III, continued by his successors, and extended by them to combat others marked down as common enemies of Christendom: Greek schismatics, German and Italian rebels (Hohenstaufen supporters, for example). Not least important was a sense of challenge to papal authority — in an overt way by the Hohenstaufen from the time of Henry VI and also implicitly, by the rise of national states, potentially autonomous units whose existence had to be comprehended within Christendom.

In the order of ideas, certain trends of thought can be singled out for their especial relevance to the new interest in the unity of the existing Christian political order. The synthetic trend of scholasticism brought to the concept of *ecclesia*, if not a wealth of profundity at least a breadth of discussion among different sorts of ecclesiastical writers who were trying to gather together the whole subject matter of their disciplines. Theologian, philosopher and lawyer, each in his different way was concerned with the *ecclesia* and its inherent unity: they have in common a view of the Church as forming in some sense a body politic. Historians of theology have shown in some detail how the concept of the Church underwent a very significant change in this period, whereby the meaning of the term *corpus mysticum Christi* became, so to say, politicized.[98] A term which earlier had been charged with liturgical, sacra-

---

[97] Cf. Boniface VIII, *Extrav. Comm.* 2.3.1.

[98] Cf. especially H. de Lubac, *Corpus Mysticum* (2nd. ed. Paris 1949) and E. H. Kantorowicz, *The King's Two Bodies* (Princeton 1957) 193-206.

mental and transcendental meaning was transformed into a 'relatively colourless sociological, organological or juristic notion' denoting merely the Christian polity or Christendom.[99] More philosophical notions in the shape of concepts of order — the *ordinatio ad unum*, so brilliantly analyzed by Gierke — both neo-Aristotelian and neo-Platonist, reinforced this concept of the Church as a *politia Christiana*.

Too little is as yet known of the interaction of theological and canonical thought to be able to say with precision just what the canonists contributed to this development among more abstract thinkers and what they received from it. That they may have been primarily responsible for initiating it is not impossible, for the penetration of juristic ways of thinking into theological speculation was probably deeper than is often suspected. But that they shared to the full in this particular movement of ideas is beyond question. From the beginning of the thirteenth century, canonists were increasingly inclined to stress a unitary view of Christian society which twelfth-century canonists, on the whole, had been content to take for granted. It underlay their thought without ever being made very explicit.

By the time of Innocent IV, however, it was very explicit. The unity of the Christian body which theologians expounded by way of *corpus mysticum* and philosophers by *ordinatio ad unum* was expounded by canonists as *regimen unius personae*. The logic behind this expression of Innocent IV's was very simple. Christ had given tutelage over the whole agglomeration of Christian organizations, clerical and lay, to His vicar to ensure that all, individuals, office-holders, organizations, should contribute each according to his due measure to the preservation of the means whereby life on earth was organized to ensure life after death. The end of Christian society was the attainment of salvation. He who had the supreme responsibility for the welfare of souls had within his authority sufficient power to ensure that the organization of Christian society was a means to salvation and not an obstacle. Canonists had justice as their particular concern. They therefore emphasized particularly the papal power of safeguarding the justice of Christendom. This the pope might do typically in two main ways — by punishing those who ruled unjustly, which he would judge for himself since justice is a moral concept: and secondly, by providing remedy when justice was impeded. *Plenitudo potestatis* and *iudex ordinarius omnium* meant, to Innocent IV and Hostiensis, besides the notion of papal sovereignty in the purely ecclesiastical hierarchy, possession of power sufficient to uphold the justice and therefore, general welfare of Christendom as a whole. It was in this sense, and this sense only, that Hostiensis could call the pope 'dominus spiritualium et temporalium.'

---

[99] Kantorowicz, *op. cit.* 202.

PART III

HOSTIENSIS AND THE PAPAL POWER IN TEMPORAL AFFAIRS

In attempting to describe the evolution of canonist thought, and in analyzing two of its major formulae, the focus of attention was Innocent IV, the first of the two thirteenth-century canonists who made of earlier canonist theory something approaching a complete logic of the papal power in temporal affairs. It is time now to turn to the second of these writers, his particular follower, Henry of Susa, perhaps the most interesting thirteenth-century canonist and certainly the author of the most complete analysis of papal power, up to his date.

Hostiensis was one of the great churchmen of a century when such were not rare. Few others, however, combined so signally as active a life both pastorally and in the diplomacy of the highest European political circles, with high academic distinction and notable personal sanctity.[1] As an academic he ranks as the first to furnish a great synthesis of ecclesiastical jurisprudence; his works denote the final achievement of its maturity as an autonomous sacred discipline, nourished by both theology and Roman law, but yet consciously distinct from them.[2] His political views reflect this balance of canon law between theology and law: they are in themselves distinctively canonist in their expression, but Hostiensis did not hesitate to borrow from theolo-

---

[1] Hostiensis's career has been in part thoroughly investigated by N. Didier, 'Henri de Suse en Angleterre (1236?-1244),' *Studi Arangio Ruiz* (Naples 1952) 333-51; 'Henri de Suse, prieur d'Antibes et prévôt de Grasse (1235?-1245),' *Studia Gratiana* 2 (1954) 595-617; 'Henri de Suse, évêque de Sisteron (1244-1250)' *Rev. hist. dr. franç. et étrang.*[4] 31 (1945) 244-70, 409-29. For his later life and an assessment of his work, C. Lefebvre in DDC 5.1211-1227 is especially valuable. Hostiensis became archbishop of Embrun *c.* 1250 and was made cardinal in 1262. His *Summa* was finished in 1253 and his *Apparatus* shortly before his death in 1271.

[2] Hostiensis discussed this question at some length in the *Proemium* to his *Summa* and adverted to it at other points in his work, e.g. *App.* 1.1.1 s.v. *quasi communem.*

gians and especially civilians if his positions might thereby be strengthened.

His outstanding position in Christendom gives his political views a particular interest. Based on an extremely thorough knowledge of canonist and civilian literature, they were written by a man with long and intimate experience of political affairs both in the curia and outside. There is therefore a vein of actuality running through his work which gives it an immediacy often felt to be lacking in more purely academic writers of the period. Further, his work was an immense influence on later thought, and directly or indirectly his mark is to be discerned on much of later ecclesiastical political thought. It was as if he typified the canonist writing of the thirteenth century. For the modern student there is a third reason for giving special attention to Hostiensis. His work has the great virtue of comprehensiveness. Hostiensis wrote with considerable clarity and at length, even verbosely. After the laconic commentary of Innocent IV, in whose writing ambiguities are often caused as much by his omissions as by any inherent complexity of the matter at issue, the repetitiveness of Hostiensis is a welcome aid to understanding.

Hostiensis' views on the papal power in temporal affairs were a compound of three main elements. The whole was rested on the decretals of Innocent III, for whom he had a special veneration — *Novit, Per venerabilem* and *Solite* in particular. It will be recalled that these decretals had a decretist background, of which Hostiensis was fully aware. On this basis, lines already well indicated by Innocent IV were developed, specifically those which emphasized the unity of Christian society and a 'temporalized' view of the kingship of Christ exercised by His vicar over Christendom. There was, thirdly, much additional support to be drawn from the commentators of the *Compilationes Antiquae* and the *Gregoriana* of whom Tancred, Bernard of Parma (*glossa ordinaria*) and Goffredus de Trano would appear to have been the most influential in the context of papal power. On only one occasion did Hostiensis include political material from non-legal sources — from Alexander of Hales, whose opinion in the particular context was drawn almost directly from Hugh of St. Victor. It goes almost without saying that whenever possible, Hostiensis supported canon law and canonist opinion with Roman law and civilian opinion.

The examination of Hostiensis' views of papal power might well begin by noticing that political writers of a slightly later period had radically different interpretations of the nature of his opinions. The existence of this conflict serves as a warning of the need to exert great care in deciding what was his real view of any matter. A detailed examination of the nature of the conflict reveals the double interpretative trend that runs throughout Hostiensis' writings. For each view represents a part of the total content of his thought.

To anti-papalists, Hostiensis was an extremist, one who professed views which over-circumscribed the independence of the secular power by an exaggerated view of papal supremacy. Thus the anonymous treatise *Rex pacificus* could formulate the charge against him:

> Quidam enim dixerunt dominum papam esse dominum omnium, non solum in spiritualibus, sed etiam in temporalibus. Et istius opinionis multum adhaesive fuit dominus Hostiensis qui fecit Summam Iuris, quae dicitur Summa copiosa. Specialius tamen hoc probat in Apparatu suo super decretales, Extr. Qui filii sint legitimi, per venerabilem, super § rationibus.[3]

On the other hand, for some papalists, as for example Aegidius Spiritalis de Perusio, he seemed to err in exactly the opposite direction in maintaining an undue limitation on the papal power in temporal affairs:

> Sed maxime miror de domino Ostiensi, qui nescio quo ductus iudicio rationis dixit: dico quod papa non habet se intromittere de temporalibus in alterius preiudicium, extr. qui filii sint legitimi, per venerabilem, § versu. insuper, nec regulariter nisi in casibus, extr. qui filii sint legitimi, per venerabilem § rationibus, prout idem Ostiensis notat, extr. qui filii sint legitimi, in c. causam que, ii.[4]

Our problem is to decide which of these interpretations — each based, it is to be noticed, on the same text of Hostiensis — was correct or at least the nearer to the essential Hostiensis. It is a problem which goes wider and deeper than the work of one canonist, no matter how important in himself. For it would be possible to go to the canonist tradition as a whole and by selective reading urge each of these positions. The collective work of the thirteenth-century canonists could be, and was, exploited by political writers of a later age to argue each of these antithetical opinions. Which represents the authentic canonist position? Was Hostiensis an extremist as *Rex pacificus* so roundly asserted? Or did he represent something nearer to a middle position between extremes as the formulation of Aegidius Spiritalis suggests?

Both writers cited the same texts of Hostiensis as the basis of their contentions — his commentaries on *Per venerabilem*. And it can be admitted at once that both writers were accurate enough in their reporting of his words. Whether their deductions from those words were accurate is, however, another story and can only be decided after first examining these particular commentaries *in toto* and then placing them within the whole composition of Hostiensis' political logic.

---

[3] This treatise, a product of the controversy between Philip the Fair (whose case it is arguing) and Boniface VIII, has been analyzed by W. Ullmann, 'A Medieval Document on Papal Theories of Government,' EHR 61 (1946) 180-201. I cite from the edition of Dupuy, *Histoire du différend d'entre le pape Boniface VIII et Philippe le Bel, Roy de France* (Paris 1655).

[4] *Libellus contra infideles et inobedientes et rebelles sancte Romane ecclesie et summo pontifici*, ed. R. Scholz, *Unbekannte kirchenpolitische Streitschriften aus der Zeit Ludwigs des Bayern (1327-1354)* II (Rome 1914) 105-29 at 111. The tract was written before 1334.

The glosses on *Per venerabilem* in the *Apparatus* and its discussion in the
Summa formed the lengthiest single chapter in Hostiensis' treatment of the
papal power in temporal affairs. He himself obviously held it as his major
exposition, as his frequent cross-references to it indicate. It is not an easy
chapter to read. When one of its passages can give rise to diametrically op-
posed interpretations, it is clear that careful reading is necessary; it must
therefore be considered in some detail. But *Rex pacificus* and Aegidius Spiritalis were right in giving emphasis to it, for it holds the key to Hostiensis'
final opinions on the nature and exercise of papal power in temporal affairs.

1. *The Commentary on 'Per Venerabilem'*

There were two main issues involved in *Per venerabilem*, the one reacting
on the other. The first, the narrower, was concerned with whether the pope
had the power to legitimize for the purpose of dynastic succession, and whether
he should, given the particular circumstances of the case, accede to William
of Montpellier's petition to exercise the power. The second, ranging more
widely, was concerned with the basis in divine law for papal intervention
de temporalibus and with the circumstances of the exercise of that power.
Hostiensis, among decretalists, had something new to say on each of these
issues. The different levels of his argumentation might for convenience of
analysis be put in this order: statement of the principle of *plenitudo potestatis*;
the legitimation problem reformulated; the principle of imperial *plenitudo
potestatis*; the legitimation problem solved; general considerations of the three
aspects of Church-State relations — the distinction of the powers, the supremacy of the spiritual (with particular reference to the exercise of *plenitudo
potestatis* in Christendom), and the cooperation of the powers.
Reverence for papal primacy was a pronounced feature of Hostiensis'
writings.[5] The commentary on *Per venerabilem* was his chosen place for some

---

[5] Two characteristic statements on the topic might be noticed: 'Summa sede sedet, in
illa videlicet quam Dominus sibi in personam Petri specialiter elegit, ut infra, qui fil. sint
legi. Per venerabilem, § rationibus, vers. sane; haec est navis quae licet fluctuat non pericli-
tatur, 24.q.1. Non turbatur et c. preced. et seq. et ad idem 19, 20, 21, 22 di. per totum; ideoque summus pontifex appellatur, infra de stat. monach. Cum ad monasterium, in fi. Ple-
nusque vicarius extat: quamvis enim quilibet episcopus dici possit vicarius Jesu Christi,
33.q.5, Mulierem, et supra de sacra unctio. c.i § ad exhibendum v. caput iungitur et § seq.
v. ad quod etiam, est tamen particularis, sed papa est vicarius generalis unde omnia gerit
de omnibus prout placet iudicat et disponit, 9.q.3. Cuncta per mundum et c. Per principalem, 2. q. 6. Ideo 1 et 2, et de hoc satis not. supra de translation. episcopi § cuius auctoritate v. patet, et ex praemissis et praecedentibus et sequentibus; est etiam plenus, id est,
habens plenitudinem potestatis, ad quam vocatus est, alii vero in partem sollicitudinis, supra
de usu pal. Ad honorem, 2.q.6. Decreto et c. Qui se scit. Ideo breviter dic quod dummodo
contra fidem non veniat in omnibus et per omnia potest facere et dicere quicquid placet,
auferendo etiam ius suum cui vult, quia nec aliquis audet ei dicere, cur ita facis? 19 di.

of his most characteristic interpretations of it. The term *plenitudo potestatis* (which was used in the decretal itself) gave his interpretation its unifying theme and was exploited in each of its main canonistic significances: as the generic term for the expression of papal sovereignty in the hierarchy of ecclesiastical jurisdictions and as comprehending, by extension, the headship of Christian society as a whole. The Petrine texts cited in the decretal gave Hostiensis an opportunity to synthesize the traditional view of the primacy as known to canonists through the *Decretum*.

Rome, the 'altera hierusalem' in that it had been sanctified by a second crucifixion when Christ's 'primus vicarius' was martyred, was the 'caput et domina et princeps omnium ecclesiarum . . . mater et magistra cunctorum fidelium,' divinely empowered with the fulness of power. Such was this power, Hostiensis concluded, that

> Dicamus igitur cum domino Innocentio iii. quod quicquid facit papa Deus facere creditur, dumtamen evidenter non peccet, nec faciat contra fidem.[6]

Hence Hostiensis was extremely anxious not to comment *contra textum*. He had sharp things to say about the standards of scholarship and weakness of faith of some earlier canonists who seemed to him to have done so, thereby derogating from 'tantum imperium potestatis.'[7] Hostiensis set himself to extract the full force of Innocentian doctrine.

All decretalists before Hostiensis, with the exception of Alanus, had to a greater or less extent demurred at the claim that the pope could legitimize for temporal purposes. As has been seen earlier, a series of reservations had been entered, even by men like Tancred and Innocent IV, who were far from being apathetic about strengthening the compass of papal monarchy. Hostiensis had little sympathy for such hesitations and struck out along a new path which, he considered, brought canonists back to the real mind of the legislator.

All his predecessors had begun their discussion with the premise that the pope could legitimize in the spiritual order and the emperor in the temporal

---

In memoriam, de poen. dist. 3 para. ex persona, et omne ius tollere, et de iure supra ius dispensare, infra de cog. spirit. Capite, infra de concess. preb. et eccles. non vacan. Proposuit, quia veri Dei vicem gerit in terris, supra de translat. episcopi, Inter corporalia, respons. 1 et c. Quanto, respons. 1, infra ut bene. eccles. Ut nostrum § 1 v. porro': *Summa* 1.32 § 3. 'Consistorium Dei et pape unum et idem est censendum, Ex. domini nostri (i.e. Innocent IV), de appell. Romana, quia et locum Dei tenet, infra ut benefi. eccl. c.1 § 1 et in ligando et in solvendo ratum est quicquid facit clave non errante, sic intelligas 24.q.1 Quodcunque ligaveris. . . . . . Et breviter excepto peccato quasi omnia de iure potest ut Deus . . . ': *App.* ad 1.7.3 s.v. *veri Dei vicem*. For further references of this type see my paper, 'The Use of the Term *plenitudo potestatis* by Hostiensis,' cited p. 86, n. 41, *supra*.

[6] *App.* ad 4.17.13 s.v. *casualiter.*

[7] *Ibid.* s.v. *quod non solum.*

order. Hostiensis denied this. For him, the pope alone had power to legitimize; the emperor had no power of legitimation. Marriage, a sacrament, acknowledged to be a spiritual matter, was the concern of the Church alone, and its jurisdiction — with its 'accessoria' such as legitimation — was a matter for the ecclesiastical court. The emperor might allow a bastard previously disinherited to succeed, but this would not be legitimation in the strict sense. The dispensed would merely be being admitted to the inheritance '*tanquam legitimus.*'[8]

It followed then that the pope within the limits of divine law certainly had the power to legitimize in temporal matters. But Hostiensis was not prepared to go on immediately to argue that therefore he could legitimize for all secular purposes. Fifty years of canonist contention warned him that there was no straightforward application of the principle of sole papal legitimation to inheritance of temporal possessions. Further, there was his own very real appreciation of the imperial *principatus* (his own term)[9] and his recognition that the emperor was in some sense at least a sovereign ruler, holder of *plenitudo potestatis* (again, his own term)[10] in temporal affairs. For Hostiensis the emperor was 'Dei vicarius in terris in temporalibus,'[11] with a greater power in temporal affairs than the pope:

> imperator praeest omnibus temporalibus immediate . . . sed et quamvis persona imperatoris subsit pape et temporalia per quamdam consequentiam, tamen imperator *magis* potest in temporalibus que a Deo immediate tenet ut supra dictum est, et ideo dummodo caveat a peccato, de ipsis potest disponere prout placet.[12]

Hence the sole papal right of true legitimation had to be balanced against this imperial immediate jurisdiction in such matters as hereditary succession.

---

[8] 'Dicunt tamen Vincentius, Laurentius et Tancredus quod papa non potest legitimare quo ad hereditatem temporalem nisi in patrimonio B. Petri . . . . Johannes (Teutonicus) dicit quod hoc uerum est directe, sed indirecte hoc potest, sive per consequentiam: quia eo ipso quod aliquem legitimat quo ad seculares actus, videtur per consequens legitimatus quo ad temporales, nam si maiora conceduntur, ergo et minora . . . sed illud certum est, quod imperator legitimare potest quo ad temporalia, non quo ad spiritualia . . . Salva reverentia aliorum mihi videtur, dominum papam habere potestatem legitimandi quo ad spiritualia et temporalia et ipsum solum . . . nam causa matrimonialis spiritualiter pertineat ad ecclesiam, adeo quod secularis iudex de ipsa cognoscere non potest etiam si inciderit, nec de legitima filiatione . . . dicas tamen quod imperator legitimat, id est tanquam legitimum etiam spurium ad hereditatem suam admittere potest . . . ': *Summa* 4.17. § 11.

[9] *Apparatus* ad 1.23.10 s.v. *sit situm.*

[10] ' . . . et quod solutus est princeps legibus . . . appellationem ad ipsum factam poterit recipere de plenitudine potestatis, contra quam non intendimus disputare . . . ': *Summa* 2.28. § 4.

[11] *Apparatus* ad 4.17.13 s.v. *recognoscat.*

[12] *Ibid.* s.v. *casualiter.*

Hostiensis' attempt to reconcile these two positions, though not without its ambiguities, constituted one of the most nuanced discussions of the relations of the two powers in thirteenth-century canonist writing.

The problem resolved itself into this: Hostiensis wished, on the one hand, to preserve the principle of papal monopoly of general legislation concerning marriage, and on the other, to give real meaning in practice to his principle that 'de ipsis [temporalibus imperator] potest disponere prout placet.'

Only the pope could declare a universal law concerning marriage. Putative marriage afforded an example: only the pope could promulgate a general law that a marriage invalid in itself, if contracted in good faith, was to have the same effects as a valid one. No emperor might make a law of this sort which laid down rules governing the validity of marriage. But the result of a judgment given of putative marriage legitimated the children, and Hostiensis clearly intended that such ecclesiastical jurisdiction should have this effect. But he did not consider it a power in temporal affairs similar to that of the emperor; it was legitimation for temporal purposes, 'casualiter,' indirectly.

This different nature of the papal power from the imperial power in temporal affairs led Hostiensis to make a distinction which gave practical consequence to the principle. According to Hostiensis, Roman law established that in exceptional circumstances the emperor might deprive a subject of his *ius acquisitum*. The pope too might do this in the ecclesiastical order, but Hostiensis would not grant him an unreserved right to do it in the temporal order. He therefore compromised and made use of the distinction established by his predecessors between legitimation *quoad hereditatem* and legitimation *quoad honores seculares et actus legitimos in quibus non vertitur privatum interesse*. Hereditary right was a 'private interest' because there was already some one in possession. Only the emperor could dispossess the existing possessor in favor of the newly legitimated and he could only do it in grave circumstances. But the pope could only do it 'eo qui ius habet consentiente'[13] In brief, the

---

[13] 'Potest tamen dispensare seu legitimare si vult idem papa quo ad ecclesiastica et secularia ubi habet temporalem iurisdictionem, et in aliis casibus, ut supra dixi . . . quod intelligas sic: ne fiat preiudicium illi ad quem iam devoluta est hereditas, verum eo qui ius habet consentiente, proderit legitimatio quo ad omnia . . . alias non proderit nisi quo ad spiritualia et honores seculares et actus legitimos in quibus non vertitur privatum interesse . . . . . Imperator autem potest auferre etiam acquisitum ius, sed forte non sine peccato, nisi ex magna causa fieret . . . vel nisi donandi animum habeat . . . sed papa non potest nisi casualiter, licet per generalem constitutionem solus papa legitimet vel illegitimet et sic generaliter potestas solius papae est specialis; quo ad secularia in quibus vertitur privatum interesse solius imperatoris, nisi in casu; sed quo ad ecclesiastica, solius papae; communis autem est utriusque quo ad secularia in quibus non praeiudicatur alicui: hoc salvo, quod per papam vere legitimatur aliquando, sed per imperatorem nunquam, licet aliquis per ipsum tanquam legitimus admittatur': *Summa* 4.17. § 11.

pope could only legitimize for succession to property if the holder of the title to it agreed to his doing so.

Clearly this was not an altogether satisfactory discussion, leaving many points unanswered and making use of a distincton between 'public' and 'private' interests which in this context seems artificial. Nevertheless, it was a genuine attempt to apply principles to cases and it resulted in an attempted solution which, for all its defects, was hardly an extreme one since it contained a limitation on papal powers and was prepared to recognize a degree of secular autonomy in temporal affairs. The opinion was implicit in Hostiensis' argument that legitimation for purposes of succession was primarily a matter for the temporal power. What emerged from this aspect of Hostiensis' thought as a general principle, was the consideration that the pope could not intervene in the temporal order *in preiudicium alterius*. It was a principle that Hostiensis was to use in all circumstances when he was relating general considerations of the supremacy of the spiritual to a specific problem of intervention in the temporal order. In the overall assessment of his final positions concerning the relations of the two powers, it is an important one. The hierocrat Aegidius Spiritalis was right to single out this view of Hostiensis as a sensible modification of papal absolutism in temporal affairs.

Nevertheless, despite a clearly dualist vein discernible in the solution of the legitimation problem, the tenor of his commentary as a whole on *Per venerabilem* was strongly monist. He took the opportunity of rehearsing most of the characteristic canonist arguments in support of papal power in temporal affairs; the derivation of imperial power from the pope's authority demonstrated through a 'two swords' discussion, the papal right of deposition, the *imperium spirituale*, the ancillary nature of secular power when the clergy demanded help — all were asserted in somewhat inflated language. What is of real interest in all this, is to see his return to the theme introduced by Innocent IV, and adopted by Hostiensis in his commentary on *Licet ex suscepto:* the vicariate of Christ as a preordained fact of Christian history and the one stable feature of the *regimen Christianum.* It was above all the unitary nature of Christendom which he emphasized, and its consequential subjection to its ruler,[14] the 'unus vicarius legitimus generalis in terris' who

> superest et preest omnibus . . . et hanc maioritatem et potestatem et auctoritatem summam et excellentem in omnibus et per omnia et super omnibus christianis totius mundi indistincte sibi datam concedo . . . Habet enim papa ipse plenitudinem potestatis . . . Et maior et superior est omnibus christianis.[15]

---

[14] ' . . . . cui omnes homines debent esse subiecti, et ei in omnibus obedire, cuius nauis stabilis est et immutabilis, nam etsi quandoque fluctuet non mergeretur': *App.* ad 4.17.13 (*Per venerabilem*) s.v. *plenitudinem potestatis.*

[15] *Loc. cit.*

All Christians form one body — 'una ecclesia generalis simul collecta.'[16] The identification of the traditional Pauline notion of the unity of the Church with the unity of the society of Christian nations forming Christendom was complete. The vicar of Christ was the sole head of the Christian body politic:

> ergo quo ad maioritatem unum caput est tantum, scilicet papa: unus debet tantum esse caput nostrum, dominus spiritualium et temporalium, quia ipsius est orbis et plenitudo eius ut de dec. c. Tua nobis (3.30.26: Ps. 23. 1), quia omnia commisit Petro . . . [17]

It was this text which the author of *Rex pacificus* had retained from Hostiensis' commentary. Yet as a statement of Hostiensis' final position on the *plenitudo potestatis* in Christendom it was not altogether accurate. For when it came to considering the practical circumstances of the actual exercise of this power, Hostiensis was more restrained and his final position was a sensible qualification of 'dominus spiritualium et temporalium.'

It will be recalled that Innocent III in *Per venerabilem* had contended, in general and ambiguous terms, that in cases of doubt recourse should be had to the apostolic see. Hostiensis had no doubt as to what Innocent III intended in citing Deut. 17.8;

> officii nobis commissi debitum non debemus alicui petenti denegare: hoc autem pertinet ad officium nostrum etiam in temporalibus, ubicumque super dubio quoque requirimur.[18]
> in omni foro et in omni casu difficili et dubio, standum est diffinitioni domini pape.[19]
> quo ad ecclesiastica indistincte et regulariter: quo ad secularia casualiter . . . spectat ad papam declaratio dubiorum.[20]

Thus Innocent III has given expression to a principle of critical importance for the canonist understanding of the actual exercise of the *plenitudo potestatis* in Christendom; the pope had a discretionary power to supplement the defects of temporal justice. Hostiensis formulated the principle with great clarity, giving detailed attention to the instances known to the law (canon and civil) of the supplementation of temporal defects by the spiritual power. This formulation was fully representative of the canonist tradition and was based on the *glossa ordinaria* which itself derived from early decretalist work:

> *certis causis inspectis temporalem iurisdictionem exercemus.* puta quando requirimur et alii non preiudicamus, ut dixi et notavi supra, et propter defectum iusticie ius reddimus etiam in temporalibus, et in causa misera-

---

[16] *Loc. cit.*
[17] *Summa* 4.17 § 10.
[18] *App.* ad 4.17.13 s.v. (*preiudicare velimus*) sed.
[19] *Ibid.* s.v. *inter causam et causam.*
[20] *Ibid.* s.v. *ad iudicium.*

bilium personarum; . . . et vacante regno vel imperio ; . . . et ratione cuiuslibet peccati notorii et iuramenti; . . . et ratione connexitatis, et ratione diversarum opinionum ut sequitur; et ubicunque dominus iniuste tractat hominem suum vel iniuste iudicat et ubicunque civitas iudice caret; et si recusetur iudex ordinarius ut suspectus. Nam et hi quattuor premissi casibus etiam secundum leges imperatoris communes sunt omnibus episcopis per suas civitates et dyoceses, ut in aut. ut differentes iudi. resp.i. et §i, et § si tamen contigerit et § in civitatibus, coll. ix.[21]

The pope, then, might exercise jurisdiction in temporal affairs when such exercise was required of him to remedy defects of justice, providing — important reservation, springing from concern for the separation of the powers — he did not thereby himself commit an injustice by prejudicing the rights of another.

This last cited gloss had significant things to say both about the practical nature of papal supremacy in temporal affairs and also about the distinction of the powers. Implicit in it was the third aspect of Church-State relations, the necessary cooperation of both powers. The spiritual authorities were called upon to cooperate in the government of civil society by providing justice when otherwise it would be wanting and by punishing those guilty of injustice. *Per venerabilem* suggested a further aspect of cooperation to Hostiensis which he discussed explicitly, though in a very general and somewhat exaggerated way.

Medieval political argumentation by way of symbol and simile is at best inconclusive and at worst absurd. Hostiensis used both methods and achieved both results when discussing what *Per venerabilem* taught about the cooperation of the powers.[22] Coronation ceremonies provided the symbolism. A prelate was anointed on the head, a king on his arm — thus was designated *auctoritas* as against *potestas* (with the latter deriving from the former), *scientia* and *potentia*, the directing brain of the Christian body politic and its defending

---

[21] *Ibid.* s.v. *certis causis* etc.

[22] 'Non multum discrepant (scil. sacerdotium et imperium) quo ad principium, unde procedunt, sed multum discrepant quo ad majoritatem, inde est quod caput episcopi inungitur, sed armis regis et episcopus chrismate, rex oleo ut scias quod episcopus est vicarius capitis nostri id est Christi et ut ostendatur, quanta sit differentia inter authoritatem pontificis et principis potestatem . . . quia quanta est differentia inter solem et lunam, tanta est inter sacerdotem et regalem dignitatem . . . Quae verba licet per doctores diversimode exponantur: tu tamen dic, quod sicut luna recipit claritatem a sole, non sol a luna, sic regalis potestas recipit authoritatem a sacerdotali, non e contra: sicut etiam sol illuminat mundum per lunam, quando per se non potest, scil. de nocte, sic sacerdotalis dignitas clarificat mundum per regalem, quando per se non potest, scil. ubi agitur de vindicta sanguinis . . . unde et lex secularis debet servire canonicae . . . Per hoc etiam innuitur quod septies millies et sexcenties et quadragesies quater et insuper eius medietatem est major sacerdotalis dignitas quam regalis': *Summa* 4.17 § 9. The metaphor was also discussed in generally similar terms, *Apparatus* ad 1.33.6 s.v. *ut quanta.*

arm were thereby distinguished.[23] Hostiensis had to admit that in practice most kings were not anointed on the arm but on the head. But his main point was that kings provided the material force that spiritual jurisdiction needed.

His simile was the old one which compared the spiritual power to the temporal power as the sun to the moon and he elaborated in some detail, even to calculating the arithmetical difference between the two. A conclusion emerged, however, from this politico-astronomic discussion. It served to make the same point extracted from coronation symbolism in a different and rather more specific way:

> sacerdotalis dignitas clarificat mundum per regalem quando per se non potest, scil. ubi agitur de vindicta sanguinis . . . unde et lex secularis debet servire canonicae.

The cooperation of the two powers, then, meant to Hostiensis especially the employment of the secular power when the spiritual power was not able to accomplish its objectives without the use of physical force. It was a principle which underlay all canonist thought about the relations of the powers and elsewhere Hostiensis had much to say about it.

Thus the analysis of *Per venerabilem* had led Hostiensis to discuss in some detail the three major components of the Church-State relationship: the distinction of the powers, where he emphasized that the pope might not intervene in the temporal order *in preiudicium alterius;* the cooperation of the powers, where he underlined the duty imposed on the spiritual power to supplement the defects of temporal justice where such action was required and also stressed the necessity laid on the secular power to give support whenever the *sacerdotium* wanted it. More strongly sounded, however, than these two notes was that of the supremacy of the spiritual power, the extension of its guardianship of morals into a jurisdiction *per consequens* in temporal affairs, the reign of Christ the king, embodied in His vicar, in the Christian polity. Each of these three threads of argument which Hostiensis disentangled from the difficult case of the bastards of Montpellier can be examined further as they were spun out in other contexts.

---

[23] The distinction between the *auctoritas* of priests and the *potestas* of secular rulers was Gelasian in origin and had been used by Innocent III in his decretal on the anointing of kings (1.15.1). Hostiensis commented: '*auctoritatem*: hic no. ius. *potestatem* hic no. factum; quod dicit officium episcoporum potius consistit in iure quam in facto, officium vero principum econverso. Primi habent verba, secundi facta; primi scientia, secundi potentia, et ideo etiam dicitur quod unus gladius alio semper eget . . . sed et hic no. quod auctoritas non dependet a potestate sed potius potestas ab auctoritate': *Apparatus* ad 1.15.1.

2. *The Distinction of the Powers*

There were several strong forces at work in the shaping of ecclesiastical jurisprudence which kept the principle of the distinction of the powers in the forefront of the canonist mind.

It could not be ignored. It was a principle of divine law as *Per venerabilem* itself had stated very definitely; and justice, supreme good in human affairs, demanding that to each be given his own, compelled the rendering to Caesar of what was his. Innocent III thought the matter important enough to be the subject of a canon of the Fourth Lateran Council.[24] That the Lord had spoken 'indistincte' in ordering the distinction of the powers, as some canonists thought, discussing the exact degree of Caesar's subjection to the pope, did not alter an essential postulate of canonist thought. There was a field of activity proper to Caesar:

> Nam et iurisdictiones distincte sunt, ut notavi infra, Qui fil.s.leg. § Qualiter, et reddenda sunt que sunt Caesaris Caesari, supra, de cler. coniug., Ex parte.[25]

The law of Caesar was well-known to canonists. As has been seen, the theory of papal sovereignty was clothed in garments borrowed from the Roman wardrobe. It could hardly escape the canonists' notice that the prerogatives they attached so enthusiastically to papal power were formulated originally by emperors about their own power. It would be absurd to suggest that canonists could place such value on Roman law analyses of the principles and techniques of supreme power whilst remaining unaware of its theory of secular sovereignty. In fact in the course of commentary on such titles of the *Gregoriana* as *De constitutionibus*, *De appellationibus*, *De privilegiis*, where the 'parallelism' of the two sovereigns, ecclesiastical and civil, was particularly marked, canonists recognized the supreme legislative and judicial authority of the emperor. As has been seen, the term *plenitudo potestatis* as interpreted by Huguccio owed something to Roman law and civilian commentary. It was

---

[24] Canon 42 forbade clerics to extend their jurisdiction 'praetextu ecclesiasticae libertatis' to the prejudice of secular powers, and ordered them to be satisfied with positions that had been fixed by law and approved custom, 'ut quae Caesaris, reddantur Caesari; et quae sunt Dei, Deo recta distributione reddantur.' (An earlier use of this exact form of words is pointed out by C.R.Cheney and W.H.Semple, *Selected Letters of Innocent III concerning England* [London 1953] 205, with other Innocentian usages of Matt. 22.22). This canon did not find a place in *Comp.* IV, cf. A. García y García, 'El Concilio IV de Letrán (1215) y sus comentarios,' *Bulletin of the Institute of Research and Study in Medieval Canon Law, Traditio* 14 (1958) 485-6. Innocent's concern to avoid trespass in the secular sphere is noted by Cheney and Semple, *op. cit.* 106 where attention is also drawn to the importance in this regard of his decretals X.2.2.10, 11.

[25] *Summa* 2.28 § 4.

entirely characteristic of the canonist approach that Hostiensis should attribute *plenitudo potestatis* (*in temporalibus*) to the emperor. For he was sovereign in the temporal order, holder of a supreme legislative and judicial power, not lightly to be overborne by the spiritual power:

> Verumtamen quod rite factum est per imperatorem, non debet infringi per papam, nec debet se intromittere de subditis imperatoris, nisi forte in casibus.[26]

A third force keeping the distinction of the powers within the canonist tradition was the influence of the twelfth-century decretists. They had been especially interested in distinguishing the powers, largely because they had been much concerned to decide which was the area of activity that definitely was not Caesar's. They wished to define sound norms by which the autonomy of the Church in its own concerns could be established. The principles on which the clergy and clerical business and property could be emancipated from lay control were laid down. And though the object and substance of the discussion were orientated to ecclesiastical interests, yet it inevitably carried with it at least an implicit view of the proper object and area of operation of the secular power. For the powers could only be distinguished accurately if the correct decisions were made as to what constituted the right ends and means of the activity of each power. Decretist commentary on D.10, discussed earlier, affords a good illustration of how mature decretist scholarship could delimit the powers quite precisely. The canonist work based on the *Decretum*, as a general tendency, gave a distinct 'dualist' flavor to the canonist tradition and the *glossa ordinaria*, the major representative of the work of roughly the first half of our period, fully reflected this trend. A concern for distinguishing the powers was thus built into the canonist work of the later thirteenth century. If it was less conspicuous than in the earlier period, it was nonetheless part of Hostiensis' stock-in-trade:

> Quis possit constitutionem facere? . . . Item imperator in temporalibus, C. de leg. l. 2 et l. humanum, non tamen in spiritualibus seu ecclesiasticis, quia non subsunt ei, in authen. quomodo op. episc. in princ. coll. 1, 96 dist. Duo sunt, et c. Si imperator: tamen legibus suis in ecclesiasticis utimur quando adiuvant et non offendunt, 10 dist. c.1, et c. In adiutorium et precedentibus, infra, de no. ope. nuncia. cap. 1 et sic sunt distincte iurisdictiones, 10 dist., Quoniam.[27]

The fourth and last feature of canonist methodology tending to emphasize the distinction of the powers was perhaps the most important of all. Decretalist writing, concerned above all to integrate the *ius antiquum* and its attendant decretist commentary with contemporary legislation, was occupied espe-

---

[26] *Summa* 4.17. § 10.

[27] *Summa* 1.2. § 8.

cially with practical issues. The decretists worked from the texts of traditional authority; the decretalists, however, worked from cases. All the 'political' decretals of Alexander III and Innocent III were issued as attempts to solve practical problems arising from actual political circumstances. *Ex tenore, Ex transmissa, Causam, Si duobus; Novit, Venerabilem, Licet ex suscepto, Per venerabilem, Excommunicamus,* were all formulated in response to problems that men had experienced in the contemporary world. They therefore reflect the reality of a political situation where emperors, kings, communes and others did exercise real power and were often resentful of what they considered as the interference of the papacy in their own business. Though an important part of canonist activity was to draw principles of universal application from these decretals — principles which had their validity independently of the particular circumstances which had caused the issuing of the decretal — nevertheless their commentary, in turn, inevitably reflected something of the political realities. So much of canonist theory sprang from the attempted solutions of problems which had arisen in the day to day business of governing Christendom and so much of it was led by men like Innocent III, Innocent IV, and Hostiensis who were not primarily academics. No matter how abstract or divorced from practical considerations individual canonist opinions came to be, the canonist tradition as a whole found its *raison d'être* in those matters which were *practiciora et quotidiana.*[28] It was always directed towards the concrete situation, problem and solution. It could not, therefore, at least in the last analysis, avoid taking careful note of an existing political situation in which emperors, national kings, and communes, jealous of their established rights, kept the reality of a distinction of powers before the eyes of popes and canonists.

Philip Augustus provides a ready example of how the determination of a king to preserve his feudal rights uncompromised by papal action left a clear mark on the *Corpus Iuris Canonici* and the formation of canonist theories. *Novit, Per venerabilem,* and *Excommunicamus* — the three Innocentian political decretals *par excellence* — were each in their different contexts framed and phrased to accomodate the French king's resistance to any apparent infringement of his rights.[29] They therefore inevitably contained along with their

---

[28] As Hostiensis put it, *Summa* proemium § 1.

[29] *Novit* was of course a reply to Philip's challenge that his dispute with John was a feudal matter and did not pertain to the pope. Innocent granted that a feudal matter 'ad ipsum spectat.' *Per venerabilem* acknowledged that William of Montpellier was subject to others and therefore could not claim legitimation *in temporalibus* from the pope without their assent ('In aliis autem nosceris subiacere. Unde, sine ipsorum forsan iniuria, nisi praestarent assensum, nobis in hoc subdere te non posses, nec eius auctoritatis existis ut dispensandi super his habeas potestatem': PL 214.1132; the second sentence was omitted in the version of the letter used in the *Gregoriana*). The provision in *Excommunicamus* whereby the lands

definitions of sacerdotal superiority, a 'dualist' element — a recognition of the primacy of feudal suzerainty — and this element became an essential part of canonist theory:

> Item cognitio feudi non ad ecclesiam pertinet, sed ad dominum feudi, et quo ad talia, nihil ad papam de feudo, nisi ratione violentie vel negligentie vel peccati: sic loquuntur iura supra alleg. de for. comp. Et est ratio, quia in his non privilegiavit princeps ecclesiam: ergo nec papa debet ei iniuriari nec forte posset sua constitutione.[30]
> Nec invenies decretum, vel ius canonicum quod in feudalibus imperatori vel regi legem imponat.[31]

Thus in principle, Hostiensis was very emphatic that, though the spiritual power was superior, each of the two powers had its proper sphere of activity. This principle he put forcibly at the very beginning of his *Summa*:

> quidquid autem dicatur, hec est veritas quod distincte sunt iurisdictiones, quamvis una maior sit reliqua, et qualibet secundum legem suam iudicabit.[32]

But it was one thing to insist on the principle of the distinction of the powers and quite another if the superiority of the spiritual power came to be so insisted on that the distinction was virtually abolished. Statements about there being two powers might be of the order of pious platitudes if they did not have practical content. The reality of Hostiensis' professions must be tested by examining the extent to which he gave them proper force in the actual conduct of affairs.

The *ratione peccati* argument opened a breach in the wall of secular autonomy, How far was Hostiensis prepared to widen it?

Both Innocent IV and Hostiensis recognized that the logical extension of that principle could lead to the virtual abolition of secular jurisdiction. They therefore tried to find a principle with which to restrict the *ratione peccati* jurisdiction to prevent all manner of cases becoming ecclesiastical *per viam denunciationis iudicialis ad ecclesiam*. It was not an altogether satisfactory attempt, but it is clear that neither of these alleged 'hierocrats' wished to extend it beyond the particular cases specified in the decretal itself. Neither was prepared to use the argument as a lever to expand the competence of the ecclesiastical courts.[33] This conclusion emerges clearly from a further discus-

---

of a convicted heretic were open to occupation by the orthodox only 'salvo iuris domini principalis' is to be seen as a reservation imposed by Philip's strong stand that only he had the right to dispose of forfeited fiefs in France. About Philip's view, cf. A.C.Shannon, *The Popes and Heresy in the Thirteenth Century* (Villanova 1949) 37.

[30] *Summa* 3.49 § 13.   [31] *Ibid* § 4.

[32] Proemium § 3.

[33] Hostiensis: 'Tamen iudex ecclesiasticus hanc denunciationem non debet admittere indistincte, nisi in defectum iusticie vel ratione pacis vel iuramenti vel secundum dominum nostrum (Innocent IV) quando alias non audiretur in foro civili, puta quando obligatio

sion of *ratione peccati* jurisdiction which Hostiensis wrote when examining the types of case that properly belonged to the ecclesiastical court.

All that the canonists knew as *crimina* were sins. Did it follow therefore that only the ecclesiastical courts had cognizance of crime? How did the principle that the Church exercised jurisdiction *ratione peccati* apply in this context? Did laymen have to answer for their crimes in ecclesiastical courts? What was the competence of ecclesiastical courts over the laity in matters of sin?

Hostiensis answered these questions by making a distinction which adequately covered the claims of both *fora* to have jurisdiction in one and the same crime. The ecclesiastical courts would concern themselves with the crime as sin and punish it especially, inflicting penance. If it happened to be a crime unknown to civil law — fornication was instanced — then there would be no further proceedings in the civil court. If the civil court was interested in the crime, as of course it was in the majority, then the appropriate temporal punishment by the appropriate temporal authority might be inflicted, and it was for the temporal power to concern itself with any necessary *satisfactio temporalis* involved (as would be the case in perjury or usury for example). The ecclesiastical court did not concern itself directly with these temporal aspects but judged and punished sin. The judgment of sin might have an indirect effect on the secular aspect, in that sin could not be forgiven until satisfaction had been made. Thus if the sin was theft or usury, restitution was an essential precondition of forgiveness. But the ecclesiastical court was not judging temporal satisfaction as such, about which the lay court had full competence.[34]

This was a note of realism, a doctrine which reflected broadly the system prevailing in the various parts of Christendom, a distinction which could be applied to the satisfaction of both Church and State. Hostiensis' examination

---

naturalis tamen est . . . . . vel quando notorium est peccatum . . . . vel quando hanc proponit persona miserabilis et depressa . . . . Alioquin si hoc generaliter intelligeres hec absurditas exinde sequeretur quod periret iurisdictio temporalis gladii, et omnis causa per hanc viam ad ecclesiam deferetur': *Apparatus* ad 2.1.13 s.v. *corripere*.

[34] 'Unde proprie et vere loquendo, crimen ecclesiasticum dici potest illud quod est crimen secundum canones et non secundum leges: ut crimen usurarum et crimen fornicationis, quod secundum leges non est crimen . . . . ideo dic quod ubicunque quaeritur de peccato, cognitio pertinet ad ecclesiam quo ad diffinitionem peccati, nam multa iudicat ecclesia fore peccatum, et in multis casibus in quibus seculares et mundani contrarium iudicarent. Item ad ecclesiam pertinet poenitentiam dare et sic per consequentiam cogere ad satisfactionem, quia non dimittitur peccatum etc. infra, de usuris, Cum tu, et sic potest intelligi quod dicitur, ratione peccati cognoscit ecclesia supra tit. 1, Novit resp. 1, ad fin. Potest etiam adiri ecclesia in defectum iustitiae principaliter, alias cognoscit iudex secularis principaliter de satisfactione temporali, si sit quaestio inter laicos: vel si clericus impetat laicum de rigore iuris . . . . ': *Summa* 2.2. para. 11.

of this practical problem of the respective competences of ecclesiastical and secular courts was marked by a conspicuous absence of that abstract dogmatism which marred his commentary on *Per venerabilem*. There was no place here for metaphors about two swords or the sun and moon, no extravagant exegesis of the Old Testament. Hostiensis had recalled his own maxim — *generalitas parit obscuritatem* — and kept his attention strictly on specific matters. It was so in other contexts where he dealt with the practicalities of the mutual accomodations which the two powers were forced to make. The clerical contribution to the needs of civil society has been noticed as one such context.[35] So also was his discussion of appeals.[36] Another, that concerned with the very important question of lay participation in episcopal elections, deserves closer examination, for it affords further proof that Hostiensis (and the canonist tradition generally), despite occasional florid verbiage about spiritual supremacy, had a realistic view of the double and joint interests of both powers.

The importance of lay investiture as an issue of discord between the two powers needs no emphasis here, nor is it necessary to recall the various stages of its settlement in mutually accepted compromises. These solutions, differing in detail in different parts of Christendom, were broadly similar, and that achieved between Innocent III and King John of England affords typical illustration of how the respective claims of both powers in the elections of bishops were adjusted[37] in a system that worked, on the whole, without friction.

On the one hand, the king was accorded his place in the proceedings by papal acknowledgement of the obligation of the electors to seek royal license to hold an election and also to present their candidate to the king for his assent. On the other hand, elections themselves were to be 'free,' that is to say, without any degree of lay participation, and 'canonical,' that is, according to the universally valid norms of the common law of the Church.

This Anglo-papal concordat, though recalled in *Magna Carta*, was not in the *Corpus Iuris Canonici*. Nor indeed was there any decretal to give a comprehensive statement of the 'canonized' *de facto* position in any country. Some decretals had incidental reference to the presentation of the bishop-elect for royal assent, but there was nothing for the early decretalists to work on which approached the clarity and fulness of Innocent's letter to John. Early decretalist references to the participation of kings in episcopal elections tended therefore to be somewhat vague and academic, and this deficiency was reflected in the *glossa ordinaria*. Nevertheless the appearance of canonist monographs on elections put the canonist tradition in direct contact with the realities of the

---

[35] By G. Le Bras, *L'immunité réelle* (Paris 1920).
[36] Cf. *Summa* 2.28 § 4 *A quo et ad quem appellatio debet fieri*.
[37] Text with notes in C. R. Cheney and W. H. Semple, *op. cit.* 198-201.

existing situation and posed some of the questions involved in the mutual accommodation of both powers which the early decretalists had avoided.

Hostiensis' commentary on the title *de electionibus* and the treatise of Lawrence of Somercote[38] were the outstanding products of mid-thirteenth century concerning episcopal elections. In a sense, they were complementary works, at least as far as English electors were concerned: Hostiensis' a detailed analysis of the existing law of elections, the canon of Chichester's more an electoral formulary and practical guide to procedure. Together they give the sum of the canonist understanding of the distinction of the powers in the matter of episcopal elections.

One question demands an answer if the solidity of the distinction of the respective spheres is to be properly tested. Did the canonists allow real weight to royal participation by giving it a genuinely *de iure* position, or was the king's place merely tolerated *de facto*? Put more concretely: was the election valid if the electors chose not to ask for royal license to elect? If the king refused his assent to the elect, had there to be a fresh election? Or did the canonists allow electors to evade the king if they could?

The final answers to these questions are to be sought in papal and royal correspondence dealing with them as they actually arose, rather than in the writings of jurists. Nevertheless they are questions which enable us to see both how far the jurists were conscious of the realities of political life and to test the weight they were prepared to give to the principle of the distinction of the powers in a specific matter of practice.

It was about these questions that the early decretalists and the *glossa ordinaria* were noncommittal. Lawrence of Somercote attempted a concise statement of the strict law governing the king's place:

> *aliqui de canonicis ad dominum regem eant petituri ab eo licenciam eligendi.* Hoc utitur omnino contra iura, X de elec. c. Cum terra et c. Quod sicut [1.6.14,28]. Papa tamen scit hec omnia et tolerat, per litteras approbavit . . . [*littera*] *mittatur domino regi per eundem electum et aliquos canonicos pro assensu regio.* Hoc expressum est iure, X de elec. c. Quod sicut et c. Cum inter universas, in fine, et c. Sacrosancta [1.6.28, 15, 51].[39]

---

[38] A. von Wretschko, *Der Traktat des Laurentius de Somercote, Kanonikus von Chichester über die Vornahme von Bischofswahlen, entstanden im Jahre 1254* (Weimar 1907).

[39] 'Corpore autem defuncti sepulturae tradito de consuetudine ecclesiae Anglicanae actenus est obtentum, quod sollemnes nuntii, aliqui scilicet de canonicis, ad dominum regem eant petituri ab eo licentiam eligendi' (*ed. cit.* 28). A gloss on the two last words (von Wretschko thought the author might be Lawrence himself) reads: 'Hoc utitur omnino contra iura, de elec. c. Cum terra et c. Quod sicut (1.6.14, 28). Papa tamen scit haec omnia et tolerat, per litteras approbavit' (*ed. cit.* 51). On the request for royal assent, Laurentius: 'Post haec (scil. the election itself, consent of the elect, publication of the result) fiant tria paria litterarum: unum quod mittatur domino regi per eundem electum et aliquos de canonicis *pro assensu regio* requirendo . . . .' (*ed. cit.* 33). The gloss on the words in italics reads:

This was a fair statement of the information available directly from the *Decretales*. If royal license was asked for, this was against the law and only tolerated, but the presentation of the elect for royal assent was quite legal. This was the nearest Lawrence got to discussing the legal significance of royal participation.

Innocent IV and Hostiensis, however, together provided the answers to the questions and were strongly in favor of the king. Basing himself on the *Decretum*, Innocent asserted that, where by custom or privilege the consent of a prince to an election was required, the election was void if that consent was not sought.[40] Hostiensis repeated this view. He also added another of his own to make it clear that an election was not canonical if the king's role, as legally established, was not recognized. The consent of the king to the elect was also required for canonical validity. If the king objected to the elect — 'etiamsi dissentiat sine causa' — the election was *irrita*, and this held good whether or not there were temporalities involved.[41]

This concern to delineate the respective places of Church and State in the creation of a bishop showed a firm regard for the reality of the dualism of the powers in matters where the interests of each power converged. It was an attitude of Innocent IV and Hostiensis, as indeed of all canonists, at least as characteristic as their insistence on the superiority of the spiritual power. It is quite clear that the principle of the dualism of the powers was a positive factor in canonist thinking, not to be easily ignored or lightly circumvented.

3. *The Cooperation of the Powers*

Hostiensis had little that was original to say about the cooperation of the powers. In substance, the question had not altered very significantly from the days of the later decretists. In one of his central texts dealing with it, he enunciated the traditional decretist principle, learned from Gelasius, that

---

'Hoc expressum est iure, de elec. c. Quod sicut et c. Cum inter universas, in fine et c. Sacrosancta (1.6.28, 51)' (*ed. cit.* 51). This gloss was an adaptation of the *glossa ordinaria*: ' . . . electio facta praesentari debet patrono ut suum praestet assensum, supra eo. Cum terra, et c. Cum inter universas et infra eo. tit. c. Sacrosancta': ad 1.6.28 s.v. *impedire*.

[40] Innocent IV: 'Mors autem defuncti potest nunciari principi et eius consensus requiri si de consuetudine vel privilegio hoc habet princeps et si fiat electio contra consuetudinem vel privilegium cassabitur, lxiii.dist. Lectis, xviii.q.ii. Abbatem': ad 1.6.28 s.v. *nominatio;* Hostiensis, *Apparatus ad loc.*

[41] Hostiensis: 'Sed et electione facta, potest requiri consensus patroni, tamen irritabitur, etiamsi dissentiat sine causa, infra eod. Cum terra, et c. Cum inter universas, in fine et c. Quod sicut; "sine causa" ideo dixi, quia si a principe temporali, temporalia teneat, et suspectus est, vel infidelis, merito audietur, sicut in illustris regis Anglorum privilegio continetur quod comprobatur infra de iur. pat. Nobis fuit § 1: idem videtur etsi temporalia non teneat, arg. in utroque, de iureiur. Nimis et c. Petitio': *Summa* 1.6 § 5.

each power needed the other, each was bound to help the other. From Isidore and the decretists he drew another maxim to establish the same general principle: 'scientia ecclesie eget potencia secularis.'[42] D.10 and C.23 q.5 supplied Hostiensis with the groundwork.

For the more practical content of the Gelasian and Isidorian generalities, his immediate source was Innocent IV. The secular power could be compelled to give help to the spiritual power as was appropriate to its inferior status, but the converse was not true. The superior could not be forced into action by the inferior. Certainly the ecclesiastical authorities would entertain secular requests for spiritual action but the actual decision to act was purely ecclesiastical. The king might ask pope or prelates to excommunicate his enemies but this could not be more than a request. On the other hand, if pope or prelates asked a ruler to proceed against, say, heretics or ecclesiastical rebels or despoilers of church property, this was an order, to disobey which brought ecclesiastical penalties. Mutualism of the powers might be the doctrine, but the mutuality was not equal. The secular power could be coerced into cooperation; the spiritual power could not, for that would be to violate ecclesiastical autonomy.[43]

Thus the superiority of the spiritual power conditioned the principle of the cooperation of the two powers in two ways and the priesthood had both the advantages. If it ordered the secular power to act in its support, there was no refusal, but if the secular power wanted cooperation it was for the priesthood to judge whether it should be given or not. Spiritual supremacy involved two things: power to command and power to reject — to exact obedience and to repel interference. The underlying assumptions of the whole principle emerge clearly in the microcosm of the analysis of the conditions of the cooperation of the two powers. Hostiensis was but reproducing in his own words a more up to date statement of the decretist interpretation of D. 10 in making these points:

---

[42] Cf. p. 30 n. 43 above.

[43] 'Una enim potestas alia semper eget, et ideo tenentur se ad invicem adiuvare, ut xcvi. dist. Cum ad verum, c. Duo sunt, x.di. Si in adiutorium, et c. seq. (Quoniam idem) et c. in lombard. ut episcopi et comites invicem sibi auxilium dent, in rubro et in nigro. Sed secundum dominum nostrum (i.e. Innocent IV) hec est differentia: quod secularis iudex potest cogi ad prestandum auxilium, sed per secularem ecclesiasticus non cogetur, ut infra c. Ad reprimendum, secundum dominum nostrum et melius, infra de iud. Qualiter. Quidni? Secularis enim inferior est, ut patet in eo quod leg. et no. infra, de mai. et obed. Solite. § potuisses: ergo in superiorem potestatem non habet, infra, de mai. et obed. Cum inferior. Et est secunda differentia, quod secularis non habet examinare processus ecclesiastici. Ecclesiasticus nunquam ad peticionem secularis excommunicabit, nisi ex causa rationabili et canonica forma observata, infra de sen. excomm. Sacro, extra. domini nostri, Cum medicinalis (= VI° 5.11.1) . . . et scientia ecclesie eget potencia secularis': Apparatus ad 1.31.1 s.v. fuerit.

Ideo et ad leges recurrimus tanquam ad ancillas nostras in materiis civilibus, et ex eis sumendo argumento ubi ius non habemus expressum canonicum vel divinum, x dist. ca. i, ii et per totum . . . Sic et ad ministros ipsarum recurrimus etiam imperando et cohercendo quando ipsorum auxilio indigemus . . . non sic e converso, quia nec leges possunt preiudicare canonibus tanquam inferiores . . . nec ministri ipsarum tanquam inferiores possunt vel debent ministros canonum cohercere . . . nisi ratione temporalium quo ad ipsas res temporales.[44]

In the context of the ecclesiastical order, then, the secular power was 'ministerial' (Huguccio) or 'ancillary' (Hostiensis). As to precisely when recourse was to be had to the servant or handmaid, Hostiensis held much the same doctrine as had Huguccio. Papal legislation after Huguccio's time had ordained that in one case in addition to incorrigibility and heresy, abandonment to the secular arm was the penalty for criminous clergy, namely, the forging of papal letters.[45] In these contexts, according to Hostiensis, the secular power acted as a 'pars ecclesie' to provided the appropriately radical degree of punishment inflicted by the Church on a delinquent cleric.[46]

Nor was Hostiensis outside the stream of canonist tradition when examining the place of the secular power in the suppression of heresy. His *de hereticis* was anchored securely to that *compendium* of anti-heretical legislation issued by Innocent III, notably in the Lateran Council. The secular authority was stringently bound to its duty to cooperate in the extermination of heresy. Its role was merely executive, supplying police services under the direction of ecclesiastical judges, liable to stern punishment for dereliction of duty. Such was demonstrated clearly by the exaction of an oath binding it to loyal service and by the duties laid on it of producing suspects, destroying or confiscating the property of the guilty, inflicting the final hideous penalty on the condemned.[47]

---

[44] *Apparatus* ad 5.32.1 s.v. *adiuvantur.*

[45] X. 5.20.7 (Innocent III).

[46] '*Et non habeat ultra quid faciat.* Ex hoc no. expressum quod nullo modo est utendum temporali gladio nisi premisso spirituali. Tunc enim demum recurrendum est ad secularem potestatem quando ecclesia proficere non potest et non habet ultra quid faciet, ut hic et infra, de here. Excommunicamus, § 1, et de homici. Postulasti, infra, de cler. excom. min. c. ii, cum suis concordantiis. Nec dicas aliud in iudice seculari nam et ipse et gladius suus pars ecclesie sunt. Unde si sane vult procedere primo recurret ad gladium spiritualem antequam et ipse utatur suo, ut no. in summa, de treuga et pa. § quid sit iustum bellum': *Apparatus* ad 2.1.10.

[47] 'Ergo cognitio, examinatio et condemnatio istius criminis ad ecclesiasticum iudicem pertinet principaliter, non ad secularem, licet secularis executionem habeat . . . nam et ratione peccati ecclesia iurisdictionem habet, etiam in temporalibus . . . hoc enim indubitandum est, quod Deus est omnibus praeponendus . . . ergo et est eius vicarius . . . unde Dominus ad Hieremiam: "Ecce constitui te etc." (Jer. 1.10) secundum Goffredum, et ideo seculares tanquam inferiores, sive sint temporales sive perpetui in principio administra-

It was revealed most clearly in the ultimate sanction to be imposed for secular negligence or disobedience in carrying out instructions. The penal section of Hostiensis's treatise *de hereticis* achieved its point of culmination in considering deposition. No heretic was fitted to hold office in Christian society. Deposition was part of the punishment of any convicted heretic, 'sive sit clericus sive laicus: papa vel imperator vel alius inferior'. It was also the appropriate punishment for those who gave tacit or overt support to heretics. There was a general principle that any ruler who was negligent in performing his function of providing justice to his subjects might be deposed. *Alius item* was an illustration of it and the context of heresy provided a practical application of it. To permit heresy to be taught and followed was to allow evil to flourish and thus to violate Christian justice and betray the duty of a Christian ruler. To tolerate heretics was a gross failure of the function of a ruler whose 'totum studium est ut subditi Deum recognoscant et honeste vivant' and who 'cupit augmentari fidem catholicam'. Not only should he be deposed for his fault but his territory should be exposed to occupation by true believers.[48]

---

tionis suae tenentur iurare publice quod a terris suae iurisdictioni subiectis, universos haereticos ab ecclesia denudatos, studebunt exterminare bona fide totis viribus, ut infra eod. Excommunicamus itaque, § Moveantur. Debent etiam iurare, ut requisiti iudicibus ecclesiasticis ipsos bona fide et efficaciter iuxta officium suum adiuvent contra haereticos: quod sacramentum si praestare renuerint, vel praestitum transgressi fuerint illo quo potiebantur honore, privari debent: intelligas quando erat temporalis potestas, nec ad alium eligitur: civitas autem quae his institutis restiterit, si ad comminitionem episcopi non emendaverit, aliarum carere non debet commercio civitatum et episcopali dignitate privari, ut infra eod. Ad abolendam § Statuimus et § Civitas. Sed si dominus temporalis, id est secularis, perpetuus monitionem ecclesiae spreverit, per metropolitanum et comprovinciales episcopos est excommunicandus et si nec sic resipuerit, sed in excommunicatione per annum steterit, significandum est summo pontifici qui anno elapso vasallos suos a fidelitate denunciet absolutos et terram exponet catholicis occupandam, salvo iure domini principalis, si ipse particeps non sit, nec aliquod obstaculum supradictis opponat, alias eandem poenam patitur, etiamsi nullum dominium super se recognoscat, ut infra eodem, Excommunicamus itaque § si vero dominus. Si ecclesia contra rebelles brachium invocat seculare . . . ideoque manu militari sunt haereticis bona omnia auferenda: quia secundum Isydorum et Augustinum et alios sanctos, et ipsa bona nullo iure possunt haeretici possidere, naturali non quia secundum ipsum sunt communia . . . nec iure divino, sicut filius Dei ostendit dicens "Auferetur a vobis regnum, et dabitur genti facienti fructum eius" (Matt. 21.43). Item "Labores impiorum iusti edent" (Prov. 13.22). Item "Ora sunt iustorum" (citation not identified) secundum Goffredum et Raymundum, idem nec civili, nec canonico . . . ' *Summa* 5.7 § 4.

48 'Deponitur etiam haereticus sive sit clericus, sive laicus papa vel imperator, vel alius inferior ab omni dignitate, 40 dist. Si papa, 24 q.1. Qui contra pacem, infra eod. Ad abolendam § 1 et 2, et degradatus traditur curiae seculari, ut ibi . . . Et nota quod domini temporales non solum propter suam heresim, sed etiam aliorum quos dum possunt admoniti exterminare negligunt, excommunicari possunt, et terrae ipsorum exponi catholicis occu-

4. *The Superiority of the Spiritual*

On each occasion that Hostiensis asserted his belief in the principle of divided jurisdiction he added the qualification that the spiritual power was 'maior' or 'superior.' The consideration of the principle of papal *maioritas* and its full implications in practice will form a summary of Hostiensis' final position on papal superiority in temporal affairs.

The essence of his justification of the papal position was a foreshadowing of the central argument of *Unam sanctam*. It was an article of faith that all were subject to the 'unus generalis vicarius in terris' whose undivided headship of the Church was the surety of her indivisibility, stability and immutability. But the 'ecclesia generalis' or 'unum corpus' from which obedience was exacted comprehended Christian society in its totality: communes and kingdoms as well as parishes and dioceses. It was not merely society in its ecclesiastical ordering that was to be ruled; Christian public life generally was under God and the law institutionalized in the papacy. Hostiensis, no less than Innocent IV, believed that sacred history demonstrated this subordination of God's people to its divinely appointed guardian and, no less than Aquinas, that all the kings of the *populus Christianus* should be subject to the pope as to the Lord Jesus Christ Himself.

The due fulfilment of the spiritual charge laid on the vicar of Christ demanded a degree of control over the temporal,

> anima facta est ad servitium Dei, cetera omnia ad servitium anime . . . sic per quamdam consequentiam qui habet regere animas non est omnino exclusus ab his que subiecta sunt animabus, et qui habet quod maius est habet et quod minus . . . [49]

The ruler of souls was 'not altogether excluded' from exercising direction over those non-spiritual matters which might promote or hinder spiritual well-being. What in concrete terms did this imply?

Expressed in strictly juridical terms, the papal function, according to Hostiensis, was to make provision for the 'communibus utilitatibus.'[50] Whilst

---

pandae, infra, eod. Excommunicamus § si vero dominus temporalis. Idem si princeps negligens inveniatur, circa regni regimen et iustitiam faciendam, 17.q.4. Si quis deinceps, 11.q.1. Nullus, 32.q.5. Praeceptum. Unde Zacharias Papa Ludovicum (*sic*) regem Francorum, praedecessorem Pipini patris Caroli, deposuit hac de causa, 15.q.6. Alius': *Summa* 5.7 §§ 9-11.

[49] *Apparatus* ad 4.17.13 s.v. *plenitudo potestatis*. The dictum 'qui habet quod maius est habet et quod minus,' which was Innocent III's basic argument in claiming a power to legitimize *in temporalibus* since he had the power *in spiritualibus*, derived from an axiom of Roman Law: 'In eo quod plus sit, semper inest et minus' (*Dig.* 50.27.110). It was later to find a place in the *Liber Sextus* as the *regula iuris*: 'Cui licet quod est plus, licet utique quod est minus' (5.13.53). As a philosophical principle it had an important role in the political thought of Aegidius Romanus and other extremists, cf. A. Gewirth, *Marsilius of Padua* 1 (New York 1951) 14-20.

[50] *Apparatus* ad 3.38.17 s.v. *Romano pontifici*.

it was not 'fitting' for the pope to use his *plenitudo potestatis* or prerogative power excessively,[51] it was by its virtue that he could make such provision for the common necessities of Christendom when only by its exercise could justice be maintained. Papal authority contained that reserve of power in the constitution of Church and Christendom which could be used exceptionally and adventitiously to make due provision for those cases for which established laws and procedures had no remedy.

In these terms, Hostiensis, in common with all thirteenth-century canonists, recognized a number of circumstances where the power might be, or indeed had already been, exercised in the temporal order. It was the pope's function to listen to any who petitioned him with a complaint of injustice. He might resolve legal doubts and ambiguities 'etiam in secularibus,' act in vacancies in the succession to kingdoms as well as to the empire, pronounce on the justice of a war, supplement and punish temporal negligence and defect.[52] These were the typical occasions when Hostiensis envisaged the pope exercising his discretionary power. But there might be other occasions when the pope was required to act. Every body politic needed an authority endowed with sufficient power to make provision in necessities and Hostiensis in his theory of the *plenitudo potestatis* was applying to the context of Christendom a principle drawn from Roman law:

> in omnibus et in singulis specialibus que occurrunt, necesse fuit saltem per unum rei publice provideri, arg.ff. de orig. iur.l.ii. § novissime, ii.colu.[53]

Put in this way, it was not perhaps an unreasonable case. Certainly the papacy had been acting on it for a considerable period and equally certainly, the political powers of Europe made use of papal authority when it suited them. Hostiensis was not theorizing *in vacuo* but attempting to formulate principles from data which an existing situation presented to him. It is, however, true that Hostiensis on occasions overstated his case — when, for example, he asserted that the pope had been given full power, 'in omnibus et per omnia . . . indistincte.' But on closer examination of all the texts in which he discussed papal power, it becomes clear that his real position concerning the operation of papal power in temporal affairs was somewhat less trenchant. Hostiensis did not in the last analysis believe that the pope had full power in temporal affairs *indistincte.* His true position was more nuanced.

---

[51] *Apparatus* ad. 1.21.2 s.v. *dispensare.*

[52] This is the case argued in the context of *Per venerabilem* especially s.v. *certis causis inspectis* (see above, p. 112) and in relation to *Licet* substantially reproducing Innocent IV's commentary (cf. above p. 68-69 nn. 22, 23).

[53] *App.* ad 4.17.13. s.v. *casualiter* and s.v. *sed*: 'verum, quia officii nobis commissi debitam non debemus alicui petenti denegare: hoc autem pertinet ad officium nostrum etiam in temporalibus ubicumque super dubio quocumque requirimur'.

In this particular text Hostiensis had not entered a series of qualifications that elsewhere in his work he was fully prepared to admit.[54]

The pope did not have power in temporal affairs in the same way as did the emperor (here personifying the temporal power as such) nor did he have as much power in them as the emperor. In principle Hostiensis admitted that the emperor had *plenitudo potestatis* in temporal affairs. The pope only had power over *temporalia* when they had given rise to sin, doubt, negligence or injustice. In these circumstances his power was direct and comprehensive: it was in this sense that Hostiensis could speak of the pope as 'dominus temporalium.' He was not asserting that the pope had any right to intervene in the temporal order when it was being properly conducted. Indeed Hostiensis expressly said that he had no right to do so. Put in its most concrete terms, this principle meant to Hostiensis that the pope was precluded from *feudalia*. This was the proper field of activity of the prince and the pope could only act in it by virtue of privilege granted to him by the prince. The spiritual power must not usurp that sphere of activity which Christ Himself had decreed belonged to another power.

Papal intervention in temporal affairs was only 'in casibus' or 'casualiter' — that is to say, when such intervention was necessary for the direction of the faithful, the correction of sin, the preservation of peace in the *respublica Christiana* — in a word, the maintenance of spiritual welfare. When it came to stating the principle which justified this intervention *in ordine ad spiritualia*, Hostiensis resorted to arguments based on the kingship of Christ conferred on the pope and the comprehensiveness of his quasi-divine jurisdiction and on the unitary nature of Christian society. Such arguments of high principle considered alone might suggest that there could be little place in the system for a meaningful distinction of the powers. But argued on the level of practice, papal power in temporal affairs was seen by Hostiensis as to some real degree limited by the God-given right of the secular power *in temporalibus*.

A double principle was maintained by Hostiensis, and by canonists generally, of 'iurisdictio distincta' and of a papal 'generalis et suprema manus super omnes,' that is, of the powers distinguished whilst yet allowing for a general, overall discretionary power for the papacy to act at need for the good of Christendom. What has to be decided is the extent to which canonists could reconcile these two positions. This problem is a fundamental one for it is the question of how canonists faced the existence of the two-fold tendency which ran

---

[54] Thus 'Sed et quamvis persona imperatoris subsit pape et temporalia per quamdam consequentiam, tamen imperator magis potest in temporalibus que a Deo immediate tenet ut supra dictum est, et ideo dummodo caveat a peccato, de ipsis potest disponere prout placet': *ibid.* s.v. *casualiter.* But this position went along with the principle that the pope had power *indistincte* in temporal affairs where the common welfare of Christendom was concerned.

through all their discussion of the relations of the powers: one which stressed the papal monarchy of the 'kingdom' of Christendom and the other which attempted to give Caesar his proper due. It can be examined in microcosm in the context of appeals, and from the examination of a specific point there can be isolated the ultimate assumption wherewith the canonists solved it.

It was strict law, defined by Alexander III, accepted by all canonists, not least by Hostiensis, that appeal did not lie from a secular to a spiritual court.[55] The jurisdictions were distinct; it was a violation of divine law and a usurpation of the right of another to permit a purely temporal case decided by a temporal judge to be appealed to the court christian.

It was hardly less a canonist principle, however, that the pope was *debitor iusticiae in omnibus* — an essential part of his function was to ensure that justice prevailed on all levels of Christian society. It followed therefore, and Hostiensis explicitly said so, that anyone might petition the pope if he felt he had been denied justice.[56] And it was in the light of this understanding of the papal function that Hostiensis could say that an ill-treated vassal could petition the pope against his lord.[57]

How were these positions reconciled? It is here that we arrive at the very heart of the thirteenth-century canonist view of papal superiority in temporal affairs: the resolution of the conflicting claims of the dualistic and monistic principles.

If a vassal did complain to the lord of Christendom that his overlord had denied him justice, it was open for the overlord to assert a principle accepted by the canonists, namely that there was no appeal from a feudal to an ecclesiastical court. This was essentially what Philip Augustus did claim when Innocent III sought to intervene in favour of King John. *Novit* was basically the justification for an exception to the accepted dualist principle, an attempt to demonstrate the circumstances in which an appeal from a feudal to the papal court was valid. But his justificatory line of argument, pushed to its conclusion, as Innocent IV and Hostiensis pointed out, would allow any appeal from secular to spiritual — to their mind, an 'absurdity,' for

> sic pereat iurisdictio temporalis gladii et omnis causa per hanc viam ad ecclesiam deferetur.[58]

Innocent IV and Hostiensis as their discussion of this very practical matter showed clearly saw the logical difficulty inherent in balancing the double principle of distinction of the powers in appeals and the papal duty of hearing petitions from the allegedly oppressed. But they could not formulate any

---

[55] Cf. *Comp.* I 2.20.7 = X. 2.28. 7 § 2.

[56] Above, n. 53.

[57] Above, p. 112, *gloss.* ad 4.17.13 s. v. *certis causis.*

[58] Above, n. 33.

principle which removed the tension between the dualistic and monistic aspects of the problem.

In the absence of a stated solution we must look for the assumption that lay implicit in the analysis of the whole question. The solution was allowed to rest in the practical circumstances of particular cases rather than in neatly logical academic constructions. It was a matter for the judgment of the intervening pope whether the case called for the exercise of his discretionary power. He had the final decision as to whether the dualist or monist principle should apply. In the last analysis, the canonist position depended on upholding the principle that if the pope decided that a matter concerned spiritual welfare whether of an individual or of Christendom as a whole and demanded a particular course of papal action to preserve it, the principle of divided jurisdictions was overruled. If the pope decided that the exercise of his *plenitudo potestatis* was called for, his judgment should be accepted unquestioningly, and obeyed implicitly because he was the vicar of Christ.

It was to be for this principle that Boniface VIII contended. He could maintain even with passion and with particular reference to what forty years canonistic experience had taught him, that the powers were distinct.[59] But he stood fast for the principle that no consideration of the autonomy of a prince's power in the temporal order could either impede papal right to pass judgment on royal actions, and to impose penalties if he decided such were needed, or confer any right on the secular power to question such judgments and penalties:

> Spiritualis homo iudicat omnia: ipse autem a nemine iudicatur . . . quicunque huic potestati a Deo sic ordinatae resistit, Dei ordinationi resistit.[60]

Unam sanctam enshrined the Hostiensian and canonistic logic: one community, a *christianus populus*, unique and single because it was the Body of Christ, united as a juridical society under a divinely appointed custodian. From this premise followed the fundamental principles in the application of power within this society — that its head possessed whatever right over the temporal which the good of that community demanded, that secular power was established to collaborate in the achievement of the end of that society and therefore could not allege its independence when the end was in question. In the final analysis, the thirteenth-century papal-canonist system depended on the principle of unquestioning obedience to the voice of God speaking on earth through the vicar of Christ. He was indeed 'dominus temporalium' since he alone could decide where and when the political order ceased to be merely of temporal concern, and against such a decision there was no appeal.

---

[59] 'Quadraginta anni sunt quod nos sumus experti in iure, et scimus quod duae sunt potestates ordinatae a Deo. Quis ergo debet credere vel potest quod tanta fatuitas, tanta insipientia sit vel fuerit in capite nostro?': Dupuy, *Histoire du différend . . . Preuves*, 78.

[60] *Extrav. comm.* 1.2.1 (*Unam sanctam*).

PART IV

CONTINUITY AND CHANGE

In the period between Gratian and Hostiensis canonist thought changed significantly in both method and doctrinal content. Within that time, the period of Huguccio, Innocent III and Alanus emerges as the period when the canonist tradition registered both a conclusion and a new beginning. It concluded a period when the forms in which political problems should be analyzed had been fashioned, the language of their discussion formalized and the areas of debate delimited. It was a period of beginnings also because the work of these three remarkable analysts of papal monarchy, abetted by a cluster of others, produced a framework of canonist thought about the papacy which in depth and breadth was almost completely adequate for all the needs of the thirteenth century canonist tradition.

What were the characteristic features of this analysis? It began with a thorough and systematic exegesis of the Petrine texts, scattered generously through the *Decretum*, and which was synthesized behind a number of technical terms of which *vicarius Christi, plenitudo potestatis* and *iudex ordinarius omnium* were the most important. It proceeded to use this terminology to discuss the relationship of the papacy to other jurisdictions — conciliar, cardinalitial, metropolitan, episcopal, imperial, royal. It continued with the listing of the *maiores causae* which were ordinarily reserved solely for the sovereign and of the occasions when the pope intervened in temporal affairs. It concluded with an analysis of the general principles regulating the relationship of *imperium* and *sacerdotium*. The analysis, therefore, was both theoretical and practical; it considered both principles and applications.

Examination of the relevance of papal jurisdiction to the temporal order ranged through specific practical problems to be integrated with the technical language of the general analysis. The positing and solution of the problem of the juridical bond between pope and emperor, a thorough review of deposition theory which amounted to a penal code against errant, negligent and recalcitrant lay rulers, the role of the curia as a supreme international court of first instance and appeal, formed the basic issues involved in the adaptation to the context of Christendom, of the doctrines of *vicarius Christi, plenitudo potestatis,* and *iudex ordinarius omnium.*

This process of adaptation threw up two important principles which had to be related to sacerdotal superiority: the distinction of the powers and their cooperation. Concerning the first, the powers were distinguished for both negative and positive purposes — negatively in order to decide what the secular power was not allowed to do in the ecclesiastical order; positively in order to decide what it should do as its own proper function. The detailed treatment of this positive aspect was not primarily the concern of ecclesiastical lawyers. It belonged rather to the civilian and other secular jurisprudences. But the function of the prince was of prime concern to the canonists in one important matter. In certain circumstances the secular power was an instrument for ecclesiastical service, a *brachium seculare* and this was the principle and terminology canonists used in considering the cooperation of the powers. The processes of distinguishing the powers and giving precision to the conditions of their cooperation were determined by a view of sacerdotal superiority which gave the *sacerdotium* the voice of final decision and the power to enforce it under sanction.

The totality of the canonist analysis of papal power here outlined amounted to change on a considerable scale in comparison with the theory produced by earlier writers, canonist or otherwise. The comprehensive examination of dualism, of the circumstances of cooperation between the powers and, above all, of the *imperium sacerdotis* gave a solidity, born of the intermixture of principle and application, to thirteenth century political thought, which was unknown to the twelfth century. Yet it should not be overlooked that with this change there was an important degree of continuity with earlier thought.

One strand of traditional belief, often (misleadingly) called Gelasian, was concerned with that essential of Christian justice which ordained that as God had intended the power to be distinct, neither power should usurp the function of the other. It has been argued by some historians that the thirteenth-century canonist tradition moved away from this position. Rather, however, it should be seen as fostering that belief and imprinting on it a characteristic canonist impress that was to be of some significance for the future. In canonist hands it was a living principle, the better appreciated for their knowledge of Roman law and of the contemporary European political scene.

From the former, they learned the attributes of monarchy. Of course they were learning them in order to style their own concept of papal monarchy. But incidentally to their main purpose, there emerged in canonist writing a whole concept of imperial or royal *plenitudo potestatis*. The typical content of this concept could be stated as a list of the occasions of its exercise — the making of war and peace, the levying of taxes and the granting of exemption from them, the hearing of final appeals. It could be shown to be inalienable and imprescriptible. But above all, the holder of the fulness of power was known in his law-making capacity. He was the unique possessor of what was still, to Bodin, the *primum caput* of sovereignty, comprehending all its other marks, the power of making and breaking positive law. 'It may have been the Aristotelians who extracted from the *Politics* an extended concept of the State as a collective entity, born spontaneously from the nature of man, but it had already been Roman law which had yielded the lesson that political authority originated in human reason, in natural law.'[1] By the mid-thirteenth century the canonists, in learning that lesson, had clearly defined the essence and scope of the royal *principatus in temporalibus*.

From the latter they learned especially the strength of the authority of an overlord over his vassals. It was such that only *casualiter*, for grave moral reasons or in more directly juridical language, for the general welfare had the spiritual power any right of intervention. Thirteenth century canonists discussed this principle sufficiently significantly to evolve a new term — *potestas indirecta* — which many generations of ecclesiastical theorists of Church-State relations were to find of considerable value to them.

Yet when all has been said about the dualistic emphasis which canonist thought inherited, rephrased and transmitted, it has to be recognized that canonists inherited also traditional beliefs about sacerdotal superiority which amounted to a not inconsiderable qualification of that emphasis. It was of course that sacerdotal pre-eminence which determined the conditions of dualism and co-operation. 'Quis dubitet sacerdotes Christi regum et principum omniumque fidelium patres et magistros censeri?'[2] What, for the canonists, were the basic effects of this paternal and magisterial position? Three deductions represented the fundamentals of their concept of the pre-eminence of the spiritual power.

The first concerned those privileges, generically the *libertas ecclesiae*,[3] by which the superior position of the clergy was marked by certain rights to be

---

[1] L. Génicot, *Les lignes de faîte du moyen âge* (Louvain 1951) 351.

[2] Gregory VII to Hermann, bishop of Metz: *Reg. Greg.* VII, 8.21 (p. 553 ed. Caspar); *Decretum* D.96 c.9.

[3] Hostiensis followed Innocent IV in giving this definition: '*ecclesiae libertatem*: que consistit in privilegiis super spiritualibus sive temporalibus generaliter vel singulariter sive a Deo sive a papa sive ab aliis principibus concessis. A Deo multa concessa sunt ecclesie sancte Dei; hic tangimus tamen tria. Primum est illud, quodcunque ligaveris etc., xxiiii.q.i. Quodcunque ligaveris: et quantum ad personam pape extendit ad omnium dubiorum solucionem, qui fil.s.leg. Per venerabilem § racionibus. Secundum est illud quod decime, primicie et oblaciones ad clericos spectent. Hoc enim a Deo concessum intelligimus, xvi.q.i. Revertimini, quod dic ut le. et no. supra, de decimis, A nobis et c. Tua, et infra. Est et tercium a Deo concessum scil. quod ecclesia sola res ecclesiasticas administret, xcvi. dist. Si imperator, supra de re. ecc. non alien. Cum laicis, et quod de spiritualibus ius condere et iudicare potest, xcvi. dist. Denique et c. Cum ad verum. Multa et alia privilegia sunt concessa a Deo clericis quod continentur in novo et veteri testamento': *Apparatus* ad 5.39.49.

recognized by the laity — the *privilegia fori et canonis*,[4] the payment of tithe, clerical immunity from secular exactions. Since these were allegedly concessions of divine, not human, law they ought not to be revoked by secular rulers. Neither ought the 'mixed' matters involved with them to be determined by secular rulers. The second concerned the requisitioning at will of the secular power for ecclesiastical purposes. The third concerned what came to be called the *imperium sacerdotis*, that power over the souls of men which in practice, on one level, brought cases of sin into the ecclesiastical courts, and, on another, held every ruler accountable for his misdeeds, even to the point of deposition. These three themes supplied the broad framework within which canonists considered the practical applications of the superiority of the spiritual power. They were present in canonist thought from the earliest decretists onwards. For the most part, they were not new, and on the whole, they did not change substantially. They were the essential bases of the continuity of canonist thought.

The elements of continuity throughout this formative period should perhaps be emphasized. It has often been asserted that at some stage in the opening decade or so of the thirteenth century, the canonists began to forsake an earlier established 'moderate' position in favor of an increasingly uncritical 'extremist' position. The view seems no longer acceptable. Whether it is thought that the early canonists were moderate or extreme in their views, it can scarcely be maintained that their successors were substantially different. There were changes — in terminology, in systematization, in emphasis, in length of treatment — but the really fundamental positions, at least as far as applications were concerned, remained the same.

Perhaps the most striking illustration of this continuity that can be made is in the matter of the papal deposing power. Few categories of papal action demonstrate more fundamentally the nature of papal authority in temporal affairs, and the deposition of Frederick II by Innocent IV in 1245 was perhaps

---

[4] The justification for the privilege was argued by Innocent IV on the basis of glosses by Laurentius and Tancred: 'Sed quis eximit (clericos) de iure imperatoris cum prius ei subessent? Respondeo, quod papa consentiente imperatore, xi. q.iii c. iii. in aut. de sanc. epis. § si quis contra. in aut. ut cler. apud proprios epis. § vl. infra, de iur. cal.c.i. This was the solution of Laurentius: to it Tancred added: Sed hec non plene eximunt, unde dicimus quod exempti sunt a Deo, xcvi. di. Si imperator.' Innocent added: 'vel dic quod papa eciam sine consensu imperatori bene potuit eos eximere a iurisdictione imperatoris per suas constitutiones, quia cum clerici spirituales res sint, et ex toto corpus et animam dederunt in servitium et in sortem Christi transtulerunt, xii.q.i.c.iii: per consequens pape in iudicio et constitutionibus subsunt, x. di. Imperium, Suscipitisne, et infra c. Solite': *Appar.* ad 1.34.2 s. v. *principi.* Hostiensis repeated substantially the same gloss, *App. ad loc.* s.v. *abiiciatur,* pointing out, however, that this was a 'privilegium personale' and not 'reale' and also that there were exceptions to the former. These exceptions which, he was careful to indicate, were 'de licentia ecclesie,' are given *Apparatus* ad 3.30.25.s.v. *de spiritualibus.*

the most drastic of all applications of it. Whatever view might be taken of the prudence of that act, there can be no doubt that, as far as the canonists were concerned, it contained no doctrinal novelty. Innocent IV based his action on a deposition theory drawn from the *glossa ordinaria* of the *Decretum*, itself the compressed summary of the common opinion of the early decretists. And, taking continuity further back, it is to be observed that the decretists case for papal deposition made no doctrinal additions to the case advanced by Gregory VII when he deposed Henry IV; with which action the decretists had a direct textual link. In the light of this sort of continuity in so fundamental a matter, it is difficult to believe that canonist thought changed radically in any of its essential positions.

There is a second train of thought, however, which suggests the same conclusion more powerfully, a train of thought which clarifies the whole notion of papal superiority in canonist thought, and its relation to non-canonist writers both before and after our period.

Anyone who seeks to understand the fundamentals of medieval political thought must inescapably treat of the theme of unity, that principle, which, as Gierke so finely saw, was the source and goal of the medieval view of human society. But Gierke's brilliant sketch of the medieval *ordinatio ad unum* was basically the analysis of a philosophical system; his sources Augustine and, to a great extent, the medieval Aristotelians. Some of the most interesting of recent research has been devoted to the theme of unity as a policy, actually pursued by the popes, particularly in the early middle ages. From the ninth century, it has been made clear, the popes were deliberately directing men's thoughts to the idea that Christendom, the universal society of the faithful, should be regarded as an organic whole, that it should be considered the noblest of communities, that to belong to it was the first and most natural duty of a Christian ruler and his people. The terms *Christianitas, Christianus populus* and the like, though lacking theological precision, were specific enough to disseminate the idea that the spiritual solidarity of the practice of the same faith constituted the bond of an external visible community. The Roman Church, it was postulated, was not merely the 'mother of churches'; it was also 'mother of nations.' Again the term was ultimately somewhat vague, but the papal intention in using it is clear enough. It was to evoke recognition of the principle that the diversity of Christian peoples formed a unity because the papacy existed to promote a common good of all Christians, transcending the particular goods of individual rulers and peoples. Thus this society, Christendom, existed because there was in the Roman Church a focus of institutional unity, both spiritual and temporal. The pope, it was claimed, as pope, by right of his apostolic mission itself, was the foundation of a single Christian *respublica*, exercising a charge over all Christian nations.

If then, the idea of unity is the key idea in medieval political thought, it was born not so much of the abstractions of the *De civitate Dei*, much less of the philosophical concepts of order, derived from Plato and Aristotle, as of the travail of a particular historical context. The papal insistence on a unity of Western Christian nations in Christian solidarity under the *principatus* of the Roman Church was the papal reaction to a century of disintegration — the period of the break-up of the Carolingian empire, of Arab and Scandinavian invasion, of rupture between Rome and Constantinople. If Christianity remained the one light in this darkness, Christianity (it was asserted) lived solely through the Roman Church. The papal guardianship over a universal Christian society in its temporal aspect was, therefore, only the corollary of the popes' spiritual function.

The second half of the eleventh century was of crucial importance in the development of this line of thought about the papal headship of Christian society. This was the period of completion in the sense that it was now brought to maturity, and of new beginning in that its scope of application was widened. Gregory VII laid down the characteristic political attitude of the twelfth-century papacy: its role as *princeps super regna mundi*,[5] its *cura totius Christianitatis*,[6] its function as *debitor iusticiae in omnibus qui in Christo sunt*.[7] Such phrases, expressing the notion of a supreme judge of Christian society, conventionalized in the phraseology of the papal chancery, became the terms of reference of twelfth-century political thought.

These terms were sufficiently well-established for the canonists to rest content in assuming them. They formed the context within which canonist political ideas were worked out, but for the most part it was a framework which they took for granted. Their task was not to speculate about the nature of this Christian society, a line of thought left to other types of writer to develop. Canonist concern was with the more prosaic work of registering the occasion of the exercise of the papal headship of *Christianitas*. This work they did assiduously and in general agreement.

It was especially in the early decretalist phase of canonist scholarship that the canonists reached a common opinion as to the occasions on which the pope intervened in temporal affairs. In listing them, they were drawing on what had actually happened. Their work was not speculative; it was a recording of the acts (or some of them) of the pope fulfilling his function as judicial head of Christendom. The catalogue of such acts became a standard feature of canonist political writing for the rest of the thirteenth century, and represents, perhaps, its most characteristic expression. What received special

---

[5] *Reg.* 1.63 (p.92 ed. Caspar).

[6] *Reg.* 1.15; 1.29; 5.2 (pp. 24, 46, 349).

[7] *Reg.* 2.44; 6.13 (pp. 180, 416).

emphasis was the principle that the pope intervened in temporal affairs to ensure that no individual Christian or people should be denied due measure of justice for lack of recourse to a superior tribunal. The thirteenth-century canonists agreed that redress could be had from the pope either by application to him, or on his initiative, when the normal judicial machinery was obstructed through the negligence or culpability of a secular ruler, or through a vacancy in the office of ruler, or when the matter in question was especially difficult, or existing law made no adequate provision, or when the impartiality of judges was suspect. Thus the canonist fashioned a distinctively juridical formulation of the papal *cura totius Christianitatis* in a theory of prerogative power, based on the known instances of its exercise.

This was the uniquely canonist contribution to medieval thought about the papacy as an international power, and it passed into all future discussions of the problem.[8] Yet it developed very slowly. Canonists of the early part of the thirteenth century were content to assume much. They took for granted the idea of the papacy as the constitutive principle of Christendom. They applied a notion of prerogative power without stopping to try to disentangle the notion as such from the circumstances of its exercise. It was the prick of controversy, the propaganda attacks of Frederick II on the whole notion of a papal power in temporal affairs which stimulated the first canonist examination of these two basic features. The major canonists of the century, Innocent IV and Hostiensis, did not add occasions on which the power was exercised to the number listed by their predecessors; but they did attempt to consider the fundamentals in themselves. It was urged, by way of a theology of history, that, from the creation of the world, God had not ceased to rule it. After a brief period of direct divine government, the divine charge had been entrusted to a succession of vicars, the rulers of the chosen people, continuously through the Old Testament to the New, through the history of the *populus Dei* to its transformation into *Christianitas*. Divine law thus reached the world through a visible head, charged to rule as divine vicar, empowered with all things necessary for the welfare of Christian society. To the pope then, as wielder of the plenitude of spiritual power, had been given sufficient power in temporal affairs, to the extent of supplying defect of secular justice, punishing culpable negligence in the actions of any king, and generally upholding the harmony, security and peace of Christendom. Thus there emerged the central tenet of whole theory of the papal power in temporal affairs, whatever subordinate justificatory arguments might be involved: with the pope resided a pleni-

---

[8] It was this notion which Aegidius Romanus drew from the canonists in a key chapter of his *De ecclesiastica potestate*, 3.9: 'Quid est plenitudo potestatis et quod in summo pontifice veraciter potestatis residet plenitudo' (ed. R. Scholz 90-95), whence to James of Viterbo, *De regimine Christiano* 2.8 (ed. H. X. Arquillière 251).

tude of power extending to all that was necessary and expedient for the *salus reipublicae Christianae.* It is perhaps significant that the papacy had long been acting on the principle before the canonists arrived at its conscious formulation.

It was the search to find a foundation in divine law for an *officium pastoralitatis* of this type which was to give thirteenth-century papal and canonist thought a coloring which many modern historians have found extreme. Essentially the principle was based on the power of the pope as *vicarius Christi* exercising the kingship of Christ. What received especial emphasis was his sovereignty over a juridical society concretely realised as Christendom — 'une réalité territoriale, démographique, politique et religieuse.'[9] It was this monarchy over a specific society situated in time and place that was envisaged. Hence the fundamental ecclesiological notions in which it was argued — the unity of the Church, the Mystical Body, the kingship of Christ — lost much of their purely spiritual and charismatic meaning and became politicized. No doubt there was always a tendency for this to happen whenever ecclesiastical writers wished to discuss the Christian body politic. But it was more than a tendency once the term *vicarius Christi* became generally accepted. By its means a whole argument could be summarized whereby the mystical unity of the Church was equated with the unitary structure of Christian society and its mystical headship was construed as the temporalized kingship of the pope over this community. Hence such exaggerated and unspecific language as: 'Jesus Christus preest toto orbi ita et papa';[10] '(papa) solus dominus universalis in toto mundo':[11] this theme is already discernible in canonist thought before the pontificate of Innocent III. But he gave it great impetus and thereafter it was a continuous thread in the canonist tradition — Boniface VIII was linked to Alanus Anglicus and Tancred through Hostiensis, Innocent IV, the *glossa ordinaria* on the Decretals and such canonists as Henry of Cremona and the anonymous commentator of *Clericis laicos*, who wrote apologetic treatises.

The coexistence within the canonist tradition of this unitary theme with a dualistic one gave it a certain disharmony. From the early decretists to the early decretalists, and continuously to the post-Gregorian commentators,

---

[9] G. Le Bras, *Histoire du droit et des institutions de l'Église en occident*, I: *Prolégomènes* (Paris 1955) 239.

[10] *Summa Reginensis* (c. 1191): 'Dicebat cardinalis sanctorum Johannis et Pauli quod inde dominus papa dicitur Christi vicarius quia Jesus Christus preest . . . ': ed. Stickler, in *Studia Gratiana* 3 (1955) 393.

[11] Henry of Cremona: 'Hoc etiam est de necessitate nature, scilicet quod papa sit solus dominus universalis in toto mundo, quia omnes fideles sunt una ecclesia . . . ': *De potestate papae* ed. R. Scholz, *Die Publizistik zur Zeit Philipps des Schönen und Bonifaz' VIII* (Stuttgart 1903) 469.

canonist thought knew a two-fold tendency, a tension between two lines of thought, the reflection, in its purely medieval form, of the perennial precariousness of the balance between Church and State. It was dualist whenever it was nearest to particular practical problems and to the lessons of Roman law. It was monist when it wished to emphasize the existence of a single Christian society under a single head. For much the greater part of canonist writing, it was the dualist emphasis which had the more significant place. But emphasis on unitary Christian society was the almost automatic canonist and papal reaction to attacks on the papal power in temporal affairs. This reaction was already discernible in the time of Frederick II. It was the distinctive note of the works of Innocent IV and Hostiensis. It was not a new note in itself, but the prominence given to it by these writers was new to the canonist tradition. It reappeared, in strengthened form, in the time of Philip the Fair and Boniface VIII gave it the seal of official approval in *Unam sanctam.*

The twofold tendency remained: Boniface VIII himself gave it expression in one of his best known *cris de cœur.*[12] One trend emphasized the separation of the powers, knew the natural political order, paid adequate regard to what was due to royal rights, solved particular points of mutual interest quite realistically. The other trend made the unity of Christendom its overriding concern. The two trends were never harmonized. Perhaps harmony was impossible to come by. At any rate, the attempt was not made, and a major thirteenth-century canonist, such as Hostiensis, will often seem to a modern student of his work to have advanced at one place positions inconsistent with positions advanced in another part.

There are few things more instructive about the thirteenth-century canonists than the study of how their views were used by the polemical writers of all sides in the days of Philip the Fair and Louis of Bavaria. Papal, royal and imperial propagandists were all to find in the standard canonist commentaries important material to advance their cases. The champions of the papacy would claim Hostiensis and his predecessors for their contribution to the logic of the papal headship of Christendom. The champions of the secular power would claim them for their contribution to the logic of dualism. It is exceedingly difficult to say definitely which side was guilty of the more serious misrepresentation. Modern historians have remembered the canonists for their service to papal theocracy. Before making this the whole story, however, they should bear in mind that Aegidius Romanus, perhaps the most extreme papalist of all, devoted a substantial part of his treatise to demolishing the dualist position as made by the thirteenth century canonists, while on the other hand William of Ockham, the most penetrating of anti-papalists (writing

---

[12] Above, p. 129 n. 49.

at a later date), consistently used that same dualist position as a major weapon. It was often the fate of the moderate aspects of canonist thought to be ignored or attacked by the papal apologists. But they were put to constructive use in helping to re-establish a new theoretical equilibrium between the two powers. It was ironical that this was a canonist service sometimes more appreciated by the anti-papalists than by the orthodox. But the real significance of the thirteenth-century canonists' work is thereby brought out. Not merely did it record the distinctively medieval political idea, that of Christendom, but it looked also towards the more distinctively modern one, that of the sovereign ruler.

Contradiction

LIST OF WORKS CITED

I. Sources: law and legal literature

(a) *Manuscripts*

(i) Commentary on the *Decretum*

ALANUS ANGLICUS, *Apparatus 'Ius naturale'*. B[ibliothèque] N[ationale] 15393

Apparatus 'Ecce vicit leo'. BN Nouv. acq. 1576

Glossa Palatina, Durham Cathedral MS C.III.8

Glossae anonymae, B[ritish] M[useum] MS Stowe 378
        Durham Cath. C.I.7
        Durham Cath. C.II.1
        Gonville and Caius College, Cambridge MS 676

HUGUCCIO, *Summa* Pembroke College, Cambridge MS 72 (to D. 56)
        Lincoln Cathedral MS 2 (Pars Ia, IIIa)
        BN 15396-7
        BN 3892

JOANNES FAVENTINUS, *Summa* BM MS Royal 9.E.VII

RICARDUS ANGLICUS, *Summa Quaestionum* Zwettl MS 162

SIMON DE BISIGNANO, *Summa* Lambeth Palace MS 411
        Summa 'Elegantius in iure' BN 14997
        Summa 'Tractaturus Magister' BN 15594

(ii) Commentary on the *Quinque Compilationes Antiquae*

Compilatio Ia: Tancred, BN 3930; Durham Cath. MS C.III.4

Compilatio IIa: Damasus, BN 3932; BM Roy. 11.C.VII

Compilatio IIIa: Laurentius Hispanus, BN 3932; BN 3930
        Joannes Teutonicus, BM Roy. 11.C.VII; Caius MS 17.28
        Tancred, Durham Cath. MS C.III.4; Caius MS 17.28
        Vincentius Hispanus, BN 14611; Caius MS 17.28

Compilatio IVa: Joannes Teutonicus, BN 3932; BM Roy. 11.C.VII

Compilatio Va: James of Albenga, BM Roy. 11.C.VII.

DAMASUS, *Brocarda, Quaestiones* BN 14320

PAULUS HUNGARUS, *Notabilia* BN 14320

(iii) Commentary on the *Gregoriana*

HOSTIENSIS, *Summa* Trinity College, *Cambridge* MS B.16.46.

(b) *Early Editions*

BENINCASA OF AREZZO, *Casus ad Decretum*, printed with,

BERNARD OF PARMA, *Glossa ordinaria* printed with *Decretales Gregorii IX*
(Paris 1561)

Corpus Iuris Civilis quo ius universum Iustianianeum comprehenditur. . .
(Cologne 1624)

GUIDO DE BAYSIO, *Rosarium super Decretum* (Venice 1578)

GUILELMUS DURANTIS, *Speculum iudiciale* (Basle 1574)
Rationale divinorum officiorum (Venice 1609)

GOFFREDUS DE TRANO, *Summa super titulis Decretalium* (Venice 1586)

HOSTIENSIS, *Summa aurea super titulis Decretalium* (Cologne 1612)
*Apparatus (Lectura) in quinque Decretalium
Gregorianum libros* (Paris 1512)

INNOCENTIUS IV, *Commentaria super libros quinque Decretalium* (Venice 1491)

JOANNES TEUTONICUS, *Glossa ordinaria* printed with *Decretum Gratiani*
(Paris 1561)

JOANNES MONACHUS, Commentary on *Unam sanctum* in *Extravagantes Ioan-
nis XXII cum apparatu Zenzelini de Cassanis* (Paris 1561)

MARTINUS POLONUS, *Margarita Decreti seu tabula Martiniana* printed with
Decretum Gratiani (Paris 1561)

(c) *Modern editions*

BONCOMPAGNI, *Rhetorica novissima*, in *Bibliotheca iuridica Medii Aevi*:
Scripta anecdota Glossatorum ed. A. Gaudenzi II (Bologna 1892)

Corpus Iuris Canonici, ed. A. Friedberg
I. *Decretum Magistri Gratiani* (Leipzig 1879)
II. *Decretalium collectiones* (1881)

Corpus Iuris Civilis, ed. P. Kruger (Berlin 1908)

Curialis, ed. L. Wahrmund, *Quellen zur Geschichte des römisch-kanonischen
Processes im Mittelalter* (Innsbruck 1905-28) I. 2

JOANNES BASSIANUS, *Libellus de ordine iudiciorum* ed. Gaudenzi, *op.cit.*

LAWRENCE OF SOMERCOTE, *De electionibus* ed. A. von Wretschko, *Der Traktat des Laurentius de Somercote, Kanonikus von Chichester über die Vornahme von Bischofswahlen, entstanden im Jahre 1254* (Weimar 1907)

PETER OF BLOIS, *Speculum iuris canonici* ed. T. A. Reimarus (Berlin 1837)

RAYMOND OF PEÑAFORT, St, *Summa iuris* ed. J. Ríus Serra (Barcelona 1945)

RUFINUS *Die Summa Decretorum des Magister Rufinus* ed. H. Singer (Pader-
born 1902)

Sermo habitus in Lateranensi concilio sub Alexandro Papa III ed. G. Morin, 'Le discours d'ouverture du concile général de Latran (1179) et l'œuvre littéraire de Maître Rufin,' *Atti della Pontificia Accademia Romana di Archaeologia* ser. 3, mem. 11 (Rome 1928)

STEPHEN OF TOURNAI, *Die Summa des Stephanus Tornacensis über das Decretum Gratiani* ed. J. F. Schulte (Giessen 1891)

TANCRED, *Ordo iudiciarius* in F. Bergmann, *Pillii, Tancredi Gratiae libri de iudiciorum ordine* (Göttingen 1842) 87-316

II. Sources other than legal

(a) *Papal Sources*

CHENEY, R. R. AND SEMPLE, W. H., *Selected letters of Innocent III concerning England, 1198-1216* (London 1953)

DUPUY P., *Histoire du différend d'entre le Pape Boniface VIII et Philippe le Bel* (Paris 1655)

Gesta Innocentii III, PL 214. xvii-ccxxviii

GREGORY VII, *Das Register Gregors VII* ed. E. Caspar (MGH Berlin 1920)

HOROY, *Honorii III Rom. Pont. Opera omnia in Medii Aevi Bibliotheca Patristica* (Paris 1879-82)

INNOCENT III, *Opera omnia* PL 214-7
> *Regestum super negotio Romani imperii* ed. F. Kempf (*Miscellanea Historiae Pontificiae* 12, Rome 1947)

LUCIUS III, *Epistolae* PL 201.1069-1378

MANSI, J. D. *Sacrorum conciliorum nova et amplissima collectio* 24 (Venice 1770)

MONUMENTA GERMANIAE HISTORICA, *Sectio epistolarum*:
Epp. s. XIII e regestis Pont. Rom. selectae. I. *Honorii III, Gregorii IX* (Berlin 1883) II. *Innocentii IV* (Berlin 1887)

POTTHAST, A. *Regesta Pont. Rom. inde ab anno post post Christum natum MCXCVIII ad annum MCCIV* (Berlin 1874-5)

WINKELMANN, E. *Acta imperii inedita seculi XIII et XIV* (Innsbruck 1885)

(b) *Theological literature*

ALBERTUS MAGNUS, *Commentarium in evangelium D. Matthei* in *Opera omnia* 8 (Lyons 1651)
> *Summa theologiae* in *Operae omnia* 18 (Lyons 1651)

ALEXANDER OF HALES, *Glossa in IV libros Sententiarum* (*Bibliotheca Franciscana Scholastica Medii Aevi* 15: Quaracchi 1957)

AQUINUS, ST THOMAS, *Catena aurea super quattuor evangelia* (Paris 1611)
Contra errores Graecorum ed. M. de Maria
Opuscula philosophica et theologica 3 (Rome 1886) and P. Glorieux, *S. Thomas d'Aquin: Contra errores Graecorum* (*Monumenta Christiana Selecta* Paris 1957)
In libros Politicorum expositio ad. R. M. Spiazzi (Turin 1951)
Scriptum in IV libros Sententiarum ed. P. Mandonnet et M. F. Moos (Paris 1929-47)
Summa contra Gentiles: editio leonina manualis (Rome 1934)

BELLARMINE St Robert, *Tractatus de potestate summi pontificis in rebus temporalibus adversus Guilelmum Barclajum* (Rome 1610): *San Roberto Bellarmino: Scritti Politici* ed. C. Giacon (Bologna 1950)

BERNARD OF CLAIRVAUX, St, *De consideratione* PL 182.727-808

BONAVENTURE St, *In quinque libros Sententiarum; Opuscula theologica* in *Opera omnia* (Quaracchi 1882-92)

GROSSETESTE, Robert, *Epistolae* ed. H. R. Luard *Rolls Series* (1861)

HUGH OF ST. VICTOR, *De sacramentis* PL 176.173-618

HUMBERTUS DE ROMANIS, *Opusculum tripartitum* ed. E. Brown, *Fasciculus rerum expetendarum* 2 (London 1640)

NICHOLAS OF COTRONE, *Libellus de fide sanctae Trinitatis*, ed. P. A. Uccelli, *Anonymus liber de fide sanctissimae Trinitatis*. . . (Rome 1880) 377-442 and P. Glorieux *op. cit. s. n.* Aquinas

PETRUS COMESTOR, *Historia scholastica* PL 198.1054-1722

Tractatus contra Graecos ed. P. Stevart, *Tomus singularis insignium auctorum tam Graecorum quam Latinorum*. . . (Ingolstadt 1616) 535-631

(c) *Political literature*

AEGIDIUS ROMANUS, *De ecclesiastica potestate* ed. R. Scholz (Weimar 1929)

AEGIDIUS SPIRITALIS DE PERUSIO, *Libellus contra infideles et inobedientes et rebelles sanctae Romanae ecclesiae ac summo pontifici* ed R. Scholz, *Unbekannte Kirchenpolitische Streitschriften aus der Zeit Ludwigs des Bayern, 1327-54* (Rome 1911-14) 2.105-29

HENRY OF CREMONA, *De potestate papae* ed R. Scholz, *Die Publizistik zur Zeit Philippe des Schönen und Bonifaz VIII* (Stuttgart 1903) 459-71

HOBBES, Thomas, *Leviathan or the Matter, Forme and Power of a Commonwealth ecclesiasticall and civil* ed. M. Oakeshott (Oxford n. d.)

HONORIUS OF AUTUN, *Summa gloria de apostolico et augusto* MGH *Libelli de Lite* 3. 63-80

JAMES OF VITERBO, *De regimine christiano* ed. H. X. Arquillière, *Le plus ancien traité de l'église, Jacques de Viterbe, De Regimine Christiano (1301-2)* (Paris 1926)

JOHN OF SALISBURY, *Policraticus* ed. C. C. J. Webb (Oxford 1909)

JOHN OF PARIS, *Tractatus de potestate regia et papali* ed. J. Leclercq, *Jean de Paris et l'ecclésiologie du xiiie siècle* (Paris 1942)

Non ponant laici, ed. R. Scholz, *Die Publizistik* 471-84

PTOLOMY OF LUCCA, *Determinatio compendiosa de iurisdictione imperii,* ed. M. Krammer (Hannover 1909)

Rex pacificus, ed. P. Dupuy, *Histoire du différend* 663-83

III. Secondary Works

AMANN, E. *Innocent IV* DThC

BAYLEY, C.C. *The Formation of the German College of Electors in the Mid-Thirteenth Century* (Toronto 1949)

BARRACLOUGH, G. 'The Making of a Bishop in the Middle Ages,' *Catholic Historical Review* 19 (1933-4) 275-319

BRYS, J. *De dispensatione in iure canonico praesertim apud decretistas et decretalistas usque ad medium saeculum XIV* (Bruges 1925)

CANTINI, J. A. 'De autonomia iudicis saecularis et de Romani pontificis plenitudine potestatis in temporalibus secundum Innocentium IV,' *Salesianum* 23 (1961) 407-80

Sinibalde dei Fieschi DDC

CARLYLE, R.W. AND A.J. *History of Medieval Political Theory in the West* (Edinburgh-London 1909-36)

CHENU, M. D. 'Dogme et théologie dans la bulle *Unam Sanctam,*' *Mélanges J. Lebreton* (Paris 1952) 2.307-16

CONGAR, Y.M.-J. 'Ecce constitui te super gentes et regna (Jér. 1.10) "in Geschichte und Gegenwart"', *Theologie in Geschichte und Gegenwart: M. Schmaus zum sechzigsten Geburtstag dargebracht. . .* (Munich 1957) 671-96

'L'ecclésiologie de S. Bernard.' *S. Bernard théologien* (*Anal. Sacr. Ord. Cist.* 9 [1953] 136-90)

DE LUBAC, H. *Corpus Mysticum* (2nd. ed. Paris 1949)

DIDIER, N. 'Henri de Suse, évêque de Sisteron (1244-1250),' *Revue historique de droit français et étranger* ⁴ 31 (1945) 244-70; 409-29

'Henri de Suse en Angleterre (1236?-44)', *Studi Arangio-Ruiz* (Naples 1952) 333-51

'Henri de Suse, prieur d'Antibes et prévôt de Grasse (1235?-45),' *Studia Gratiana* 2 (1954) 595-617

DONDAINE, A. '"Contra Graecos": Premiers écrits polémiques des Dominicains d'Orient,' *Archivum Fratrum Praedicatorum* 21 (1951) 320-446

DUGGAN, C. 'The Becket Dispute and the Criminous Clerks', *Bulletin of the Institute of Historical Research* 35 (1962) 1-28

FOLZ, R. 'La papauté médiévale vue par quelques-uns de ses historiens récents,' *Revue historique* 218 (1957) 32-63

GARCÍA Y GARCÍA, A. 'El Concilio IV de Letrán (1215) y sus commentarios', *Bulletin of the Institute of Research in Medieval Canon Law: Traditio* 14 (1958) 484-502

GAUDEMET, J. *La formation du droit séculier et du droit de l'Église au ive et ve siècles* (Paris 1957) and review, A. Boon, *Bulletin de théologie ancienne et médiévale* 8 (1958) 178

GEANAKOPLOS, D.J. *Emperor Michael Palaeologus and the West, 1258-1282* (Harvard 1595)

GÉNESTAL, R. *Histoire de la légitimation des enfants naturels en droit canonique* (Paris 1905)

GÉNICOT, L. *Les lignes de faîte du moyen âge* (Louvain 1951)

GEWIRTH, A. *Marsilius of Padua* (Columbia 1951-6)

GIERKE, O. VON (transl. F. W. MAITLAND) *Political Theories of the Midlde Age* (Cambridge 1900)

GILLMANN, F. 'Von wem stammen die Ausdrücke *potestas directa*, und *potestas indirecta papae in temporalibus*?' *Archiv für katholisches Kirchenrecht* 98 (1918) 407-09

'Zur scholastischen Auslegung von Mt. xvi, 18,' AKKR 104 (1924) 40-53

'Romanus pontifex iura omnia in scrinio pectoris sui censetur habere,' AKKR 106 (1926) 156-74

GOEZ, W. *Translatio imperii* (Tübingen 1958)

HAGENEDER, O. 'Exkommunication und Thronfolgeverlust bei Innocenz III,' *Römische historische Mitteilungen* 2 (1959) 9-50

'Das päpstliche Recht der Fürstenabsetzung: seine kanonistische Grundlegung (1150-1250), '*Archivum historiae pontificiae* 1 (1963) 55-95

'Studien zur Dekretale "Vergentis" (X, V, 7, 10): Ein Beitrag zur Häretikergesetzgebung Innocenz.' III,' *Zeitschrift der Savigny-Stiftung für Rechtsgeschichte. Kan. Abt.* 49 (1963) 138-73

HEFELE, C.-J. and LECLERCQ, H. *Histoire des conciles* 5-6 (Paris 1913-14)

HOF, A. 'Plenitudo potestatis und imitatio imperii zur Zeit Innocenz' III,' *Zeitschrift für Kirchengeschichte* 66 (1954-5) 39-71

JACQUELINE, B. 'Bernard et l'expression "plenitudo potestatis",' *Bernard de Clairvaux* (Paris 1952) 345-48

JORDAN, K. 'Die Entstehung der römischen Kurie,' ZRG *Kan. Abt.* 59 (1939) 97-152

JUNCKER, J. 'Die Summa des Simon von Bisignano und seine Glossen,' ZRG *Kan. Abt.* 15 (1926) 326-500

KANTOROWICZ, E. H. *The King's Two Bodies: a Study in Mediaeval Political Theology* (Princeton 1957)

KEMPF, F. *Papsttum und Kaisertum bei Innocenz III: die geistigen und rechtlichen Grundlagen seiner Thronstreitpolitik* (*Misc. hist. pont.* 19; Rome 1954)

KUTTNER, S. *Repertorium der Kanonistik (1140-1234), Prodromus corporis glossarum* I (*Studi e Testi* 71; Città del Vaticano 1937)

'Bernardus Compostellanus Antiquus: a Study in the Glossators of the Canon Law,' *Traditio* 1(1943)277-340

'The Scientific Investigation of Medieval Canon Law: the Need and the Opportunity,' *Speculum* 21(1949)491-501

LADNER, G.B. 'The Concepts of "ecclesia" and "christianitas" and their Relation to the Idea of Papal "plenitudo potestatis" from Gregory VII to Boniface VIII,' in *Sacerdozio e Regno da Gregorio VII a Bonifacio VIII* (*Misc. hist. pont.* 18: Rome 1954) 49-77.

LE BRAS, G. *L'immunité réelle* (Paris 1920)

Histoire du droit et des institutions de l'Église en Occident, I : Prolégomènes (Paris 1955)

Institutions ecclésiastiques de la chrétienté médiévale Préliminaires et I*re partie* 1 (*Histoire de l'Église* 12.i Ed. Fliche et Martin, Paris 1959)

'Le droit romain au service de la domination pontificale,' *Revue historique de droit français et étranger* [4] 27 (1949) 377-98

'Boniface VIII, symphoniste et modérateur,' *Mélanges Louis Halphen* (Paris 1951) 383-94

LECLERCQ, J. *Jean de Paris et l'ecclésiologie du* xiiie *siècle* (Paris 1942)

L'idée de la royauté du Christ au moyen âge (Paris 1959)

LEFEBVRE, C. *Hostiensis* DDC 1211-27

MACCARRONE, M., *Chiesa e Stato nella Dottrina di Papa Innocenzo III* (Rome 1940)

Vicarius Christi: Storia del titulo papale (Rome 1952)

McNALLY, R.E. 'The History of the Medieval Papacy: a Survey of Research, 1954-59,' *Theological Studies* 21(1960)92-132

MAITLAND, F.W. *Roman Canon Law in the Church of England* (London 1898)

MESNARD, P. *L'essor de la philosophie politique au* xvie *siècle* (Paris 1951)

MICHIELS, G. 'Pouvoir spirituel et pouvoir temporel,' *Bulletin de theologie ancienne et médiévale* 8 (1958)

MOCHI ONORY, S. *Fonti canonistische dell'idea moderna dello stato* (Milan 1951)

PACAUT, M. *Alexandre III. Étude sur la conception du pouvoir pontifical dans sa pensée et dans son œuvre* (Paris 1956)

La théocratie: l'Église et le pouvoir au moyen âge (Paris 1957)

'L'autorité pontificale selon Innocent IV', *Le Moyen Age* 66(1960) 85-119

POST, G. 'Two Notes on Nationalism in the Middle Ages,' *Traditio* 9(1953) 281-320

POWICKE, F. M. *Henry III and the Lord Edward* (Oxford 1947)

REUSCH, E.H. 'Die Fälschungen in dem Tractat des Thomas von Aquin gegen die Griechen: Opusculum contra errores Graecorum ad Urbanum IV,' *Abhandlungen der Bayerischen Akademie* 60 *Hist. Kl.* 18 (1899) 675-742

RIVIÈRE, J. '*In partem sollicitudinis. . .* Évolution d'une formule pontificale,' *Recherches de science religieuse* 5(1925)210-31

Le problème de l'église et de l'état au temps de Philippe le Bel (Louvain 1926)

RUPP, J. *L'idée de chrétienté dans la pensée pontificale des origines jusqu'a Innocent III* (Paris 1939)

SCHRAMM, P. E. 'Sacerdotium und Regnum im Austausch ihrer Vorrechte,' *Studi Gregoriani* 2(1947)403-57

SHANNON, A.C. *The Popes and Heresy in the Thirteenth Century* (Villanova 1949)

SOUTHERN, R.W. *The Making of the Middle Ages* (London 1953)

STICKLER, A. 'Der Schwerterbegriff bei Huguccio,' *Ephemerides Iuris Canonici* 3(1947)1-44

'Sacerdotium et Regnum nei Decretisti e primi Decretalisti,' *Salesianum* 15(1953)575-612

'Sacerdozio e Regno nelle nuove richerche attorno ai secolo XII e XIII nei decretisti e decretalisti,' *Misc. hist. pont.* 18(1954)1-26

'Imperator vicarius papae: Die Lehren der französisch-deutschen Dekretistenschule des 12. und beginnenden 13. Jahrhunderts über die Beziehungen zwischen Papst und Kaiser,' *Mitteilungen des Instituts für Österreichische Geschichtsforschung* 62(1954)

'Decretisti bolognesi dimenticati,' *Studia Gratiana* 3(Bologna 1955) 377-410

'Alanus Anglicus als Verteidiger des monarchischen Papsttums,' *Salesianum* 21(1959)346-406

TIERNEY, B. 'Some Recent Works on the Political Theories of the Medieval Canonists,' *Traditio* 10 (1954) 594-652

Foundations of Conciliar Theory (Cambridge 1955)

'Pope and Council: Some New Decretist Texts,' *Medieval Studies* 19 (1957) 197-218

'"Tria quippe distinguit iudicia. . .": A note on Innocent III's Decretal *Per venerabilem,*' *Speculum* 37(1962)48-59

TILLMANN, H. *Papst Innocenz III* (Bonn 1954)

TROMP, S. 'De evolutione doctrinae potestatis indirectae Romani Pontificis circa res temporales in controversiis S. Roberti Bellarmini,' *Acta Congressus iuridici internationalis* 3(Rome 1934)97-107

ULLMANN, W. 'A Medieval Document on Papal Theories of Government,' *English Historical Review* 61(1946)180-201

Medieval Papalism: the Political Theories of the Medieval Canonists (London 1949)

The Growth of Papal Government in the Middle Ages (London 1955) 'Some Reflections on the Opposition of Frederick II to the Papacy,' *Archivio Storico Pugliese* 13 (1960) 3-26

'Leo I and the Theme of Roman Primacy,' *Journal of Theological Studies* 11 (1960) 25-51

VAN DEN BAAR, P. A. *Die kirchliche Lehre der Translatio Imperii Romani bis zur Mitte des 13. Jahrhunderts* (Rome 1956)

VAN HOVE, *Prolegomena ad Codicem Iuris Canonici* (2nd. ed. Rome-Malines 1945)

VERNET, F. *Lyon* (*IIᵉ Concile œcuménique de*) DThC 1384-89

WATT, J.A. 'The Early Medieval Canonists and the Formation of Conciliar Theory,' *Irish Theological Quarterly* 24 (1957) 13-31

ZERBI, P. *Papato, impero e 'respublica christiana' dal 1187 al 1198* (Milan 1955)

INDEX

Aegidius Romanus, 129n., 141n., 143
Aegidius Spiritalis de Perusio, 109-10, 114
Alanus Anglicus, place in canonist thought, 33n., 46-9, 56, 62, 111, 142; on distinction of the powers, 13, 20-1; vicariate of Christ, 49-52; papal primacy, 81n., 83n., 95; deposing power, 50-1; *plenitudo potestatis, iudex ordinarius omnium*, 50, 95, 98
Albertus Magnus, St, 89, 96n.
Alexander III, Pope, 3, 24n., 28, 120, 132
Alexander of Hales, 57n., 89, 108
Alexis III, Emperor, 39n.
Ambrose, St, 14
Anastasius I, Emperor, 14
Antonius de Butrio, 37n.
Aquinas, St Thomas, 82n., 90-2, 96-7
Arcadius, Emperor, 14
Aristotle, 96n., 105, 137, 139
Augustine, St, 30, 128n., 139
Azo, 82n.

Bellarmine, St Robert, 52, 55
Benincasa of Arezzo, 13-4, 18-9
Bernard, St 2, 40, 51n., 60, 78, 79
Bible, Gen. 3.16-7; 5-9: 68n.
    14.9: 57n.
    Exod. 27.21; 38.1: 57n.
    Deut. 17.8: 38n., 115
        17.12: 41
    1 Kings 8.22; 10.1: 57n.
    Ps.   8.8: 8
        23.1: 115
        45.3: 96n.
        103.105: 2n.
    Prov. 13.22: 128n.
    Cant. 6. 8: 96
    Is. 33.22: 68n.
    Jer. 1.10: 39-41, 65, 86, 127n.
    Matt. 16.18-9: 15n., 26, 41, 64-6, 67n., 68, 83, 86, 88n., 89n., 137n.

    18.17: 17n., 41
    21.43: 128n.
    22.22: 13n., 118
    26.52: 37
Luke 5.4: 88n.
    22.38: 23n., 25n., 66
    23.34: 23n.
Jo.   1.42: 86
    19.11: 25n.
    20.23: 86
    21.17: 90n.
Acts   4.32: 29n.
1 Cor.   2.15: 58n.
    4.4: 16n., 86
    6.3: 26, 38, 58n., 65n.
2 Cor.   11.28: 9
Eph.   1.22: 8
Heb.   7.7: 57n.
Bodin, Jean, 84, 137
Bonaventure, St, 82, 89
Boncompagni, 93n.
Boniface VIII, Pope, 12, 34, 49, 51n., 59-60, 104, 109n., 133, 142, 143.
Brachium Seculare 31, 128n., 136

Celestine III, Pope, 85n.
Charlemagne, Emperor, 27
Childeric, King, 15, 26, 42, 48, 63
Christendom, 2, 7, 43-4, 51, 56-7, 63, 66-71, 83, 102-5, 114, 129-33, 139-42
Clement IV, Pope, 75n.
Clericis laicos, anonymous commentary on, 142
Code of Justinian, *see Corpus Iuris Civilis*
Coronation rite, 66, 116-1
Corpus Iuris Civilis
    Code 1.1.1: 87
        1.3.1: 20n.
        1.3.10: 53n.
        1.13.2,8: 119
        1.17.1: 20n.
        1.17.4: 88n.
        3.1.3: 54n.

3.7: 82n.
4.20.10: 83n.
5.13.1: 87
6.43.2: 87
7.39.8: 20n.
Dig.   1.2.2.11: 130
1.16.2: 54n.
26.8.1: 54n.
49.3.1: 83
50.1.3: 83
50.27.110: 129n.
Inst.   1.2.4: 82n.
1.2.6: 87
Nov.   6.pr.: 25n., 47n., 119
83.: 138n.
86.1.2: 49, 69n., 116
123.21: 138n.
131.11: 69n.
Councils, General, 3 Lateran, 1n.
31n., 80n.; 4 Lateran, 31n., 42,
48, 94n., 118, 127; 1 Lyons, 63
(see also, Frederick II, Innocent IV);
2 Lyons, 6, 75, 90-2; 1 Vatican, 75
Curialis, 96
Cyprian, St 13
Cyril of Alexandria, St 91

Damasus, 21, 26n., 53n.
Decretals, see Licet, Solite, Per venerabilem, Venerabilem, glossa ordinaria ad Decretales
Decretum, 2, 5, 10, 11, 13, 22, 26,
30, 76, 93, 111, 119, 125, 135.
Quoniam (D.10 c.8), 13, 18, 21,
24, 29, 54n., 99n., 119
Cum ad verum (D.96 c.6), 12, 16,
24, 28, 29, 50n., 62, 126n., 137n.
Duo sunt (D.96 c.10), 12, 14, 16,
17, 22, 28, 29, 39, 41, 64n., 119n.,
126n.
Si imperator (D. 96 c. 11), 18n.,
24n., 25, 29, 64n., 119n., 137, 138n.
Alius item (C.15.q.6.c.3), 12, 14-6,
22, 28, 48, 63-4, 128, 129n.
Principes (C.23.q.5.c.20), 30-1,
Administratores (C.23.q.5 c.26), 30-1,
49, 69n.
see also, Gratian
Deposing power, see Decretum (Alius
item), Huguccio, Alanus Anglicus,

Joannes Teutonicus, Innocent IV,
Hostiensis
Digest of Justinian, see Corpus Iuris
Civilis
Donation of Constantine, 25n.
Dualism, 7-8, 13, 21-2, 28-9, 32-3,
43-4, 54-5, 58, 114, 119, 121, 131
'Ecce vicit leo,' Apparatus, 20n., 23n.

Episcopal elections, 101-2, 123-5
Electoral college of German princes, 35
Emperor, homo papae 26 ; advocatus
papae, 36, 66n., 100n; defensor
Romanae ecclesiae, 36; plenitudo
potestatis of, 83, 112; Dei vicarius
in terris in temporalibus 112; solutus
legibus, 112n. See also Translation
of Empire Theory— Venerabilem
Eugenius III, Pope, 40
Extravagantes communes, 104 see also,
Unam sanctam
Extravagantes Innocentii IV, 63n.,
67n., 126n.

Frederick II, Emperor, 5, 9, 12, 62-4,
70, 99, 138, 141

Gandulphus, 27n.
Gelasius I, Pope, 'Gelasian doctrine,'
5, 10, 11, 41; in the Decretum,
9-11, 25; and the decretists, 12-34,
39; supreme judicial power of the
pope, 65n., 94-5; influence on Innocent III, 39, 117n.; on Hostiensis,
125-6
Glossae anonymae ad Decretum, Caius
MS. 676, 20n., 21n., 24n., 26, 84.;
BM. MS. Stoke 378, 15n.; Sidney
Sussex MS. 101, 15n.; Durham
Cath. MS.C.I.7, 15n.; Durham Cath.
MS.C.II.1, 27n., 77n.
Glossa ordinaria ad Decretales Gregoriana (Bernard of Parma), 22, 39n.,
41n., 108 142; two swords quaestio,
46-8, 72; indirect power, 52-3, 55;
certis causis inspectis, 55, 56n.
115; papal legislative authority, 87;
iudex ordinarius omnium, 95, 99; legitimation, 99; lay rulers and episcopal elections, 123

Glossa ordinaria ad Decretum, 14, 72, 119, 139 *see also* Joannes Teutonicus, Benincasa of Arezzo

Glossa Palatina, 23n., 25n., 36n., 81n.

Goffredus Tranensis, 5, 60, 95, 108, 128n.

Gratian, 9, 10, 12, 26. *dicta*: on the function of secular rulers, 30; papal judicial authority, 51n.; *Tu es Petrus*, 80-1; using the term *plenitudo potestatis*, 76

Gregory I, Pope, 9

Gregory VII, Pope, letter to Hermann of Metz, 12-3, 32, 64, 137; on deposition of kings, 15, 26, 63-6, 139; *debitor iusticiae*, 42n., 140; on papal primacy, 140; Christendom, 140

Gregory IX, Pope, 5, 70-1, 102n.

Gregory X, Pope, 75

Grosseteste, Robert, 12, 71n.

Guido de Baysio, 21n., 80n.

Guilelmus Durantis, 82n., 95, 100n.

Henry of Cremona, 8, 142

Heresy, legislation concerning, with canonist commentary, 31, 42-3, 48, 60, 120, 127-8.

History, use of, 15, 26-7, 44-5, 48, 56-7, 67-9, 71, 99-100, 114, 129, 141

Hobbes, Thomas, 78n.

Honorius of Autun, 29, 71

Honorius III, Pope, 88, 102n.

Hostiensis, place in canonist thought, 6, 107-8; sources of his political doctrine, 11, 108; use of Old Testament, 45, 68n., 130; papal primacy, 82n., 84n., 111; vicariate of Christ, 110n., 114-5, 129; *plenitudo potestatis*, 101-2, 110n., 112n., 114, 130; *iudex ordinarius omnium*, 95; superiority of spiritual power, 69n., 121-2, 129-33; on *Per venerabilem*, 109-17; deposition theory, 63-4, 128; punishment of heretics, 127-8; cases when ecclesiastical judges might intervene in the temporal order, 69n.; distinction of the powers, 7-8, 32, 112, 118-25; cooperation of the powers, 116-7, 118-28 ; *prin-*

cipatus of the emperor, 112 ; *libertas ecclesiae*, 137n., 138n.

Hugh of St Victor, 57, 60, 71, 108

Hugolinus, 77n.

Huguccio, 5, 15, 28, 34, 41, 47, 49, 51, 64n., 78, 86n.; deposing power, 15-18; distinction of the powers, 19-21, 24-5; *brachium seculare*, 31, 127; empire, 16, 23, 33, 47; papal primacy, 80n., 81-5; *iudex ordinarius*, 83n., 93-4; *plenitudo potestatis*, 82, 83n., 118

Humbert de Romanis, 97n.

Imperium sacerdotis, 38, 42, 63, 65, 71, 136-8

Indirect power, 49-56, 113, 137 *see also Novit*

Innocent I, Pope, 14

Innocent III, Pope, 3, 5, 16, 17, 27, 28, 29, 135; place in the history of canon law, 5, 11; and in the development of canonist political thinking, 9, 11-2, 34-60, 72-3; *plenitudo potestatis*, 85-6; *iudex ordinarius omnium*, 43, 93, 95; anointing of kings, 117n.; clerics forbidden to extend their jurisdiction, 118n.; Register, 2, 86n., 88n.; *Regestum de negotio Romani imperii*, 47n., 71, 102n.; *Sermones*, 2n., 51, 85-6, 88 *see also Vicariate of Christ, Licet, Solite, Novit, Venerabilem, Per venerabilem*

Innocent IV, Pope, 2, 4, 5, 9, 12, 32, 45, 52, 111, 130, 138; the decretalist, 58-73 ; legitimation, 61-2; *Ad apostolice sedis*, 62-3, 97n.; *Aeger cui levia*, 65-6 ; vicariate of Christ, 66-7, 70, 97, 99-100, 114, 129; Christendom, 66-71, 114; *libertas ecclesiae*, 69n., 138n.; *plenitudo potestatis*, 70, 99-100, 102-5; *iudex ordinarius omnium*, 95, 99; kings and episcopal elections, 123-5; on *Novit*, 132; deposition doctrine, 62-3, 139

Institutes of Justinian, *see Corpus Iuris Civilis*

Isidore, St, 30, 126, 128n.

'*Ius naturale,*' *Apparatus*, *see* Alanus Anglicus

James of Albenga, 88n.
James of Viterbo, 22n., 91n., 97n., 103, 141n.
Jerome, St, 30
Joannes Bassanus, 93n.
Joannes Faventinus, 24n., 77n., 78n.
Joannes Galensis, 53n.
Joannes Monachus, 96n.
Joannes Teutonicus, deposition theory 14, 48, 64n., 139; two swords theory, 36n.; sun-moon metaphor, 39; Church and the maintenance of peace, 41; indirect power, 53n.; legitimation, 54, 112n.; primacy of jurisdiction, 81; plenitude of power, 82n.
John VIII, Pope, 30
John, King of England, 17, 41, 123 132
John Chrysostom, St, 90n.91
John of Paris, 97n.
John of Salisbury, 29

Keys, power of the, *see* Bible, Matt. 16.18-19
Kingship, ministerial to *sacerdotium*, 29-33, 126-7, 136
Kingship of Christ, 45, 47, 66-8, 117, 131-2, 142

Laurentius Hispanus, 25, 36n., 47, 49, 54, 55n., 56n., 112n., 138n.
Lawrence of Somercote, 124-5
Licet (X.2.2.10), 34, 60, 71, 118n. 120; doctrine, 41-2; significance, 43; interpretation, 53n. (Damasus); 62n. (Innocent IV); 66, 68-9, 130n. (Innocent IV and Hostiensis)
Legitimation, *see Per venerabilem*
Leo I, Pope, 30, 65n., 76, 79, 85
Libertas ecclesiae, 69n., 137-8
Louis of Bavaria, 143
Lucius III, Pope, 85n.

Magna Carta, 123
Martinus Polonus, 80n.
Michael VIII Palaiologos, 75, 89n.

Mystical Body, 104-5, 115, 133, 142

Natural theory of the origin of political authority, 112, 137
Nicholas I, Pope, 11, 19, 65n.
Nicholas of Cotrone, 89n., 90
Novellae of Justinian, *see Corpus Iuris Civilis*,
Novit (X..2.1.13), 34, 54, 60, 108, 120 ; circumstances of promulgation, 17, 41, 120, 132; doctrine 40-1, 52, 55; interpretation, 14n., 21 (St Raymond of Peñafort); 41n., 49, 53 (Tancred); 41n., 53, 54n. (J. Teutonicus); 41n. 53, 99n. (Bernard of Parma); 48, 53 (Vincentius Hispanus); 50 (Alanus); 52 (Bellarmine); 53 (Damasus); 61-2, 65, 71, 100n. (Innocent IV); 121-2, 132 (Innocent IV and Hostiensis); significance, 41, 43-4, 56, 58, 132

Old Testament, use of, 38, 39-41, 44-5, 47, 56-7, 66, 67-8, 71, 80, 99, 111, 115, 123, 141 *see also* Bible
Otto I, Emperor, 26
Oath, sworn by emperor to pope, 25n., 26, 100

Pars sollicitudinis, *see* Pope, *plenitudo potestatis*
Paul, St, *see* Bible
Paulus Hungarus, 95n.
Pepin, 14, 26, 48
Per venerabilem (X.4.17.13), 60, 98-9, 118, 120; circumstances of promulgation and content, 37-8, 45, 61; significance, 39, 41-4, 70, 115, 117; interpretation, 49, 53-6 (Laurentius); 50, 53-6 (Alanus); 52, 55 (Bellarmine); 53-6, 85 (Bernard of Parma); 53-6 (J. Teutonicus, Vincentius, St Raymond of Peñafort); 69, 137n. (Innocent IV and Hostiensis); 108-17, 132 (Hostiensis)
Peter, St, Decretist exegesis of Petrine texts, 80-83; *see also* Bible
Peter Damian, St, 15n., 26
Peter of Blois, 19-20

Petrus Beneventanus, 33n.
Petrus Comestor, 39n.
Philip Augustus, King of France, 17, 37-8, 40, 41, 61, 120, 132
Philip IV, King of France, 109n., 143
Pope, *antonomastice iudex*, 28, 33, 72, 94; *caput ecclesiae*, 90; *caput vel vertex Apostolorum vel apex*, 90; *Christus, Domini*, 51; *debitor iusticiae*, 42, 49, 132, 140; *Deus Pharaonis*, 51, *diligens pater familias*, 67; *dominus spiritualium et temporalium*, 8, 105, 109, 115, 131, 133; *dominus universalis*, 142; *fundamentum totius christianitatis*, 102; *generalis legatio*, 66; *imperium spirituale*, 15, 28, 56; *inter Deum et hominem medius constitutus*, 51; *iudex ordinarius omnium*, 6, 10, 26, 43, 50, 56, 83n., 92-6, 98-9, 100n., 105, 135; *iudex superior*, 35; *iura reservata*, 45, 84-5, 102; *maior et superior omnibus christianis*, 114; *plenitudo potestatis*, 5-6, 28, 43, 50, 56, 63n., 70, 75-92, 94, 99-105, 130, 136, 141-2; *primus et maximus*, 91; *princeps super regna mundi*, 140; *summus rector*, 96; *vicarius Christi*, 7, 28-9, 33, 43, 47, 49-51, 56, 63, 66-7, 70, 85, 87, 90, 97, 99-100, 114-5, 117, 127n., 129, 133, 142; *see also Romana ecclesia*
Privilegium fori, 31, 32n., 138
Prooemium, Sapientia edificavit, 29n.
Pseudo-Gregory IV, 76n.
Pseudo-Isidore, 76n.
Ptolomy of Lucca, 8, 64n.

Quaestiones Orielenses, 25n.
Quinque Compilationes Antiquae, 5, 60, 108

Rainerius, 39n., 47n.
Ratione peccati, 14, 17, 21, 52-3, 65, 121-2; *see also Novit*
Raymond of Peñafort, St, 14n., 21, 36-7, 54, 84n., 88, 128n.
Rex pacificus, 109-10, 115
Ricardus Anglicus, 23-7, 82n.

Rogerius, 77n., 82n.
Roman law, 21, 25, 78-9, 82-3, 93-4, 113-4, 118, 130, 136, 137; *see also Corpus Iuris Civilis*
Romana ecclesia, apex ominum cathedrarum, 1n., 80n., *caput et domina et princeps omnium ecclesiarum*, 111; *commune et generale forum*, 94, 98 ; *communis omnium Christiani populi nationum*, 72, 83, 104; *cura totius christianitatis*, 140-1; *genetrix et magistra aliarum ecclesiarum*, 96; *magistra omnium*, 80n.; *magistratus ecclesiasticae disciplinae*, 88n.; *mater et magistra omnium fidelium*, 111; *mater ecclesiarum omnium*, 1n., 80n; *monarcha omnium ecclesiarum*, 1n., *navis stabilis et immutabilis*, 114n.; *plenitudo ecclesiasticae iurisdictionis*, 88n.; *preeminens iurisdictio*, 88n.; *principatus*, of: 1n., 80n. (Rufinus); 1n., 78 (St Bernard); 2n., 85-6, 94n., 102 (Innocent III); 75-6, 92 (2 Lyons); 26 (Gelasius I); 80n., 81-5 (Huguccio); 88n. (Honorius III) ; 88n. (St Raymond of Peñafort); 96 (*Curialis*); 82n., 84n., 111, 114 (Hostiensis); *see also* Pope
Rufinus, 1, 24n., 77

Siricius, Pope, 9n.
Simon of Bisignano, 23n., 78, 82, 86n.
Solite (X. 1.33.6), 60, 108; doctrine, 39-41; significance, 43; interpretation, 8n., 126n., 138n., (Hostiensis), 138n. (Innocent IV)
Stephen of Tournai, 28-9, 57, 77
Summa 'Antiquitate et tempore,' 24n.
Summa Bambergensis, 24n.
Summa 'Elegantius in iure,' 77n.
Summa ' Et est sciendum,' 27n.
Summa Lipsiensis, 15n., 24n.
Summa Monacensis, 24
Summa Reginensis, 33n., 142n.
Summa ' Reverentia sacrorum canonum,' 27n.
Summa 'Tractaturus magister,' 24n., 77n.
Summa Quaestionum, see Ricardus Anglicus

Tancred, 41, 46n., 49, 53, 87, 93, 95n., 108, 111, 112n., 138n., 142

Translation of Empire theory, 27, 35-6, 42, 46, 47, 66, 100; *see also Venerabilem*

Two swords theory, *quaestio* of Ricardus Anglicus, 23-7; connexion with Translation of Empire, 27, 36; early decretalist formulation of *glossa ordinaria* position, 45-8 ; Innocent IV, 66; *see also*, Translation of Empire Theory, Bible at Luke 22.38

Unam sanctam, 51n., 58, 59-60, 91n., 96n., 129, 133, 143

Urban IV, Pope, 90n.

Venerabilem (X.1.6.34), 16, 23, 34, 60, 120; circumstances of issue, 35; doctrine, 35-6; significance, 27, 36, 43; interpretation, 36n., 48n. (Laurentius); 36 (*Gl. Palatina*); 36-7 (St Raymond); 47n. (Tancred); 48 (J. Teutonicus); 63-4, 66, 70, 100 (Innocent IV), 64n. (Hostiensis)

Vincentius Hispanus, 36n., 48, 53n., 54, 88n., 112n.

William of Montpellier, Count, 37-8, 61, 110, 120n.

William of Ockham, 143-4

Zachary I, Pope, 14, 26, 48